SKI
TOURING

Bruce Goodlad

Second edition 2018

First published in Great Britain 2015 by Pesda Press
Tan y Coed Canol
Ceunant
Caernarfon
Gwynedd
LL55 4RN

© Copyright 2018 Bruce Goodlad

ISBN: 9781906095642

Maps by Bute Cartographics

Illustrations by George Manley

Printed and bound in Poland, www.lfbookservices.co.uk

ACKNOWLEDGEMENTS

The techniques, skills and routes in this book have been gleaned from years of sharing days out on skis in the mountains with friends and clients.

I owe a huge debt of gratitude to my wife Kate who took most of the technical photographs and toiled late into the night battling with my terrible grammar and spelling. I would also like to thank Mike Austin who has helped review drafts, made valuable suggestions, then hung on a rope to be photographed. Mike and I first skied together over 20 years ago in Antarctica and have been sharing great days out ever since. We have also been developing and delivering American Avalanche Association courses to the public in the Alps and Scotland.

Brian O'Connor has been a huge help with advice, suggestions and comments.

I felt a chapter on ski technique was essential, and there was only one person I wanted to work with; Alison Thacker.

The avalanche chapter was a big challenge, we decided to re-write it for the second edition based on the knowledge we had gained teaching avalanche education over the years separating the two editions of the book. There have been large advances made in the teaching of avalanche education and the importance of the "Human Factor", this is reflected in the new chapter.

When it came to the photography Mike and Mark gave their time freely to get in front of the camera, James Thacker very kindly spent time dangling on a rope and Andy Perkins got behind the lens when Kate was unable to do so as we had just had our son Finn.

I have to thank Franco at Pesda Press who has been as supportive and understanding as I could ever dream was possible.

A final thinks to everyone not mentioned who contributed ideas and who have shared great days in the mountain.

Photographs

Most of the photographs in the book have been taken by the author or Kate Scott unless otherwise credited in the book. I would also like to thank the following who have generously donated pictures. Mark Charlton, Mike Austin, Bruce Duncan, Andy Perkins, Neil Stevenson, Andy Teasdale, Rob Jarvis and John Dallinson.

Bruce Goodlad

ABOUT THE AUTHORS

Bruce Goodlad has been an International Federation of Mountain Guides Association (IFMGA) guide since 2001 and worked as a mountaineering instructor in the UK prior to that. He has guided on skis and foot all over the world working from Antarctica in the south to Greenland in the north. He spends about 100 days a year guiding on skis; there's nothing he loves more than sharing his time in the mountains with like-minded people. He has a special interest in avalanche education and works each year on a number of avalanche courses for professional and recreational skiers.

This is the second book Bruce has written. The first was *Alpine Mountaineering* – an introduction to alpine mountaineering techniques and the routes to develop them on, also by Pesda Press. Bruce was the Technical Director for British Mountain Guides between 2012 and 2016 when he was responsible for the organisation of training for guides. He is a professional member of the American Avalanche Association (AAA) and a partner in the avalanche education business Avalanche Geeks.

Alison Thacker is a British Association of Snowsport Instructors (BASI) level 4 ski instructor – a BASI trainer working on Ski Instructor mountain safety courses. Alison comes from a background in Scottish skiing and has raced at international level representing Scotland. She is now based full-time in the Alps where she runs her off-piste instruction and coaching business. As well as coaching and instructing Alison is a passionate ski tourer and has explored mountains all over the world on skis. Alison has spent many hours trying to iron out all of Bruce's bad skiing habits!

Mike Austin is an American Mountain Guides Association (AMGA) Assistant Ski Guide. He is a Professional Member of the American Avalanche Association, a collective group of dedicated professionals engaged in the study, forecasting, control and mitigation of avalanches, and holds Level 3 avalanche certification.

Mike has guided on ski for over 18 years, primarily on the west coast of North America from Alaska to California as well as Norway and Antarctica. In addition to guiding he has worked in a professional capacity in search and rescue programs for government agencies in Antarctica and Scotland. He has made winter ascents of prominent high altitude peaks in Alaska and Antarctica and first ascents in the Pakistan Karakoram and the Cordillera Blanca of Peru.

Mike and Bruce are partners in Avalanche Geeks, a Scotland and Alps based avalanche school. Mike co-authored the avalanche and avalanche rescue chapters of this second edition.

Contents

The Author and Publisher of this book would remind the reader that:

Ski touring and ski mountaineering are activities with a danger of personal injury or death. People participating in these activities should be aware of and accept these risks and be responsible for their own actions.

Every effort has been made to ensure that the content and instructions in this book cover all aspects of personal safety skills and techniques required in ski touring at beginner and up to intermediate level. The Author and Publisher cannot accept any responsibility for any accident, injury, loss or damage sustained while following any of the techniques described within.

If you feel that you need additional instruction in order to use this book then it is advised that you employ a suitably qualified and experienced mountain guide.

Going Ski Touring

Kate Scott skiing from the Col de Bise with Lake Geneva below.

Ski touring, or ski mountaineering, is the art of travelling through, up, down and round the winter mountains on skis. When the winter arrives and covers the hills in its icy mantle, the landscape changes. Small grassy hills, which you wouldn't have given a second glance in summer, become great mountain objectives. All you need is a set of ski touring kit and a few basic skills and you have a whole new world to explore.

Lift-accessed skiing has become a pretty mainstream sport; cheap travel to the mountains, and huge improvements in kit have allowed us to enjoy the winter mountains and learn to ski like never before. Many people are happy to confine their activities to the prepared and controlled pisted ski area, enjoying the challenge of making the skis go where they want them to go, and soaking up the mountain scenery.

However there are lots of us who, having enjoyed the pisted and controlled ski areas, want more from their skiing; we want to leave the confines of the marked trails and explore the mountains. To leave the piste and the avalanche-controlled areas requires a marked increase in skill level to ski in variable off-piste snow, and there is also a marked increase in risk. The skier needs to accept, recognise and manage the risk, and they will find the rewards are worth it. Outside of the controlled ski area the skier must be able to navigate in order to return safely from their adventure. They need to have the tools and ability to look after themselves should an incident occur, and most importantly they must have the knowledge and a sound decision-making framework to allow them to operate in avalanche terrain. This is coupled with the equipment and knowledge to affect a rescue should an avalanche occur.

Off-piste skiing using lift access is often enough to satisfy the skier for many seasons and is the best way to hone your off-piste skiing skills. There is often a point when the skier wants to travel that bit further to access a patch of powder, climb a peak or look into the next valley. This is the point when we move into the world of ski touring. There needs to be a change in kit and an acceptance of the increased risk and responsibility, and there is a further increase in seriousness as we head away from the controlled and patrolled ski areas.

Andy Congleton enjoying some lift-accessed off-piste in Bruson.

Initial forays into the backcountry may be achieved on foot; short hikes with our skis on our back can give access to clean lines and great snow, however the areas you can access are limited and you don't have the option of turning around if you don't like it. By changing your ski bindings to a touring model, and buying a pair of skins that stick to the base of your ski, you are freeing yourself from the constraints of mechanised skiing, and opening the winter mountains to your imagination. It won't be long before you have left your alpine ski boots in the garage and spend the winter in touring boots, travelling through the mountains, skiing great lines, and enjoying peace and solitude that you could only imagine when using lifts.

In this book we will give you the tools to make the transition from off-piste skiing to ski touring and ski mountaineering; we will assume that you can already ski off-piste to some degree. We have a chapter written by Alison Thacker, BASI Trainer (she trains ski instructors), to help you deal with

Kate Scott enjoying
some early season
powder in St Gervais.

Kate Scott pulling a
sledge while moving
camp ski touring
in Greenland.

difficult off-piste snow and make that transition to the backcountry. We will look at all the kit you will need, some essential and some desirable, then give you the skills to use it in a practical and accessible manner.

The book will look at avalanche awareness and give you some practical ideas to allow you to make solid decisions about where and when to ski, and give you the tools to effect a rescue should disaster strike.

One of the great adventures when ski touring is to tour through the high mountains, linking peaks, passes and glaciers. We will look at all the considerations for skiing on glaciers, when to use a rope and how to deal with crevasses and crevasse rescue.

Having given you the skills, we will have a look at some of our favourite ski tours, giving you the information and top tips to have your own backcountry adventure.

The scope of ski touring

We have mentioned lift-accessed off-piste skiing and the desire to move away from the controlled area, but the scope of ski touring is vast. As a mountain guide, in one winter I may do everything, from a one hour skin from a lift to access some great powder, to spending two weeks camping on a glacier in the Arctic, ski touring everyday and pulling all our equipment on a sledge.

We can break things down into a number of styles of tour. The simplest, and in my view the best, way to start touring is to do short skins in and around a ski area. This allows you to develop the skills and confidence to venture into the backcountry, without going too far. The next step is to use the lifts to gain height then leave them behind to get to more remote spots; this often gives the greatest amount of downhill skiing for your effort. As you exhaust the lift-accessed possibilities you can choose tours that start from the road. This is the purest form of skiing; you get out of the car, put your skins on, climb to a peak or a col then ski back to the car – no mechanisation, just you and the mountain.

Kate Scott and Alison Thacker putting skins on next to the car.

To enjoy longer tours where you may be out overnight you will have to think about accommodation. In the European Alps we are very lucky to have an extensive hut network; these huts have a guardian (hut keeper) for part of the winter who will provide you with dinner, bed and breakfast (for a fee) so you can travel light, just taking your essential kit with you.

Iain Muir leaving the Chardonnet hut in the Val Claree.

Huts can often be linked together to create a multi-day tour. This is an amazing way to spend time in the mountains; you can leave the road and rejoin it five or six days later having travelled through the mountains, up peaks, over passes and enjoyed some great food, wine and company in some lovely mountains huts.

This style of hut-to-hut touring is pretty unique to the European Alps; there isn't a comparable hut network anywhere else in the world. New Zealand has huts, but they aren't guardianed, and there are some great huts in North America, but they are run in a very different style, and much of the remote ski touring in North America is done using tents.

Ski touring does not have to be extreme. You can enjoy travelling through the mountains on any number of easy, relaxing tours, or you can make it extreme by choosing to ski some steep descents. You can ski on glaciated terrain where you will have to carry ropes and crevasse rescue equipment, or you can ski on un-glaciated terrain where your pack will be much lighter.

This book is focused on touring in the European Alps, but all the skills and techniques are transferable to mountains around the world.

Ski touring – ski mountaineering, the difference?

Kate Scott ski mountaineering in the Aravis.

There is much debate about what constitutes ski touring and what is ski mountaineering; to me there doesn't seem much difference. You could argue that ski touring is travelling through the mountains and ski mountaineering is climbing up mountains using skis. It's a discussion that could go round in circles indefinitely, but to me the transition point between touring and mountaineering is when I take my skis off, put crampons on my feet, and swap ski poles for an ice axe. There are many occasions when I can skin straight onto the summit of a mountain, strip my skins and ski down. This is much less serious than climbing a classic ski mountaineering peak like the Piz Buin. Situated in the Silvretta region of Austria, the peak is climbed by skinning to the base where you swap skis and poles for an axe and crampons. You then climb to the summit and back down to the skis, and then ski home.

Kate Scott carrying
skis on her way to the
Col des Chasseurs,
Les Contamines.

Whenever I travel any distance on my skins I will always have a pair of lightweight crampons and an ice axe with me, so the kit and my approach is pretty much the same no matter where I am going. There are many days when an ice axe may be useful, you can cut a platform to make it easier to put skis on or add security in many different ways. If you don't have it with you, you can't use it.

To make life easier in this book, I will generally refer to ski touring, but to me the two terms are interchangeable.

A few other terms

It is worth mentioning a few other commonly referred to terms that crop up in ski language, most have come from our friends in North America.

Backcountry – this is the terrain away from the lifts and controlled ski areas. So no piste, lifts, avalanche patrol or ski patrol, you will need to rely on your own skills and experience.

Side or slack country – generally off-piste skiing accessed from a lift but may involve a small hike or skin to gain off-piste snow, which then usually feeds back into the ski area pretty easily. When skiing this type of terrain you need to be aware of where you are and where you are going. A set of tracks may lead into tempting terrain, but if you don't know where they lead you can get into all kinds of trouble.

How good a skier do I need to be to tour?

This is a perennial but valid question, how good a skier do you need to be to go ski touring? The answer isn't as straightforward as you might hope, but the better an off-piste skier you are, the more you will enjoy ski touring. There is no short cut to effective off-piste ski technique, modern skis and good quality ski instruction will help, but the only way to get better at skiing is to go skiing. **There is no substitute for time on snow.**

If you enjoy off-piste skiing and can get around the mountain in control, making the skis change direction where and when you want, and you can control speed and line, then you are ready to go ski touring. It doesn't matter if it doesn't look pretty; it is all about being effective in a variety of snow types, tidying up your look for the pictures will come with time. The idea that you can equate an on-piste grade to ski touring terrain is pretty ludicrous. The snow in any ski touring day can vary from perfect powder to un-skiable crust, and you must have a technique in your box to deal with it. You may be able to traverse and kick turn to get yourself down the mountain but it isn't really skiing, though there are occasions when this is the only way to deal with terrible snow.

You will also have to remember that the rucksack you are carrying will be a bit heavier than a standard off-piste sack, you will need skins and other pieces of safety kit that you may not think necessary when skiing from the lifts. I carry my basic ski touring kit with me all the time, so I am used to the weight of the rucksack and I can change plans at any point in the day.

In real terms what does this mean? If you can ski off-piste from the lifts, in control, with the odd crash, then you are ready to go touring. Go for a bit of a skin and see how it feels skiing with your touring kit and the heavier pack. If you are still in control and having a good time, let's go touring. If you are crashing lots, feel on the edge of control and not having a great time, but love the uphill and touring experience, I'd recommend you invest in a few ski lessons from a good instructor and spend a bit more time building on your downhill skills. This may feel frustrating in the short term, but in the long term you will enjoy both your off-piste skiing and ski touring much more.

Ski Touring Kit

Skis can take you to amazing places ... here camped on Brabant Island, Antarctica.

As a skier you will probably have a lot of the kit that you need to enjoy ski touring, but there are a few other essentials that you will need when you leave the pistes. The most obvious is a set of touring bindings and skins plus your avalanche safety equipment. If you already ski off-piste regularly you will probably have the latter so the easiest way to release yourself from the confines of the ski area is to change the bindings on your skis from a downhill to a touring model, buy some skins and you are off. Once you have decided ski touring is for you, you may want to invest in some more specialist equipment. Here we are going to walk you through all the kit you may consider taking on the hill. What you actually take may depend on where you are going, for example you don't need to carry glacier travel kit if there isn't a glacier.

There is a full check list in the Appendices that you can photocopy and use when packing.

The essentials

Skis

In the good old days a ski was a ski, go into any ski shop now and you are faced with such a big selection that you don't know where to start. There are all sorts of shapes from the super-wide powder skis that you need a helicopter and a back garden the size of Alaska to use, to the super-light, skinny, carbon fibre skis designed for ski randonnée racing.

Kate Scott, Greg Watts and Jane Williams enjoy modern skis in La Grave.

A selection of modern skis.

Early rise or rockered tip.

When I started ski touring, skis were long and narrow and skiing off-piste was only for really good skiers. Skis have now got shorter and wider which provides more float so you don't sink in soft snow, and the addition of some side cut makes the ski much more manoeuvrable and easier to ski. Until recently, the design and construction of skis was such that if you bought anything that had 'tour' written on it, you got a light ski that was great for going up and terrible for skiing down. This has now changed, so you can get a light ski that will give you the performance you want in ascent and descent. If you end up carrying them on your pack they are noticeably lighter and easier to manage. The downside to light skis is that they are easily deflected in cruddy snow, which can make them feel a bit twitchy. You will usually get better skiing performance from a slightly heavier ski.

It is not essential to use a ski that is designed for ski touring; any backcountry or free ride ski will do the job, but it is worth thinking a bit about size and shape before you get your credit card out.

The wider the ski, the easier it is to ski in soft snow, because you sink less deeply, making the ski easier to turn. The softer the flex the ski has, the easier the tip will ride to the surface again, making it easier to ski in soft snow. Some manufacturers now use what they call an 'early rise tip', also known as 'rocker'. This is where the front section of the ski curves up off the snow before the tip, which makes it easier to keep your tips near or on the surface of the snow.

Kate Scott skiing powder on some fat skis, St Gervais.

In a perfect world we would just ski powder all the time so big, soft skis would be great, but backcountry snow is often a long way from perfect. Skiing in the Alps you may have a 2000m vertical height difference from where you start skiing to where you reach the road. During that descent the snow will have been affected by different weather at different altitudes. It may have been really windy up high so the snow will be wind scoured; as you drop you may come into a sheltered area and enjoy some beautiful powder. You may then change aspect and have to ski some sun crust, before dropping to lower altitudes where it may be warm and the snow has turned to the consistency of porridge.

Your skis (and the skier) will have to be able to cope with all these snow types. A good all-mountain ski should help you deal with most of these conditions. Let's face it, perfect powder is pretty easy to ski no matter what you have on your feet (as long as it isn't a super-stiff race ski designed to bite on ice), so I look for a ski that will perform well on harder, more difficult snow types that I will also be able to ski in the deep, fluffy stuff. What this means in reality is a compromise between stiffness and width. A ski with a bit of stiffness in the mid section and a rockered tip seems to be the best compromise so far.

The more side cut a ski has the tighter the turn radius, and certain shapes of side cut will allow the ski to turn more easily. While having a ski that is easy to turn when skiing on-piste can be really good fun, they can feel skittery and unpredictable in difficult snow. If you end up on steep terrain with hard snow with a ski that has a lot of side cut, you will find that as the ski flexes the only part of the ski that is in contact with the snow is the tip and the tail. This can feel pretty scary.

A side effect of having really big skis is that you won't fit in the skinning track made by other skiers, and while this isn't a problem on short tours, making your own track day after day can be a real pain.

If you go the other way and get a super-skinny ski you will benefit from the weight saving in ascent, but in descent you don't have much surface area to float in soft snow, and in difficult, crusty snow the light ski can be easily deflected by the crust or other lumps and bumps in the snow. If you are a good enough skier to cope with this you could take advantage of the super-light kit that is available. If you look at the weight and size of the skis that ski touring racers are using and the speed they are moving at, there are definite advantages, but you should watch them trying to ski downhill in deep soft snow, it's quite entertaining.

I have talked a lot about wide and thin skis so it's time to talk numbers; what sort of size works? Most people talk about the size underfoot as being the key size when it comes to float. A ski with an underfoot width of between 85 and 95mm will work in most conditions, as a wide soft shovel at the front will help the ski ride onto the surface of difficult snow. Skiers from a more traditional skiing background may find this quite wide, but combined with today's lightweight construction techniques it will give you a ski that you can enjoy in both directions, up and down. I would then recommend you try a few different makes and models of skis to get a feel for how stiff they are, and go for something with a medium flex. Our friends in North America ski a lot of soft snow and often have skis wider than 100mm for touring.

Bindings

There are two real options when it comes to bindings, there is the 'pin' or 'tech' style bindings developed by Dynafit, or the 'frame' style binding. The tech binding works by using pins that locate into the toe of the boot, providing the hinge system for going uphill, and an attachment into the heel of the boot for going down, which makes for an incredibly light, secure system.

Dynafit tech or pin bindings with skin and ski modes demonstrated.

The alternative is a frame style binding where an attachment system similar to a downhill binding is mounted to a frame with a hinge at the front for going uphill and a locking mechanism for skiing downhill, e.g. Fritschi. The main advantage to this style is how easy they are to clip in and out of.

Frame binding from Fritschi in ski and skin modes.

It is worth looking at the pros and cons of the different bindings you are going to come across. If we start by comparing the two systems, generally the tech system takes a little bit of getting used to as they are more fiddly to put on. The attachment at the toe is via two pins that locate into metal inserts in the boot. This provides a pivot point at the toe that makes for a very natural skinning action. When you step into the binding a lever is pulled up to lock the toe of the binding in place for skinning, this is then unlocked for descent.

The rear of the binding has two pins that locate into an insert on the heel of the boot. This rotates at right angles to the ski for ascent releasing the heel, the binding is rotated in line with the ski and the boot locked in for descent. The only way you can adjust the level of the release (known as the DIN setting, as on an alpine downhill binding) is at the heel.

Some people consider that this system isn't as safe as there isn't any way of controlling the DIN setting at the toe. Having skied on Dynafit tech bindings for more than 10 years I have had no problems with this. The bindings are secure in ascent and descent, the binding system sits the boot much lower on the ski than a frame binding, which feels like you are really in touch with the ski, and eliminates the torsional flex that is present in some frame bindings. The attachment system for the ski crampons is also superb with these types of system. Bindings using the Tech system are now available from a number of manufacturers.

Pros: *Weight, security, feel.*

Cons: *Needs specific boots with the Dynafit inserts, these must be fac-
        tory fitted so may limit the choice of boots, although this is less
        and less the case with many manufacturers having boots which are
        tech binding compatible. There is also a perception that they are not
        as safe.*

The frame binding is typified by the Fritschi system (there are also models from Salomon, Marker and a couple of other manufacturers.). The advantage of the frame system is that it will fit any ski boot so is a good system for people starting ski touring. With this binding you can try touring with your standard downhill ski boots on some short tours. If you decide you like the activity you can think about changing to a specifically-designed ski touring boot and binding. You just need to adjust the toe height to allow for the difference in thickness between a downhill boot and a rubber-soled touring boot.

As the frame binding will work with any current boot design it is also ideal for those who want the drive, power and precision of a downhill boot when lift-accessed skiing, but want to change to the comfort and flexibility of a touring boot when skiing away from the lifts on the same pair of skis. Those of you used to skiing on downhill bindings may notice the lack of precision from some frame bindings. There are a number of reasons for this. If you are using touring boots they have a rubber sole, which absorbs some of the pressure that would be transferred directly from your foot to the ski with a hard plastic boot sole. There is a degree of flex in some frame bindings, which becomes more pronounced as the bindings get older. The boot is also mounted a small distance above the ski which decreases feel and can take a bit of getting used to. The bindings that have been released by Marker in recent years, starting with the Duke and moving through different weights and maximum DIN settings to the M10, have combated this by locking the whole binding frame onto the ski which gives a better feel than the Fritschi or Silvretta binding in descent. In ascent the Marker system has a very natural skinning action, but the transition between modes is the most difficult of any of the bindings currently on the market, and very prone to icing up.

Top Tip

If buying frame bindings to fit a number of different boots check the sizing carefully. I have had clients who have been skiing on a medium binding, then got new boots which were slightly smaller and the bindings could not be adjusted small enough for the new boots. While this could be expensive, it is also quite embarrassing to discover this at the top of a lift when about to set off for a day's touring.

Pros: *Flexibility, ease of use.*

Cons: *Heavier, bulkier, more flex.*

Skins

Originally seal skins, but fortunately now brushed nylon or mohair (or some-times a combination) with a self-adhesive back, the skins are stuck to the bottom of the skis with the bristles facing the tail. Over time the glue may need to be reapplied but this is an easy job. Alternatively you could consider Gecko skins which use some kind of silicon suction technology to attach the skin to the ski and work surprisingly well.

The base of a skin.

When the skin is attached you should be able to see the edges.

The bristles allow the ski to glide forward then when you step forward the bristles grip the snow allowing you to make uphill progress. When you get to the top of your ascent, peel the skins off the skis, lock the heel of the binding down and you are ready to enjoy the descent.

With the advent of wider shaped skis not all skins will fit all skis. When the skin is stuck to the base of the ski there should be enough of a gap down each side of the skin that you can see the metal edges of the ski. If the skin overlaps the edges you won't be able to grip hard snow with the edge of the ski. If there is too much of a gap when you pressure the edge of the ski, there is no skin to grip, and the ski will go shooting backwards. This is incredibly frustrating and tiring so make sure you get the right skin width from the start.

Top Tip

If you buy new skis make sure you check that your skins fit properly before going on the hill.

There are two ways of buying skins; many of the ski manufacturers have teamed up with a skin manufacturer to sell skins specifically cut to the shape and length of their skis. These are great, the skins are cut using a laser so the precision is superb and it saves you the hassle of trimming the skins yourself. The alternative is to buy a skin that is wide enough to cover the base of the ski then trim it to fit your ski, this is pretty easy to do with the tool provided with the skins, you just have to be very careful to get the size correct so only the edges of the ski are exposed. Most shops will trim your skins for you for no extra charge.

There are lots of different attachment systems for skins, the simplest system is a metal or wire loop that fits over the tip of the ski then the self-adhesive back is smoothed along the skin. I used this system for years without any problems, but there is the risk of the tail of the skin unpeeling if the glue gets a bit tired. This can be a disaster as snow sticks to the glue side of the skin and it won't reattach. These things always seem to happen when it is cold and windy and it is difficult to fix. A number of manufacturers use a tip loop and a tail strap; this works really well but does mean that you have to buy the skin approximately the right length for the ski. G3 use a similar idea but have two hooks at the tip that allow the skin to hook onto any odd shaped tips.

Two common skin attachment systems from Dynafit and Dynastar.

An alternative is a tail hook with a rubber tensioner and loop at the tip. I have never been very keen on this, as it is easy to kick the loop off the tip of the ski which results in snow getting between the glue and the ski. A final manufacturer-specific system like the one Dynafit use is worth considering, with a tail hook and a rubber tip that locates securely into a notch on the front of the ski.

Top Tip

If the skin gets damp at the beginning of the day, as you gain height and move into colder drier snow this may stick/freeze to the damp skin causing a build up of snow. This is known as 'balling up'. You can help prevent this by treating the skin with a waterproof silicon coating called 'skin guard'. I treat my skins at the start of every week's touring, then carry a small block of glide wax that can be applied directly to the skin should this problem occur on the hill. Black Diamond make a specific rub-on wax called Glop Stopper which does this really well.

Ski crampons

Depending on what language you speak you will hear ski crampons referred to as couteau (French for knife) or harscheisen (German for crampons); here we will keep things simple and just refer to them as ski crampons. Your ski crampons are used when the snow gets too hard, and maybe icy, to allow effective grip with your skins. By using these you can carry on uphill with your skis on your feet rather than strapping them onto your rucksack and continuing on foot.

Dynafit ski crampons.

These clever bits of metal attach to your ski or binding, and they hinge up out of the way when you slide the ski forward, then when you weight your boot the crampon is pushed down into the snow. Ski crampons are binding specific so you will only be able to use a model designed for your type of binding. You will need to check the width of your ski in relation to the ski crampon, especially if you buy new skis and transfer the bindings across from your old skis. A crampon that is too wide will work but it can feel disconcerting. Another thing to watch is that as bindings have developed within a brand, the design of ski crampons has changed so a Fritschi ski crampon from a few years ago will not fit the current Fritschi range, so make sure you check before going on the hill. Additionally don't assume that you will be able to buy things like ski crampons in resort. I have wasted hours helping people look for ski crampons when they could have just ordered them on the internet long before their trip.

Marker and Fritschi ski crampons.

Boots

The difference between downhill ski boots and ski touring boots is that a downhill boot has very limited flex in the ankle and the calf, the leg is always held forward in the cocked position. When you try to skin uphill in these, this will limit your stride length. Touring boots have a locking mechanism at the ankle that allows a big range of movement and a long stride length for uphill travel, then the ankle can be locked for downhill skiing.

The plastics used in most downhill boots are much heavier (and cheaper) than a touring boot and, finally, touring boots have a rubber-patterned sole compared to the hard plastic sole of a downhill boot, allowing you to walk about much more easily. This rubber sole means that touring boots cannot be used in most downhill bindings as the rubber sole stops the glide, or release, plate at the toe from working. I have seen many broken legs from people who have thought they would get away with this and didn't.

Sole of a touring boot.

Some downhill-orientated boots come with an interchangeable sole unit, one rubber, the other hard plastic. The plastic sole can be used in downhill bindings.

Ski touring boots used to be designed for either uphill performance (lightweight and comfort) or downhill performance (control and weight); this is no longer the case. Boot design combined with advances in plastic technology and heat mouldable liners have narrowed the gap between uphill and downhill performance.

There is still a choice to be made, as within the range of boots currently on the market, you still have to make a choice between a more downhill-orientated boot or a lightweight uphill-orientated boot. With the current popularity of ski randonnée racing, the light boots keep getting lighter, incorporating lots of carbon fibre and other high tech materials. These design features are filtering down throughout the range of available boots creating lightweight designs that can actually be skied in. Skiers used to get hung up on the number of buckles a boot has, with three-buckle boots being considered for touring performance and four for downhill performance. New designs and materials have made this concept obsolete with three-buckle boots giving great performance and a bit less weight.

Let's have a look at the pros and cons of choosing a boot from one end of the spectrum or the other.

Touring boots left to right are more uphill to more downhill-orientated.

Downhill-orientated boots

The design of these boots is orientated toward downhill performance; the boots are usually stiffer for more control and often heavier as a result. They often come with interchangeable sole units as mentioned above. The stiffer plastic used can have an impact on the comfort of the boot on long uphill days, as will the weight, so I would consider these boots more suitable for skiing close to resort where you may skin for a couple of hours but not all day. They are perfect for those wanting to mix a bit of off-piste skiing and touring but aren't prepared to sacrifice performance for weight. Having said that you will see plenty of people happy to tour on this type of boot all the time, they just have to be a bit fitter to push the extra weight, but are prepared to make the sacrifice for the downhill performance.

Do anything boots

These are the boots that you will see most people ski touring in. They give a great balance between performance and weight, with lightweight materials being used more and more regularly; these boots are also getting lighter. This is the style of boots that I will usually ski in, as they are fairly light and will cope with any conditions. In many respects they are the ultimate compromise boot, as plans and snow conditions change you will have a boot that will cope with pretty much anything.

Lightweight boots

Some of these boots are out and out randonnée racing boots while others I would say are race inspired, which means less carbon fibre so they meet certain price points. These boots are great in ascent, they are so light with such amazing flex that you will fly uphill. Downhill they will give you a bit more of a challenge, as they don't have as much support as the other boots, so you will need to be a much better skier to take advantage of their all-round performance. In consistent snow types some of these boots are so good that you won't notice the lack of support, but in variable conditions as is typical of most ski tours, with a heavy pack on you will really notice that you are fighting hard to stay on the middle of the ski.

Heat mouldable boot liner.

Boot liners

When looking at boots it is worth going for a model with thermo mouldable liners, which offer more comfort, and are lighter and warmer. They also dry faster. Injected moulded liners do give you unrivalled control and feel but they are cold, heavy, uncomfortable to skin in and very expensive.

Thermo mouldable liners will pack out a bit with use so when you have them moulded use a thin sock and with a few uses they will soon pack out to a standard sock.

Buying boots

When buying boots go to a shop that has been recommended and is a specialist; you can't decide from the marketing which boot will suit the shape of your foot. A good shop will look and measure your feet then suggest a number of models which will suit your feet and the performance characteristics you are looking for. The suggestions may be from a number of manufacturers depending on your foot shape and what you want to do with the boot.

I would recommend always buying boots as early as possible in the season when the shops have a full range of models and sizes. I would also suggest going to a ski resort to do this, so that you can get the boots fitted on arrival then ski with them for a few days. Then if you need any alterations done you can get them done there and then and check the alterations have worked. What better excuse for an early season long weekend on the skis?

Top Tip

Most specialist shops operate on an appointment system, so do your research and make an appointment before you leave home.

Poles

Off and on-piste pole baskets.

You don't need to go and spend lots of money on fancy poles, a simple one-piece, solid pole with a decent-sized basket will work in any situation. Small piste-style baskets will drive you nuts as any time you push on the pole it will vanish into the soft snow.

Grip tape makes it easier to hold the pole in different positions.

If the poles you own have small baskets it is pretty easy to change them. Some people use longer poles for touring than downhill skiing so they can get more of a push, personally I use the same length of pole for everything and haven't had any problems. As well as bigger baskets, it is worth thinking about wrapping some grip tape, like you have on tennis racquets, down the top third of the pole; this makes it easier to grip when traversing.

There are lots of really expensive carbon fibre poles out there which are lovely to use. They have a great swing weight and are really light when carried, but it's up to you how you spend your money. There are also lots of adjustable-length poles. In my experience these tend to self-adjust at the least appropriate moment, like the first turn of a steep gully or along a teetery traverse. There are two systems to lock adjustable poles, an internal screw system or an external flick lock system. The flick lock is definitely the most reliable and can easily be tightened on the hill.

Flick lock pole in action.

You may also see poles that convert to avalanche probes, which are totally pointless. If you are involved in an avalanche rescue you want a proper avalanche probe that you can get out of your pack quickly and deploy. You do not want to waste valuable time trying to take the handles and baskets off your ski pole.

Choosing avalanche safety kit

There are three essential items of kit that we should all carry if we ski off piste: a transceiver, shovel and probe. By off piste we mean not standing on a groomed ski run, there is no "it's ok I'm still in bounds, I don't need the kit". In Europe, the ski area people control and manage the mountain to keep the pisted runs safe they do not protect any off piste areas of their terrain.

Essential avalanche safety kit.

There a number of inbounds avalanche fatalities when the victim was within seconds of a groomed run but were not found until it was too late and may have survived if they had been wearing an avalanche transceiver.

There's also what we think is a fourth essential – a pair of skins. If you don't carry these you don't have the ability to turn round and climb out of avalanche danger.

Avalanche transceiver

Transceiver technology has come a long way in the last 20 years since the first digital transceivers arrived in the market. I would only consider a three-antenna transceiver and I only want to ski people who have three-antenna units, I want them to be able to save me as quickly and effectively as I can save them.

Three-antenna units have two long aerials in a cross that when in search mode give you a direction and distance to the buried victim the third antenna is a short one and comes into play as you get close to the victim. This makes the location of deep burials easier and eliminates spike points that used to be a confusing issue with some of the original digital units.

Most of the three-antenna units come with signal suppression or mark function, which makes it much easier to deal with the nightmare that would be a multiple burial situation. This uses the digital signature of an individual unit to ignore or suppress the unit that is being dug out so that you can look for the next victim.

Three-antenna avalanche transceivers.

There are great units on the market from Mammut, Ortovox, BCA and Pieps, no matter what unit you choose it is essential that you practice with it. You need to create realistic scenarios on difficult terrain preferably old avalanche debris and bury the unit deep (1.5m). This simulates a real rescue as opposed to sticking a unit just under the snow on a flat bit of ground. Beacon Parks are a great way to train and are available in lots of ski resorts. You need to be confident that you can rescue someone in less than 15 minutes and be happy that they can rescue you in the same time frame.

Probe

A transceiver will only get you so close, then you need to pin point the victim with an avalanche probe. This is done by probing outwards in a spiral from the lowest reading. A body is squidgy (probe each other to see what it feels like). When you have found the victim leave the probe in place and get ready to dig – this reassures the victim and gives you a visual reference.

Probes should be a minimum of 240cm in length and should have a wire core and a quick lock mechanism for fast easy deployment. Those with a rope core are prone to collapse during use and probes with complicated locking mechanisms should be discarded as they burn valuable time in deployment. Probes should be relatively thick so they are easy to handle and are not deflected by debris when probing in the snow. Carbon probes need to be thicker than aluminum as they are easily deflected by debris. The ones that fold up into a shovel handle are a joke and should be thrown away immediately, they are so short and flimsy that all they say is that you have no respect for the lives of the people you are skiing with. Probes with depth measures marked on them are useful as an indicator of depth; they are also useful when feeling for layers in the snowpack or probing for crevasses on a glacier. Like a transceiver you need to practice deploying your probe and using it.

Shovel

Shovelling is the slowest part of any rescue, modern transceivers are so good you should be close to your victim very quickly; once you have probed you will know where your victim is. If your victim is buried less than 1m down take a pace downhill and dig in towards the victim. If more than 1m then go 1.5 times the burial depth down hill and dig in towards the victim. You can find some great info on the most effective shovelling techniques on the internet. It's often referred to as tactical digging or strategic shovelling techniques.

The only option for a shovel is one with a metal blade, do not consider anything else. Although a plastic shovel may be strong they flex and do not cut into the debris effectively. Extendable handles are a personal preference but you should be digging on your knees so they aren't that important but they do make them easier to pack in your sack.

Like a transceiver and a probe you need to practice digging and study effective digging techniques. Make sure you are efficient and effective. Digging your partner out of an avalanche should not be the first time to put your shovel together and dig in hard snow!

Back Country Access Shaxe and Black Diamond Metal Shovel.

Collapsible metal shovel.

Skins

Imagine you are skiing down a valley, you have got your avalanche hazard evaluation wrong, and you are now in a terrain trap with unstable snow all round you. What are you going to do? Without skins you have three real options, call a helicopter rescue (only possible with a phone signal and good weather), you could walk out (which is extremely unlikely), or you can stick your head in the lion's mouth and keep on going. Alternatively if you have a set of skins with you, you can put them on and climb out (assuming you are using some kind of touring binding). Should you come across an avalanche incident and you are at the bottom of the debris it is much easier to put your skins on and climb up than it is to search the debris on foot.

Skins add very little to the weight of your pack and massively increase your options on any ski day so why not have them along.

Training

The skills needed to perform an avalanche rescue are much more involved and complex than most people think. If we think we can make ourselves ready to perform a rescue by looking for a transceiver under a pile of leafs in our local park at the beginning of the winter then we're fooling ourselves. Confusion and stress will be extremely high. Fine motor skills will disappear along with your peripheral vision and hearing. Who's in charge? How many people are missing? It can get pretty messy. Heard about tactical digging? You should have; it's arguably more important than knowing how to use your transceiver. Don't even get us started on multiple burials.

Avalanche equipment has moved on massively in recent years and your ownership and operation of this life saving equipment should reflect that. *Above all you have to train and practice regularly.*

Backcountry Access Shaxe

The BCA Shaxe in shovel and ice axe mode.

While there are many great shovels on the market I want to point out one particular piece of kit that I think is exceptional. The Shaxe is a shovel that can be used as an ice axe and a rescue sled kit. In shovel mode the single piece shaft is a strong single piece metal bladed shovel. The handle from the shovel can then be removed and an ice axe head can be inserted, making an extremely functional ice axe. If you had to construct a rescue sled then the shovel blade can be bolted onto the tips of the ski and the shaft across the tails (skis need to be predrilled, K2 skis come with inserts), your poles can then be strapped diagonally to create an extremely functional sled. In the colder winter months I carry the Shaxe in shovel handle mode, then in the touring season where I am more likely to need an ice axe I will carry it in ice axe mode on the outside of my pack. Even with the ice axe head attached the shovel is very effective in a rescue situation.

Airbag rucksacks

Airbag rucksack have been around for a number of years, but have seen a marked increase in popularity in recent seasons; more sales have lead to increased research and development by manufacturers, making the units lighter and cheaper. Most avalanche fatalities happen as a result of asphyxia, so by using an airbag, if you are caught in an avalanche you have more chance of staying on the surface and hence surviving.

The concept behind an airbag rucksack is simple; the skier wears a rucksack in which there is an integral airbag, just like in a car, that can deployed by pulling a handle in the event of being caught in an avalanche. The airbag inflates keeping the skier on the surface. This happens due to the 'brazil nut effect' or more technically 'inverse segregation'. When a group of particles are in motion, the larger objects will migrate to the top. As you move down with an avalanche the airbag creates dynamic lift, resulting in the skier being pushed to the surface.

Airbag rucksack being released.

You can prove anything with statistics, but research in has found that in avalanche incidents, where an airbag rucksack was deployed and the victim was not killed by trauma, the victim was about 50% more likely to survive an avalanche. In incidents of complete burial, when the airbag was deployed the victim was significantly quicker to be rescued, as part of the bag was often above the surface and the rescuers were able to look for a bigger target. The statistics vary significantly between North America and Europe as the tree line is much higher in North America so avalanche victims are often swept into trees. In Europe we generally ski above the tree line so trauma incidents are reduced but burials are increased.

With these statistics you will wonder why we aren't all skiing with one, the answer is twofold; cost and weight. The cost is currently between £600 and £900 (winter 2017/18). The weight of an average unit is between 2.5 and 3kg, which is an increase of about 1.5kg on an average empty ski pack.

There are two types of airbag system the compressed gas system pioneered by ABS but now used by a number of manufacturers and the battery powered fan pack developed by Black Diamond (there is now a model from Arcteryx available in North America). There are pros and cons to both systems, a gas system can only be deployed once before you have to pay for a cylinder refill, while you may not plan to be avalanched multiple times this system does not allow you to practice without a cost implication. The battery system allows you to practice without any financial penalty. It also much easier to fly with, as you need a dispensation from many airlines to fly with a compressed gas cylinder. The fan system is still heavy, in some cases up to 1kg heavier than an equivalent sized gas powered pack. There are also some doubts about the battery power in extreme cold. I'm sure in time battery technology will allow the packs to become lighter and the systems will become cheaper.

So the cost is prohibitive for many skiers and the weight will have a major impact on many skiers' day. To summarise: if you can afford it and are strong enough to carry it, an airbag rucksack would massively increase your chance of survival in an avalanche. If you can't, people have been skiing for decades without one, through good practice have been avoiding avalanches, and with good training, rescuing people from avalanches.

If you do buy one, you have to careful to avoid the subconscious process where because you have one you are more inclined to ski more risky slopes – a bit like when they introduced air bags to cars.

Avalung

The Avalung is a system from Black Diamond which allows you to extract life-giving air from the snowpack. The device requires you to have a mouthpiece in your mouth which you breathe through, air is then drawn in from the snowpack and carbon dioxide is expelled through another part of the device. Should you be buried for any length of time this prevents the creation of an ice mask around your face, which is what usually causes the build up of CO2 and death. In an average avalanche those dug out in 15 minutes, not affected by trauma, survive. The average dig-out time is about 20 minutes. The air supply within the snowpack can be stretched to over 50 minutes with an Avalung, so if you are buried and have got the breathing tube in your mouth it should extend your survival time.

An Avalung is available either as a stand-alone unit which is worn over the top of your outer layer of clothing, or integrated into a rucksack.

There is the obvious problem with this system, that you need to get the breathing tube in your mouth which, when cart-wheeling down the hillside in an avalanche, may be rather difficult. There have been recorded cases where victims have survived having used an Avalung where they probably wouldn't have without, so the system does work.

Avalung in use.

Given the choice between a stand-alone unit and an Avalung rucksack I would prefer the sack. If you keep it as your standard sack, it is easy to always have it with you and doesn't add another layer to faff with every time you change clothes. It does have the advantage of price and weight over an airbag, being on average two-thirds cheaper and a lot lighter, but it doesn't keep you on the surface. It is better than having no extra protection system, but if you have the option to save for an airbag then that would certainly be my suggestion.

The question I would ask myself if using an Avalung is if I suddenly feel that I need to have the unit in my mouth shouldn't I be questioning whether I should be skiing the slope I am standing at the top of.

Recco

Recco is a type of radar reflector system. A reflector is sewn into clothing or stuck onto boots. In the event of a burial a detector is brought on site and then used to detect the reflectors. This usually arrives with the ski patrol or by helicopter. **This is in no way a replacement for an avalanche transceiver and companion rescue.**

By the time the detector is on site you will have used the 15 minute survival window and you are probably looking at body recovery.

Mountain kit

Boot crampons

As soon as you take your skis off on hard snow you may struggle to walk comfortably in your boots. This can be potentially dangerous if you slip, and can prevent upward progress. If you want to climb to a summit that can't be reached on skis you will often need to put on boot crampons. As mentioned earlier I think that putting on boot crampons is the line at which ski touring becomes ski mountaineering. There are two different materials used in the manufacture of crampons for ski mountaineering; aluminium and steel. The advantage of aluminium is the weight. When ski touring your crampons will spend most of their time in your rucksack where weight is important, and most of the time spent wearing crampons will be on snow, rather than ice, so the fact that aluminium is soft and doesn't wear very well is not a big problem. Where aluminium crampons are a problem is when you come across really hard ice as the metal is too soft, and will bend rather than bite.

Boot crampons.

L to R aluminium, mixed aluminium and steel, then steel with different attachment systems.

Anti-balling plate.

Steel crampons have the advantage of being made with a harder metal so they bite much better into hard ice, they are also much harder wearing, so if you end up moving on rock in your crampons, the points won't wear down as quickly as they would with an aluminium model. The drawback is that they are considerably heavier. Grivel have produced a hybrid design, called the Haute Route, for ski touring where the front half of the crampon is made of steel and the back half is aluminium. This works really well and for me is the perfect solution for most ski trips. If I am heading somewhere that I know I will need crampons a lot I will consider an all steel crampon.

No matter what model you use, make sure they are fitted with anti-balling plates. These stop the build up of snow on the underside of the crampon that stops the teeth working effectively.

It is worth keeping them in a crampon bag to save the rest of your kit from their sharp points. Try and find a bag that is made of soft, robust fabric as stiff, hard cases always take up more space in your rucksack.

Ice axe

Ski touring ice axe.

An ice axe is really useful for all sorts of ski touring purposes, not just security when you don't have your skis on. An axe can be used for improving a skinning track in hard snow for your team or chopping a ledge so you can take your skis off in order to put crampons on. I will often cut a ledge with my axe to make it easier where people are going to do a kick turn.

You can get some ridiculously light ice axes made from aluminium, but I'm not very keen on them, as the aluminium head of the axe just isn't up to use in hard snow. I would look for a model with an alloy shaft and a steel head. If you are looking for an axe in a mountaineering shop you will be faced with a huge variety of different shapes of axe. For ski touring you want to keep it simple with a straight or slightly curved shaft and a classic shaped head. The shaft length may be a bit of a compromise, as 60cm is probably the most versatile for mountaineering but it is quite long on a ski pack, so I would suggest something about 50cm, then it won't stick up if it is on the outside of your pack and in many cases will fit inside your pack.

Harness

A harness is essential for all glacier skiing; if you fall in a crevasse then rescue is much easier if you are wearing a harness. If you need to wear a rope to climb a peak or protect yourself on steep ground, then a harness is much more comfortable and secure than tying the rope round your waist. There is no need to go for a full-blown climbing harness as, hopefully, you will never actually be hanging in it, but it does need to be up to the job if you do have to hang in it.

There are two basic designs; the nappy design which wraps round your waist with a piece that pulls up between your legs to engage the leg loops, and a style that has leg loops that you step your feet through. The advantage of the nappy design is that you can put it on easily if you have your skis or crampons on.

Nappy-style harness
by Petzl.

Cilao harness.

The leg loop design is probably more comfortable if you have to hang in it but is more awkward to put on, especially over ski boots. Having said that the lightest harnesses on the market use this design.

It is worth keeping a screwgate karabiner clipped into your harness when you have it on, so if you do need to use the rope you can attach it quickly and easily.

Rope

Climbing ropes stretch to absorb a fall. This isn't so important in skiing situations as we are unlikely to get into a situation where a fall may happen, so most people use pre-stretched rope. It has some dynamic properties, but not as much as a standard climbing rope. When ski touring weight is important, so you want to take the lightest rope that will do the job required. A common diameter of rope for ski touring is 8mm; this is a good balance between being able to manipulate the rope with gloves on and being light. Length is always a difficult decision as well. The longer the rope, the heavier it is, but if the rope is too short it may not reach you in a crevasse. Most people use a 30m rope as this seems to work in most situations. It is essential that there are two ropes within the party skiing on a glacier; if you only have one rope and the person carrying it falls in a crevasse it will be quite difficult pulling them out. If you have two 30m ropes and you need to make an abseil or make a long lower, you can tie the ropes together.

In some places it is useful to have more rope, for example if you are in remote areas with heavily-crevassed glaciers, or you want to cross some steep cols. You could carry a longer 8mm rope or, what I often do, carry 30m of 8mm rope and 50m of Hyperstatic Rope (this is an extremely strong lightweight rope with no stretch see next). I recommend you experiment with different dimensions of prusik and try a mechanical device like a Wild Country Ropeman or Petzl Micro Traxion (we will talk about this later) with whatever rope you chose to use.

Hyperstatic Rope

Hyperstatic ropes are ropes that do not stretch, many of them stretch less than wire. They are also extremely strong for their weight and diameter so they are a great idea for the ski tourer, being lighter and packing smaller when compared length for length with a standard climbing rope. The Petzl RAD line typifies this system.

The Petzl RAD system – a hyperstatic rope.

While there are obvious weight and size advantages the downside is that these ropes are more difficult to handle their narrow diameter means that they do not work with standard diameter prussics. You will need to use a combination of Petzl Micro Traxion and Petzl Tibloc to set up and efficient haul system.

The static nature of the rope means that it cannot be used in a lead climbing situation and care must be taken if used for short roping. There is no issue with roped glacier skiing the dynamic nature of any crevasse fall negates any risk of harm from the static nature of the rope.

Glacier travel and crevasse rescue kit

If you are skiing on a glacier you will need to take enough equipment with you so that if someone falls in a crevasse, or you come across a team with someone in a crevasse, you can rescue them. We will talk about how you may rescue someone in the glacier skiing section of the book, but for now let us just look at the standard kit you should carry. As mentioned above there should always be two ropes and a minimum of two crevasse rescue kits in the party, but it is better if there are a few extra bits of kit in the team as well.

As a minimum you will need enough kit to create an anchor (this usually involves burying skis) and set up a hauling system to pull someone out of a crevasse. In addition every member of the party should carry one ice screw and an eight-foot (120cm) sling with a screwgate karabiner. In the event of a crevasse fall they can then secure themselves to the wall of the crevasse while they wait for rescue.

Glacier travel kit.

Standard crevasse rescue kit

There should be **two** of these in the party, even if it's a party of just two:

2 x ice screws – about 17cm. These should be clipped together with a snaplink karabiner and should have rubber caps on the teeth to protect the teeth and your trousers.

2 x 8 ft slings (120cm doubled length).

3 x screwgate karabiners, at least one should be an HMS (pear-shaped) design.

2 x prusik loops and one mechanical device such as a Wild Country Ropeman or Petzl Micro Traxion.

1 x pulley-style karabiner – such as a DMM Revolver.

30m of 8mm rope – there should always be two ropes in the party.

I usually add 5m of 6mm cord, which can be used in anchor creation but also can be used to help reading the terrain in poor visibility (see navigation chapter).

Individual glacier
travel kit.

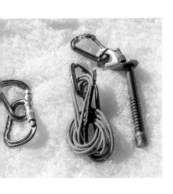

Personal minimum kit when you are part of a party where two other people are already carrying the above.

1 x ice screw about 17cm in length.

1 x 8ft sling with two screwgate karabiners.

Prusiks

A prusik is a length of 5–6mm cord that is tied in a loop using a double fisherman's knot. Take a 120cm piece of cord and hold the two ends in a loop so the two pieces are lying opposite each other with the ends facing in opposite direction. Take one end and wrap it twice round the other rope and pass the end through the loops. Do the same with the other end and pull tight – the knots will slide and tighten against each other. The loop should be about the length of your forearm.

Making a prusik.

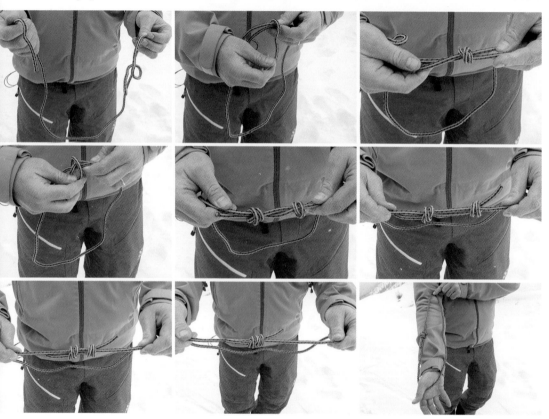

Personal kit

Here we are going to look at the clothing and personal equipment you would take for a day's touring or off-piste skiing. If you are reading this book you are almost certainly already a skier and will have a set of ski kit already, but I think it is worth sharing what works for me and looking at the various options.

The winter season can be up to six months long with huge variations in temperature, so the clothing suitable for touring in December may well be different to early May.

The layering system of clothing is the most versatile system where one layer is worn on top of another to vary temperature, as opposed to wearing one thick layer which is not so versatile. My preference is for a system where I just keep adding or removing layers from the outside. I shouldn't have to take a layer off to change what is underneath.

To make things easier let's split the body into bits; bottom, top and extremities.

Bottom half

If we start with the feet, almost every blister I have had in mountaineering or ski boots I can put down to socks. Personally pure merino wool socks are the only choice. They are expensive, and don't last as long as I would like, but they do keep my feet warm and blister-free. If you buy cheap socks and get blisters you know what to do. I generally only wear one thin pair of socks, as I want the feel and precision that gives me when skiing. The boots have plenty of insulation and thin socks dry faster in the hut in the evening.

I will generally put on my bottom half clothing and leave it the same all day. It is too much hassle to change bottom layers on the hill, so I regulate my temperature by varying my top half clothing.

No cotton. Cotton is a great fabric but not in the mountains. It absorbs water, the body then uses its valuable heat to dry the fabric, which cools your core. Wicking fabrics pull the moisture away from your body and don't absorb moisture, so it is much easier to maintain a comfortable temperature.

Early season it can be pretty cold even when going uphill, so I will usually start with a merino wool base layer. Merino is great at temperature regulation and it doesn't smell so you can wear the same garment for a number of days without offending your team mates. As the season warms up I will drop the base, merino layer from my lower body system.

Softshell trousers with a merino base layer top.

Paclite jacket and trousers.

When I'm off-piste skiing in cold conditions with lots of fresh snow about I will add a pair of power-stretch tights to the merino, then add a pair of Gore-Tex trousers on top. Gore-Tex breathes enough and has the waterproof qualities to keep me dry when getting on and off lifts with lots of snow around, which invariably melts to give a wet bum and legs. I would make sure that the trousers have good venting zips so I don't get too hot if I am hiking or making a short skin. Softshell is way more comfortable than hardshell as it is, as the name suggests, softer and more comfortable to wear. It is also more breathable so you don't sweat, consequently you don't get damp so you stay warmer; it also sheds snow surprisingly well.

If the plan for the day is touring, I will always wear softshell, this gives me the comfort, flexibility and breathability to skin, ski and climb in comfort. My favourite softshell trousers have long thigh zips to allow for ventilation.

In the early part of the season I will usually have a base layer underneath, as the weather warms up in springtime I will just use my underwear.

If using softshell I will always carry a superlight pair of Gore-Tex Paclite trousers in my sack in case the wind picks up and the weather gets bad. These weigh very little and pack incredibly small, a model with full-length side zips will allow you to put them on easily over ski boots.

Top Tip

If you unzip your trouser vents in the spring, make sure you put sun cream on your legs. I have burnt an inch-wide strip down my thigh on a number of occasions when forgetting to do this.

Top half

I will use my top half layering to regulate my temperature throughout the day. The system I prefer is to layer up progressively, with multiple layers, that way I don't have to take an outer layer off to add an inner layer so losing heat; this is also very time-consuming.

Again remember ... no cotton (see above).

I will start with a base layer, usually merino wool, as per the bottom half. This is great for regulating temperature and it doesn't smell like a synthetic garment on multi-day trips. The one drawback with merino is that it doesn't wick moisture away from your body as well as a synthetic fabric, but luckily those clever designer-types are starting to combine merino and synthetic fibres to produce wicking, low-smell fabrics.

Softshell jacket
and trousers.

Synthetic insulated
jacket with a hood.

Down jacket.

I will layer a hooded softshell on top of this. When going uphill through much of the season this is all I will need, as the hood keeps any weather off and helps regulate temperature. The softshell will keep out wind and light snow and be breathable enough for most output. In the spring when it is much warmer I will often add a lightweight Pertex-style windtop to my pack which I can wear on top of my base layer when skinning, as a softshell can often be too hot. A chest pocket is really useful for carrying navigation tools.

On top of the softshell I will have a Gore-Tex jacket; this offers weather protection but also adds warmth. I would usually choose an Active Shell or Paclite product that would be breathable, lightweight and packable. A good hood is essential. I would then add a synthetic insulation layer to this which I can pull on over everything else; this should also have a hood, which makes a huge difference to the warmth of a garment.

If I'm out on really cold days, I would also add a down jacket, this may seem excessive but I have been out skiing in sub -20°C in December and needed to wear every item described above.

Extremities

Hands – I will always have a minimum of two pairs of gloves with me, a thin pair for skinning and a thick pair for skiing, and if it's likely to be really cold I will add a pair of mitts into my sack.

I would shy away from glove models that are designed to be their own layering system as your hands will invariably get sweaty and damp, so having a completely dry pair of gloves to put on for the ski down is really nice. You would also have all your eggs in one basket, which would be a disaster if you dropped a glove when you have all the elements of the system together. If it is really cold I will add thin liner gloves inside a pair of mitts.

Thin gloves, thick
gloves and mitts.

A good pair of sun glasses protecting the eyes from reflected light.

Like socks, good gloves cost more, cheap gloves wear out really quickly and their fingers never seem to be human shaped.

Head – A warm hat for the cold and a sun hat for protection on bright days will cover most things. I usually add a headband to keep my ears warm when skiing on intermediate days, which I receive no end of stick for, but I like it. A buff is pretty useful as it can be used as so many different items of headwear or as a neck warmer. On super-cold days I will often add a fleece neck warmer.

Eyes – No matter what the conditions, you need to protect your eyes from harmful UV radiation, which means sun glasses on good days and goggles when the weather isn't so friendly.

Many people wear glasses for the up and goggles for the down. Goggles generally mist really badly if you are working hard in ascent due to the lack of airflow. Glasses steam up less, but on the descent you may be worried about planting your head in the snow and glasses take ages to clean and may get damaged. It's a decision you will have to make. No matter what you choose make sure the lenses cut out 100% of UV light, this is standard in all glasses with a CE mark.

When choosing eyewear there are four categories of protection, these represent the amount of light that is allowed to pass through the lens. Category 0 is the lowest with a clear lens and Category 4 is the darkest, which lets so little light through that they aren't really safe for driving. Goggles use the same category system. I would suggest not using anything less than Category 3 on snow.

In flat light, when the snow is difficult to see, having a yellow/orange lens can help. I always carry a second pair of glasses with orange lenses, which also serve as a spare pair of glasses and give me much better vision in poor light. My goggles also have yellow/orange lenses.

With glasses, and even more so goggles, you get what you pay for. Don't be surprised if the cheap single lens goggles you bought steam up continuously; spend a bit of money and you won't regret it. I always remember the first pair of expensive goggles I bought. I think my skiing improved by 20% as I could read the different types of snow and choose more precisely where to turn.

Helmets – Love them or hate them, there is no doubt that if you have a helmet on you are less likely to suffer a head injury in a crash or avalanche. If you are in any ski area, you will see that more and more people are skiing with helmets on. If you think about all the other outdoor activities we do, such as climbing, biking and kayaking we don't think twice about wearing a

Ski rucksack.

helmet, then we ski at high speed through trees, boulders and other skiers just wearing a woolly hat for protection. Given no penalty we would all wear one, a bit like an airbag rucksack. There are of course negatives to consider, helmets are very warm which is great when off-piste skiing in December, but not so good when skinning in early May. The end result for me is that I wear one quite a lot when I am skiing from lifts, but don't take it when doing longer tours because of the hassle of carrying it on my pack when skinning. I haven't found a helmet yet that didn't restrict my hearing when skiing down-hill, a feedback mechanism that I really like when reading challenging snow.

Rucksack – We have already discussed airbag and Avalung rucksacks. You can use any rucksack for ski touring as long as it is big enough to carry all your kit. It may be useful to have a smaller pack for off-piste skiing and non-glacial tours, then a bigger pack for glacial tours and hut-to-hut touring.

The pack will need to be big enough for your avalanche safety kit, spare clothes and your share of the group safety kit, on non-glacial days. On a glacial tour you will need space to add the rope and crevasse rescue kit (though this should be carried on your harness).

Life is much easier if you can fit everything inside the pack. This way you are less likely to lose it or have any embarrassing hang-ups on lifts. A sack of 25–30 litres will easily be big enough for non-glacial day trips, and 30–35 litres works well for everything else. The only time I have gone larger was skiing in polar regions where I needed the extra capacity for down clothing. If you are doing North American-style camping trips you will probably need some more space as well.

When looking at ski pack design I would consider the stability of the pack on your back. Load the pack in the shop with some weight and jump about, if the sack feels unstable in the shop it will affect your skiing on the hill. This is why ski sacks are a different shape to general mountain packs to create the stability. Closure is often with a big rainbow-style zip which makes it easier to pack and arrange all the weight where you want it. They also allow quick access so you don't have to rummage about like you do with a top loading sack. A pocket on the waist belt is perfect for carrying sun cream, lip salve and quick snacks to eat on the move.

Safety pocket on a ski pack.

I find a pack with a separate safety pocket where your shovel and probe can live is really useful. This keeps them instantly accessible; every second counts if someone is buried in an avalanche.

The final key feature for me is the ability to carry skis. You may think that you aren't planning any ski mountaineering, but there is always an occasion when you will need to carry your skis. Even the walk from the bottom of the Vallée Blanche to the train is more comfortable with your skis on your back.

Mike Austin carries his skis diagonally on the Trou de la Mouche, Aravis.

A frame ski carry. The author in the Mont Blanc Massif.

There are two main systems, one where the skis slide through a large loop at the base of the pack and then sit diagonally across the pack and are secured by a second, upper strap. This is the quickest and easiest loading method. The alternative system is the traditional A frame style where a ski is strapped to either side of the pack joined together at the top. You can then strap your poles on as well if you need to.

Group kit

If you are heading out for a day of off-piste skiing or touring there are some basic items of group kit that you should take with you in addition to your personal avalanche kit. If you are planning to ski on a glacier then you will need to add the two ropes and sets of crevasse rescue gear mentioned earlier.

First aid kit – (see Appendices). This doesn't have to be elaborate but some basic first aid kit between you is essential. Simple things can make a huge difference in the backcountry.

Group shelter – This is a piece of nylon fabric which looks a bit like a tent flysheet, in the event of an emergency the shelter can be pulled over the top of the group to get out of the weather. This can just be for shelter or to treat a casualty. They are surprisingly warm and pack pretty small. They come in a variety of sizes according to the number of people who should fit inside. Two, four or eight person shelters are pretty standard.

Duvet jacket – Having one extra item of really warm clothing is very useful, if a person does twist a knee and needs to wait for assistance they will get very cold, very quickly.

Spares kit – A few items of spares/repair kit are always useful should you damage a binding or a skin. A roll of cotton tape, the kind used by physios for strapping injuries is great; it stays sticky when cold unlike duct tape which goes brittle and loses stickiness in the cold. I will always have some rubber ski straps, cable ties and a Leatherman or other multi-tool to adjust any binding issues. A spare pole basket is always really useful as well.

6mm cord – I always carry 5m of 6mm cord which can be used for crevasse rescue or repairs, but also can be really useful when skiing in flat light (details later).

Scraper and wax – It's useful to carry a metal scraper and block of glide wax in case your skins are balling up. You can buy a special product called Glop Stopper but a small block of glide wax will do the same job.

Group kit.

Scraper and Glop
Stopper wax.

Communication – A mobile phone (switched off, see avalanche rescue section) with the phone numbers of the local rescue services. You can dial 112 but help will be faster if you can dial the appropriate people direct. If you are touring out of line of sight of a ski lift you may not be able to get phone reception. It is often better to assume no reception then be pleasantly surprised if you get any. If you are doing a lot of touring to remote places then it may be worth considering a satellite phone or a radio. These are becoming more and more accessible in price and smaller in size.

An alternative to direct communication is something like an EPIRB, which is a satellite rescue beacon, originally designed for sailors. These are now so small that they can easily be carried in the mountains. When activated they send out a signal which is detected by satellite, and the distress signal then sent to a rescue coordination station. The beacons are usually identifiable, so the rescue centre will know who is in trouble, and will then coordinate a rescue.

An alternative is something like a Spot Personal Tracker and Satellite GPS Messenger, which does the same job as an EPIRB but allows you to send simple messages and only costs just over £100 (2014) (some may need a service contract).

The rest

Day trips

So you have all the basics now, safety kit, ski kit and group kit. There are a few extras that I also always take along.

Sun cream – A high factor sun cream is essential even on dull days, which are often the best conditions for getting burnt. Protection for lips is essential with the same high factor, lip-specific cream tastes better but smearing standard cream works as well. Remember to do the inside of your bottom lip, this is a classic ski touring burn point when you are breathing hard going uphill. It is worth having some lip salve in your sack for application as soon as you have finished skiing, as this can often make the difference between cracked lips and not.

Top Tip

Applying the cream at least 20 minutes before exposure to the sun definitely increases its effectiveness. Keep a tube of cream in your pocket so you can re-apply easily throughout the day.

Liquid – Dehydration is always an issue in the mountains in summer and in winter. It is really easy to become dehydrated in winter, when it is cold and you don't notice how much you are sweating and don't feel much like drinking. The air is very dry in the Alps and you are losing moisture with every breath, so you need to keep taking on fluid regularly throughout the day.

Depending on the time of year I will carry a flask with warm juice or tea, or a one litre Nalgene-style bottle (plastic wide neck). In the spring when it is warm I will complement this with a one litre collapsible container. This increases my water-carrying capacity but takes up virtually no space in my sack when empty.

I am not a fan of the bladder and hose-style hydration systems, as they always seem to freeze with or without insulation round the tube, and not so easy to monitor the quantity you drink or have left. Once the hose has frozen it is incredibly difficult to get any fluid out of the bladder, and it is also really easy to catch the mouthpiece on something which can cause the liquid to leak everywhere.

A small but powerful
headtorch.

Multi-day tours

If I'm heading out overnight or for a few days I will add a few extra bits of kit and beef up my spares kit.

Headtorch – Even if this is not for skiing with, you may need to find the toilet in the hut in darkness, many huts do not have electricity throughout the night. Modern units using LED lights give a huge amount of light for their size and the batteries last a long time. Choose a model that you could ski with if you had to. If heading out for a week-long hut-to-hut trip I will generally put in new batteries rather than carrying spares.

Sleeping bag liner – Most huts require you to have a sleeping bag liner to use under their blankets or duvet, this is for hygiene reasons. Hygiene for the other users and hygiene for you as well. A silk model, although more expensive, packs incredibly small in your sack.

Socks – I always take at least one spare pair of socks just so I have a dry pair to change into at the hut.

Change of top – It is really nice to be able to change your top when you arrive at the hut. It makes you feel warmer as even if your base layer is dry it will still be encrusted with sweat. I usually just take a cotton or merino T-shirt with me; the merino is particularly good as you can use it as an extra layer if it is cold, and is lighter.

Spares kit – There is a full list in the Appendices.

On longer tours I would add the following to my spares kit:

- Araldite glue, in case I need to glue a binding screw back in.

- More cable ties.

- Some wire and a long strap.

- A Fritschi toe piece (only if there was a pair in the party) – they are very easy to replace in the field and a nightmare to cobble together if you don't have a spare.

- Extra transceiver batteries. I often carry a spare transceiver at least in the car.

- Emergency skin glue.

- Skin waterproofing.

Alternative ski/board kit

All the kit we have looked at so far has been relating to alpine technique in descent, but everything we will look at in the rest of the book can be done on Telemark ski kit or on a split snowboard. It is worth looking at what the latest thoughts are on choosing these bits of kit if you do either of these disciplines.

Telemark kit

Telemark kit has gone through a revolution in recent years; gone are the days of skinny skis and leather boots, now they have well-designed plastic boots, bigger skis and strong bindings to drive them. The big change from a touring perspective is the development of the free pivot binding, which permits the binding to pivot at the toe when in touring mode, allowing for easy kick turns and a touring action just like an alpine touring binding. This can then be locked into place to give stiffness in the boot platform for driving the ski in descent. There are also now models available from G3, Voile and Black Diamond that allow the use of ski crampons.

The only real disadvantage to touring in Telemark kit is that when you take your skis off the shape of the toe of the boot makes them more difficult to mountaineer in, and you need to make sure your boot crampons will fit the flexible boot. This has been addressed by the development of the NTN binding which allows a shorter toe section. These are a big development as they have great downhill performance as well comfort in ascent. It is worth thinking about a ski crampon system if you choose this system as they are not easily available yet.

Alexey Gorbatenkov skis Telemark in the Russian Arctic.

When touring on Telemark kit in a mixed group you also need to be aware that the binding spares are different from alpine touring bindings, so you need to source spare parts and know how to service your bindings on the hill.

Telemark kit with ski crampons.

Snowboards

Snowboards are becoming more popular in the backcountry. Traditionally if snowboarders wanted to go touring they had to use snow shoes, but since then splitboards have been developed which have got better and better. The latest versions are really easy to use, allowing the boarder to skin uphill using all the same techniques as a skier, then turn the bindings through 180 degrees and board down normally. Latest models have ski crampons available so you can go anywhere a skier can go, they are just a bit wide to fit in many skin tracks.

Duncan McCallum demonstrates the versatility of the Phantom splitboard system.

One of the traditional drawbacks is that snowboard boots are soft which is very comfortable, but are difficult to move around in without the board, as you can't kick into the snow easily. There are some systems out there that permit the use of a hard Dynafit-style boot and tech bindings for ascent which allows for an extremely versatile system. The Phantom splitboard binding is the best I have seen so far.

Packing your kit

When you assemble your kit ready for a ski tour you need to go through it meticulously and ask the question, "Do I really need that?" As you get more experienced you will be able to fine-tune what you need. If you are struggling to get all your kit in your pack you almost certainly have too much.

When buying kit think about its bulk and weight as well as its functionality. For example if you buy a lightweight thin Gore-Tex jacket (like Paclite) it will take up very little room in your pack, but if you have a heavy-duty jacket it will fill your pack. Look at the weather forecast and pack appropriately. If it's warm you don't need a down jacket and mitts, if it's cold you will have lots of clothes on but one big extra layer may be really useful.

As you are packing think about the order you will need things in, and pack accordingly. Group shelter and first aid kit can go at the bottom, then layer kit with the next least likely thing you will need on top. When packing, stuff soft items into the gaps, the smaller and more compact your sack the more comfortable it will be to ski with.

Laying your kit out can help identify anything that is missing.

Downhill Skills

Alison Thacker

Introduction

Alison Thacker
demonstrates
great technique
skiing in Bruson.

The key to skiing off-piste is to understand that it involves many different ways of skiing. Variable conditions mean that a variety of different techniques are needed. Off-piste can be anything from knee-deep powder to rock-hard ice and everything in between. They all require different techniques. Sadly the vision of off-piste skiing always being light, fluffy powder is not a realistic one. However, with the right skills all types of snow can be enjoyable. For ski touring the aim is to have efficient and effective technique for the down-hill sections so that energy levels can be maintained over long descents and for skinning uphill.

This chapter answers some of the commonly asked questions about skiing off-piste and then goes on to give some guidance for skiing in the various snow types.

Frequently asked questions

Most questions that are asked about off-piste skiing can be answered by, "It depends". The answer will depend on variables such as snow type, the level of skier, speed of travel and the steepness of the slope. These are questions that I commonly get asked that don't always have definitive answers. The answers given will get you thinking about what to do and when. You will then have the ability to play around with different variables depending on the conditions.

How far apart should my skis be?

"I have always been trying to keep my feet close together in the off-piste. When I tried putting them a little further apart I discovered I was more stable and more comfortable travelling faster."

This will vary depending on the terrain and snow but a good guide is to stand in the position that you find it easiest to balance in, without it being too strenuous. There will be some compromise in achieving this. The most efficient position to stand in is how you would stand normally, without ski boots on; with your feet hip-width apart. However when skiing off-piste this position doesn't always provide enough stability. It is easier to balance with your feet further apart (imagine a goal keeper and their dynamic stance) but this is strenuous. Does a goalkeeper stand like that for the whole match? If you stand with your feet close together it will be harder to balance when the terrain is uneven. When more stability is needed your feet should be further apart. When you find the going easier (smooth sections, spring snow) the feet can come closer together. The key is to adapt your stance throughout the day in order to keep the strength in your legs for when you need it.

Narrow stance.

Wide stance.

Where should my weight be – forward or back?

Your weight should be centred over the middle of the ski so that subtle adjustments can be made forward and back as needed. But where is the centre? A good reference point to stay centred on your skis is to be able to gently feel your shins touching the front of your boots, but also feel your heel on the bottom of your boot. A common mistake is to have an image of a static skier when thinking of a skier that is in balance. Instead this image should be a dynamic one with the skier moving as they respond to the terrain. Think of 'balancing' rather than 'being balanced'. You will need to bend and stretch joints in order to remain centred as the terrain changes.

Top Tip

Increase your range of skills and become adaptable with them. Spend time practising these skills on the piste too, so they can be applied effectively when they are needed.

Where should my
weight be?

Maintain a good
central position.

Keep a good central
position as the terrain
becomes uneven.

How do I keep my weight centred when my rucksack is pulling me back?

Ideally the angle of your back should be the same as the angle of your lower leg; tilted slightly forward. If you ski in a more upright position then you will feel that your rucksack is pulling you back. This tilt is easier to maintain if you engage your core muscles. It is also important that both legs flex (check to see that it is not just your upper one). If your lower leg is straight when you hit a bump you will get thrown backwards. You might get away with this normally but you get away with very little with a rucksack on your back!

Good balance with a rucksack on and off-piste.

"I prefer to do longer turns. For a long time I tried keeping my body facing down the hill when doing them. Once I let my body face where I was going (across the slope) I instantly felt more stable and balanced."

Should the upper body face downhill?

The upper body should face the direction of momentum. If travelling across the slope then the body should face across the slope, for instance in longer turns. When doing shorter turns down the slope, for example in a narrow couloir, and momentum is going down the slope, the body should also point down the slope.

Body facing across the slope.

Body facing down the slope.

How much weight should be on each ski?

"For years I have thought I need to do more with my inside ski. But by becoming more balanced on my outside ski my inside ski is now able to do more!"

This will vary depending on the snow type, the shape of the turn, type of ski and the steepness of the slope. Let's think of two extremes. If you are pointing straight down a slope your weight will be split equally between the two skis. If you are traversing across the slope you will have most of your weight on the lower ski. The further round the corner you come when turning the more balanced you should be on the outside (downhill) ski. Unless taking a direct line, which might be the case in powder or slush, you should be more dominant on the outside ski to stay in balance even if the weight is split 51%, 49%. Skiers often ski further round the corner to reduce speed (across, or up the slope). This is when it's key to remember to stay balanced over the outside ski. The body needs to be tilted over the outside ski to balance on it.

Top Tip

Counting as you go round the turn can be an effective but simple way to maintain a rhythm and ensure one turn links fluidly into the next.

Weight balanced equally over both skis.

Weight balanced on outside ski (yellow line indicates tilt in upper body).

People say, "Edge more". Is this correct?

Sometimes it can be, but on ice this can be a mistake. If you increase the edge angle on ice you will push the skis out from underneath you and be tilting them away from the point where the edge bites most. You need to remain balanced over the top of them. Edging skis also causes the skis to accelerate. If you require speed then use a large edge angle. A flatter ski is better for turning without gathering so much speed. Try it – go across a slope with minimal edge. Then increase the edge angle and feel the increase in speed. Skiers often struggle to ski with less edge tilt. To ski with more edge we allow our knees and hips to move away from the ski. To ski with less edge keep the knees on top of the skis. Imagine that you don't want anyone to see the bases of your skis.

Small edge angle.

Flat ski.

Large edge angle.

Using a medium edge angle for acceleration.

Is side slipping really skiing?

Yes, side slipping is a very important technique for travelling from A to B. Advanced skiers often have to relearn side slipping in order to progress further. When skiing on ice side slipping can be an integral part of linking one turn into the next and slowing your speed.

It can be done smoothly and gracefully so that it feels like skiing. Gradually release the edges of the skis so the skis become flatter and let them drift sideways down the hill while they remain perpendicular to the slope. If you find yourself drifting forwards then the tips need to be turned further up the hill. If you find yourself drifting backwards the tips need to be turned further down the hill. Practise side slipping in a straight line, and diagonally forwards and backwards so that you can manoeuvre through all types of terrain by side slipping.

Side slipping is also an essential skill for ski touring to allow you to travel on terrain that you might not be able to otherwise. It would be a shame to miss a six day ski tour because of a 20m section that you didn't want to turn on.

Side slipping.

How far ahead do you look when skiing off-piste?

Normally the primary focus should be looking into the next turn, but the wider field of vision will take in the terrain that is further ahead; very similar to driving. Look too far ahead and connection with the skis and feet will be lost. Look down too much and you'll not see what is coming up. In poor visibility or flat light the focus should change from what you can see to what you can feel. Try to feel the terrain underneath your feet.

Looking ahead.

I ski really well on-piste but struggle as soon as I get off-piste. Why is this?

It's normally a combination of three things: fitness; using only one technique; physiological issues that have arisen from the environment. Muscles work much harder to keep balancing as you ski over uneven terrain than they ever will do on the piste. Very specific fitness training is needed to prepare the muscles for this. On the piste we tend to get very good at using one technique. In the off-piste we need to get used to changing what we do to adapt to the conditions. A good off-piste skier will be a versatile one. Using positive mental imagery is a good way to help cope with challenging situations. When you have completed a good turn, log it away so that it can be replayed in the future.

What should I do if I need to turn in a small space, such as before an obstacle?

"I always used to struggle with jump turns. I don't need to battle with them anymore as now I can pivot my skis on the snow with far less effort."

Imagine if you were going to park your car in a small space; you would drive into it slowly. It is the same with turning in tight spaces; it needs to be done slowly. The actual manoeuvre might be quick but the speed being carried at the time is slow. The trick is not to gather the speed in the first place (see next page). Most people gather speed when they turn, it's natural. Spend time practising small turns where you don't pick up any speed. We rarely do this. As you'll discover when practising these turns you don't get anywhere very fast! Remember, turning using a flatter ski will mean you pick up less speed and having your skis on a large edge angle will cause acceleration.

You'll see people use a jump turn in this situation. In a jump turn you go from facing one way to facing the other without picking up speed. With a bit of practice the same thing can be achieved while keeping your skis on the ground. This is far more efficient and less risky than a jump turn.

Smiling always helps.

Top Tip

Skiers often struggle in off-piste conditions because they do what they have always done; only doing it more aggressively or more passively making it even more difficult. Rather than do more or less remember to do something different. If it's not working, change it.

How to turn without gathering speed

- Unweight the downhill ski.

- Flatten the skis so that as much of the base as possible is in contact with the snow. Moving the hips over the skis will help to achieve this.

- Once the skis are flat they can be rotated 180 degrees to point the other way. This rotation comes from both the hip and ankle joint.

- Using a strong pole plant will aid the flattening and rotation. Pole plant towards the back of the bindings, to help keep the body pointing down the hill (as shown in photo).

- Visualise the line on which the tips of the skis are going to rotate and aim to turn your skis within a box the size of your skis.

It can be helpful to practise the movement without your skis on.

Turn initiation with pole plant near back of binding.

End of the turn.

How to cope with different snow conditions in the off-piste environment

This section gives a few pointers that will assist in becoming more efficient in changing snow types.

Before setting off it is helpful to be able to predict what the conditions will be like. Then you can start thinking about the way in which you'll need to ski. For example, has the snow frozen overnight? When did it last snow? Will lots of people have skied it already? How windy has it been?

Deep powder

Powder will be enjoyed most if your skis float through it. This requires speed; imagine a water skier. Speed is needed for the skis to float on the water. Try and maintain speed around the turn; the snow will provide enough resistance for you to feel comfortable with the speed if you take your own line.

- Increase the flex at the knee allowing your weight to come more over the heels, but keep contact with the front of your boot to stop your weight coming 'back'. This will allow the tips of the skis to come out of the snow whilst remaining in control of them. If taking a more direct line then the weight will become more even over both skis.

- Using a strong pole plant will help to initiate the turn in powder.

- Although in powder we will still be balanced on the outside ski if turning away from the fall line, we want to feel that we are 'bouncing' or pushing with both skis.

Skiing powder.

Good posture in powder.

Chopped up powder

A wider stance can help maintain balance in this snow, but not so wide that each ski travels through different snow. For example if one ski goes through untracked powder, that ski will stall whilst the other ski accelerates. Try and anticipate any change of speed caused by the uneven resistance of the snow. Use bending and stretching of the legs to react to the change, as opposed to flexing from the waist.

Engaging your core muscles will ensure that you can react to the changes in terrain.

Similar to skiing in deep powder, turning with some speed will help the skis to cut through the snow. This speed can be lost after the turn by turning further up the hill. Then let the skis point down the slope and pick up speed again before going into the next turn. Using a pole plant (down-slope of you) will initiate an early edge change and help commit to the next turn. A small jump to change the edges will help bring the skis to the surface if the snow is really thick.

Skiing chopped powder.

Bumps (moguls)

When ski touring, bumps are found more frequently than people think. They will appear whenever it hasn't snowed for a while in an area where many skiers are funnelled into a narrow channel. A good example of this is on the Vallée Blanche in Chamonix.

The technique used to ski bumps is the opposite from skiing in powder and chopped up powder. Try and turn without gathering too much speed, allowing control to be maintained throughout the bumps. Turn on, or near, the top of the bump to give the skis space to pivot without applying too much edge. Remember edging will cause the skis to accelerate in an arc.

Then slide down the back of the bump demonstrating another reason why side slipping is important. From the top of the bump you will also get a view of where to go next!

Visualise the line that you want to take through the bumps. When one turn is finished a side slip can be used to get to the correct place for the next turn. Using a side slip allows progression through the bumps without gathering speed.

Top Tip

Using a snow plough is often an effective way to cope in difficult snow. It can help reduce the risk of injury at the end of a long, hard day.

Turn on top of the bump.

Spring snow

Spring snow is one of the most enjoyable types of snow to ski and skiers rarely struggle on it. This is where all your piste skills can be applied. Stand up tall, use a slightly narrower stance, and link smooth turns flowing from one into the next. Alternatively you can go for a wider stance, increase the edge angle and carve your way down it.

Ian Vokes spring snow skiing in the Queyras.

Ice

Icy slopes will often be encountered first thing in the morning when descending from a hut. It might be dark and your body will not be warmed up so it's worth gaining confidence on this type of snow. As with skiing bumps the turns want to be done without gathering speed. This is achieved by using a flatter ski.

If stood contemplating doing a turn then it's probably not the place to do one. That's the time to side slip, making progress down the slope until you feel comfortable to turn. Side slipping is a good thing!

Keep the downhill leg soft by keeping the knee flexed to reduce any juddering from the ice. Have your arms wider apart to assist with balance.

Crust

Firstly try and keep the skis on the surface by being light and spreading your weight equally between both feet. Imagine you are skiing on eggshells.

If you break through the crust your technique needs to change dramatically. You then need to be aggressive to push the snow out of the way as you go round the turn. Imagine that you are trying to disturb it, break it up as much as possible and move it out your way. Often this is easier to achieve by deliberately placing your uphill ski on its new edge to form a triangle. This could be referred to as a snowplough or a stem, but what's important is the deliberate action of placing the ski on its new edge to initiate the turn.

Using a little jump to change the edges of the skis can help start the turn, as sometimes it is difficult to change the edges of the skis when under the surface of the snow. To initiate the jump sink down and then spring up off the snow, rather than trying to lift your skis up from the snow.

Lastly, downhill kick turns are your get out of jail free card for crust snow conditions. They should be used at the point where you feel you can do nothing to make your skis turn. Forcing a turn in that situation may cause injury. However, downhill kick turns should be used with caution. If they are carried out on a steep slope there is a serious risk of falling head first down the slope. Keep them for the easy-angled slopes.

- Stand perpendicular to the slope.

- Turn your bottom ski around so that it is placed parallel to the uphill ski with your boots as close together as possible.

- Transfer your weight so that you are balanced on the downhill ski.

- Now bring your top ski around.

Skiing crust.

- Place poles out of the way, but so they assist with balance.

Downhill kick turn.
Photo – Andy Perkins.

Slush

The best techniques for slush are very similar to those needed for crust, as the principle is the same; your skis are stuck under the snow and the snow needs to be moved. A small jump can help to bring your skis to the surface to change the edges. A wider stance will help with balancing when jumping and initiating the edge change. Maintaining speed throughout the turn will help the skis to glide through the slush. Similar to skiing in powder, you will feel the weight come more over the heels, but ensure the shin is still in contact with the front of the boot.

Steep and narrow

Although this is not a snow type it is something that skiers commonly ask about. You can find all of the above snow types on steep and narrow slopes. This is when the appropriate skills will need to be blended together. For example, if the slope intimidates you then you should aim to turn without gathering too much speed. However, if there is powder you might need a little speed to allow your skis to float through the snow.

A common misconception is that jump turns need to be mastered for skiing steep slopes. Sometimes you might find a small spring helpful to initiate the turn or to get the skis to the surface, but jumping is a high risk manoeuvre, not ideal for steep slopes.

Turning without gathering speed needs to be mastered. In places where you might want to use jump turns there is usually a far more effective, efficient and safe way to turn that gets exactly the same result, going from pointing one way to pointing the other without picking up any speed. The technique is the same as for turning in small spaces; pivot a flat ski.

If you have the ability to turn without gathering much speed you will feel more confident on anything steep, icy, narrow, bumpy and in trees.

Top Tip

There's no such thing as bad habits off-piste, only we need more habits.

Kate Scott skiing
the Couloir Banane,
La Grave.

Uhill Skills

Skinning is the essence of ski touring; it's the use of skins and touring bind-ings that free us from mechanised uplift. We are going to look at how you fit skins, then use them to make upward progress. We are also going to cover fitting and using ski crampons, choosing a line, changing direction, and then as the terrain changes we will look at fitting and using crampons and an ice axe. We will then cover how to carry your skis on your pack, along with common problems associated with going uphill.

Skinning

Attaching skins

Having made sure you have the correctly trimmed skins that belong to your skis we can then have a look at attaching them. I did have a comedy incident one day when we were outside a hut fitting skins, when a client, who is an experienced ski tourer, said she had a problem, her skins had shrunk in the night. The problem seemed to be solved when she found the right combination of skis and skins.

The most vulnerable part of a skin is the adhesive side; you need to keep this clean and as dry as possible. When you buy a skin they usually come with a waxed paper on the adhesive, peel this off and throw it away, then take the plastic or mesh backing, or 'cheat sheet', out and cut it in half. You can now stick this to the base of the skin, start at one end with the skin sticking up one side of the sheet then fold the skin over and stick down the other side.

Skins folded over backing sheet.

Dry your skis before attaching skins.

If you leave it as one long sheet with a skin on each side, it is much more difficult to pack and deal with in a wind. The backing sheet will protect the glue and doesn't have any detrimental effect on its durability, it also makes the skins easier to handle. When new the glue is really strong, if the skins are left glue to glue they can be really quite difficult to separate.

Now your skins are ready to fit to your skis. Leave your bindings in ski mode with the brakes engaged (if you put the ski into skinning mode first then dropped it, the brakes would not engage and you may lose your ski down the hillside). Dry the base with a glove; if the sun is out sit the ski with the base facing the sun, this will dry and heat it making the glue stick better.

When you are ready, start at the end dictated by the skin attachment system, peel the cheat sheet off the skin just ahead of where you are sticking the skin to ski. Stick the skin to the ski, making sure that you can see both metal edges down each side of the skin and smooth it against the ski with your hand as you go, making sure there are no air bubbles. Keep going to the end of the skin. If there is no clip just smooth off the end; if there is a clip, attach it then run your hand down the length of the skin in the direction of the hairs. This will ensure the skin is stuck along the full length of the ski. I always think giving it a bit of a rub helps the glue warm up and stick better. Change the bindings to skinning mode and you are good to go.

Attaching skins.

Top Tip

If it's a really cold day stick the skin down your jacket to warm it up before applying it to the ski. If you are taking your skins off for a short descent before skinning up again, just ski with them stuffed in your jacket so they are quick and easy to put on at the bottom.

Taking skins off

Looking after the glue on the skins is every bit as important when taking the skins off as when putting them on. You may have your skins on and off a number of times in a day, so you want to make sure the glue hasn't got wet or dirty. Take the ski off and before you do anything else, engage the brakes so the ski can't take off as soon as the skin is removed. I find it easiest to do the next bit with the ski lying base side up on the snow.

Brush any snow off the skin, then detach the clip if there is one or lift the tail if not, unpeel the skin attaching the backing sheet as you unpeel. As you get to the end of the backing sheet just flip the skin over and keep on going. Press the skin onto the backing sheet and put in its bag or your sack (I usually leave the bag at home as will end up losing it otherwise) out of the way so it can't get covered in snow. This system seems to work pretty well in a wind so you don't end up with the skin wrapped round you.

Taking skins off.

Skin care

You need to look after your skins if you want them to last a long time. When you get home or to a hut in the evening, make sure you dry the skins out. This shouldn't be done using direct heat, but just hang them up somewhere warm and let the air circulate round them. In huts make sure they are clearly marked as yours, as there will be a lot of skins that look the same.

Drying skins.

Do not be tempted to dry your skins on the ski, if they get warm in the sun the glue can transfer to the ski, and the only way to get it off is with acetone.

Over time the waterproof coating on the fibres wears off, which increases the friction of the skin when gliding, so it is worth treating the skin with a product like Skin Proof. This is a silicon-based liquid that you coat the fibres with then allow to dry, which re-proofs the skin making balling up of wet snow less likely and reducing the chance of the skin becoming wet. This is a particular problem if you have a big temperature difference as you gain height. If the skin becomes wet and then you skin into colder dry snow, the cold snow will stick to the skin making progress very difficult.

Skins balling up.

If this does happen on the hill it is useful to have a metal scraper handy to take the snow off, then rub some glide wax into the skin to help it slide and reduce the chance of further balling up.

Scrape the snow off and rub on some wax.

Over time the glue on the sticky side will lose its effectiveness; if this happens on a tour wrapping tape round the offending section will usually get you home. If you are on a longer, multi-day tour, using the spray-on emergency glue from the spares kit in the evening will usually solve the problem for the rest of the tour.

Spray-on glue.

None of the above are long-term solutions, but don't worry it is really easy to re-glue a skin. Most specialist shops will do it for you for a surprisingly nominal fee. Alternatively you can do it yourself. Most glues will recommend that you remove the old glue but I have never bothered and have not had any problems. The thought of trying to remove the glue is too horrific. What I would suggest is laying some newspaper on a table and laying out the skin, glue side up, then using an old knife scrape off any bits of dirt, twigs, moss etc. making sure it is completely dry. Then take the pot of skin glue (make sure it is compatible with the glue already on your skin, shops will be able to advise or it will say on the label) then spread a thin layer of glue over the length of the skin and leave it to dry overnight. Job done.

Going uphill

Skinning is one of the most pleasurable ways of going uphill, the length of the ski smoothing out many of the undulations in the landscape allowing a steady rhythm. Although breaking trail can be hard work it is pretty pleasurable compared to breaking trail on foot.

The key to efficient skinning is to never lift your foot; gliding the ski along the ground is much more efficient. If you think of the weight of your ski and multiply by the numbers of times that you lift instead of gliding it you will realise why gliding is the best technique.

Start with your boots in walk mode, if your boots have one (if you are in downhill boots you won't have one, but don't worry). Clip into your bindings and adjust the buckles so you are comfortable. This is totally a matter of personal comfort, I usually skin with my boots undone, other people I ski with regularly have theirs done up. Slide one foot forward, don't take too long a stride at this point, then when your leg is comfortably forward pull your foot back to engage the hairs on the skin, slide the other leg forward and repeat. Practise this wherever you can, concentrate on gliding the ball of your foot along the snow then weighting your foot along the length of the ski.

Glide the ski along the snow, no lifting.

Once you have got a feel for the skin gripping the snow, point the skis up a gentle incline, think about your body position. The most effective position is to have your body in an upright position with your feet shoulder width

Skinning with an
upright body position.

apart. This is stable and will allow you to put your weight through the entire length of the ski. Skin gently uphill, just shuffle round any turns. Concentrate on an upright body position. If your weight is too far forward (most likely), or too far back (less likely), your body weight will be on the front or rear of the ski. As a result not all of the hairs on the skin will engage and the ski will lose traction and shoot out from underneath you.

If I am struggling to get my weight where I want it for maximum grip, I think about having my weight pushing down through my heels; this usually helps to spread my weight along the length of the ski. Your poles should just be for balance, so concentrate on your body position over the ski and everything else will work.

As you feel more comfortable try lengthening your stride. If you are in touring boots and in walk mode you can develop a nice long stride, if in ski boots the forward lean on the boots will limit your stride length. This is the reason that most people eventually swap downhill ski boots for touring boots (that and the weight). If the terrain is difficult you will find yourself taking shorter strides, then on easier ground you can stride out, just experiment to find a stride length that you feel comfortable with and that you can maintain for long periods of time.

Once you feel comfortable skinning around on easier-angled terrain try setting a steeper line to see what you are comfortable with. Try heading across the hillside, if the snow is soft it is easy to make a track, if the snow is hard you will need to roll the skis downhill to get the most contact between skin and snow. The best way to do this is to think about rolling your knees and ankles downhill.

Rolling and edging the
skis to get the best grip.

If the snow is really hard you will need to use a bit of a combination of rolling and edging, and this is why it is essential that the metal edge of the ski is exposed each side of the skin, so it can bite into the snow.

Top Tips for difficult skinning

When you are skinning in a good track with cold snow skinning is easy; in deep, soft snow it's hard work but you can generally go where you want.

In a skinning track that has been exposed to the sun then refrozen, or where the snow is really hard, you will have to use all the techniques described above to get as much skin as possible on the snow. Too much weight forward and the ski will shoot out from under you, while too much weight back and you may start to slide backwards. Too much edge and the ski will slide down the slope or you may end up side stepping.

The balance of rolling the ski to get the most ski contact is the trick; if you find you are exerting too much energy doing this, just stop and put on your ski crampons.

Heel raisers – As the skinning track becomes steeper then the strain on your Achilles tendon and your calves will increase. If you are flexible this is no problem but some people aren't so flexible, so they struggle to keep the weight spread out across the length of their ski because they can't hold an upright body position. If this is happening to you, there are three solutions; in the long term do more stretching, in the short term either take an easier-angled track or put up your heel raisers. Heel raisers work in different ways depending on your binding model; rotate a Dynafit, click up a Fritschi or click down a Marker. The effect is the same; you have deployed a raised platform that your heel can land on, pushing your force along the length of the ski without having to move your foot all the way down onto the ski.

Dynafit heel raiser.

If you do need to use heel raisers please use them or don't use them. Do not continuously switch between using them and not, there is nothing more annoying than skinning behind someone who is constantly engaging and disengaging their heel raisers and wasting loads of time. If you are going to use them engage them and leave them, then take them down when the terrain eases and leave them. Make sure you practise using them so the transition between modes is slick. You will probably find as you do more skinning you will use your heel raisers less. Ski touring is all about efficiency; the amount of time wasted fiddling with heel raisers is incredible.

I generally try not to use them as I find they unbalance me, make kick turns more difficult, and if I am setting a track when using my raisers the track is often too steep for those following. Where I do use my raisers is when I am breaking trail in soft snow, as the angle created by the raisers helps keep your tips up out of the snow.

A further disadvantage is if you are using ski crampons you reduce the effective length of the crampon if your foot stops at a heel raiser.

Top Tips

Solutions to most common skinning problems:

Push your weight through the heel of the boot to spread the load along the full length of the ski.

Slide the ski forward, rather than lifting it. As well as saving energy this helps keep balance.

Keep your body position upright. The most common skinning slip occurs when your weight is too far forward and the skis shoot out behind you.

In hard snow try and carve a line in the snow with the edge of the ski. If this doesn't work stamp down with your heel, then roll your ankles outwards (down the slope) as discussed earlier.

Ski crampons

When the track or the snow gets too hard for the skins to grip effectively, you can either put your skis on your back or fit ski crampons. Because of the way a ski spreads your body weight out across the snow you might not break through the surface with skis on. If you take your skis off to continue on foot then you may find you are constantly breaking through the surface, so it is often much easier to continue with ski crampons on your skis rather than putting your skis on your back.

Fitting ski crampons.

Moving with Dynafit
ski crampons on.

The one classic trap with ski crampons is that you usually leave it too late to put them on, so there is nowhere easy to stop and fit them. Get into the practice of looking ahead and trying to anticipate where you may need them, having another party ahead is always a good indicator. If they are struggling and sliding about, stop and put your ski crampons on well before you get to the point where they are struggling. It is nearly always quicker to stop, put ski crampons on, move across the awkward terrain smoothly and efficiently, then if necessary take them off again, than it is to flail around on the difficult terrain without them.

Using ski crampons

Unless you are on the flat, it is usually easier to fit the crampons to one ski at a time. I find that it is easiest to fit the downhill ski crampon first, once the ski is back on your foot this gives the most stable stance ready to fit the second crampon.

Fit the crampon then replace the ski. Fritschi have a model that you can fit on the binding and flick round into position when required, that works reasonably well. They are a bit more delicate than the old solid versions, and I would suggest taking them off the ski when skiing downhill as they do tend to catch. With a bit of practice it is possible to put Dynafit crampons on without taking your skis off which can save a bit of time.

Once you have both skis back on, make sure you disengage your heel raisers, as they effectively shorten the length of the crampon, but leave the binding in walk mode. You will now need to lift the ski and crampon with every step. The design of the Dynafit crampon means that you don't need to do much lifting, as the crampon just flops along on the surface of the snow.

If you are finding that the snow is really hard you may need a gentle stamp of the foot to set the crampon into the snow. By rolling your ankle down the slope as you are skinning, you will engage the outside teeth on the crampon as well as the inside ones increasing your security.

Moving with flick-out
Fritschi ski crampons.

Top Tip

> If there is just a short section of hard snow to cross put the basket of your ski pole under the mid point of your ski and stand on it forcing the tip down into the snow. You can lean your ski against this for support while you move your uphill foot to do the same thing. For a short section this can save you putting on ski crampons.

Cornering

Changing direction when skinning takes practice, it goes hand in hand with choosing a good line on the hillside, which we will look at later in this chapter.

Step turn

On easy-angled snow you can change direction by making small steps around a bend, this uses much less energy and is much easier than a kick turn but it is limited by the steepness of the slope and hardness of the snow. You will find that the steepness of slope you are able to step turn on will depend on the type of snow. You can shuffle round the corner on much steeper ground in soft snow or on a grippy track than you can on hard snow, where you may want to kick turn, as the skins may lose traction part way through the turn and cause you to slip.

Classic step turn.

Kick turn

Love them or hate them they are part of ski touring that you can't avoid, so the faster you learn how to do them quickly and efficiently, the more fun you will have on the hill. When referring to kick turns in the rest of the book I mean the uphill kick turn we are about to look at, as opposed to the downhill kick turn covered in the downhill chapter. There are a number of kick turn techniques, some of which I can't even achieve in the comfort and privacy of my own home. What follows is a method that works for me and is the most common method you will see. Make sure you practise this somewhere where it won't matter if you fall off; part way up the Col du Chardonnet on day one of the Haute Route is not the place to learn. Practise all the elements so they all feel natural, then put it all together so it is nice and smooth. A kick turn should not be an intimidating thing. If it is, you need to practise more in a safe place.

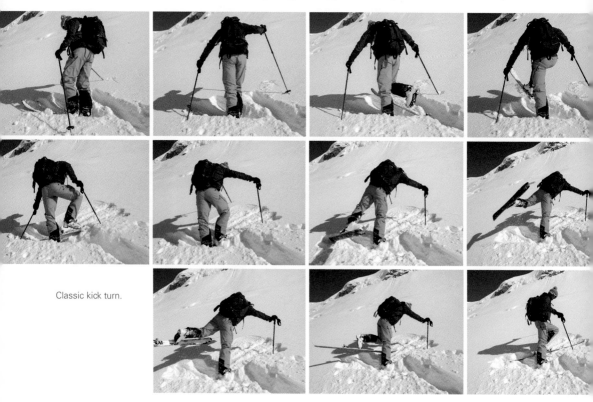

Classic kick turn.

To start a kick turn it is essential to have a stable platform. When setting a track I will level off into the horizontal before creating my platform. The platform should be horizontal so that you won't slide off it forwards or backwards. Make the horizontal platform longer than the space you need for the kick turn, then when you set off on the next section your skins will be biting on an easy-angled track to begin with. In soft snow you can just stamp a good platform, but it becomes more difficult as the snow gets harder. In really hard snow or in exposed places I will sometimes cut a ledge with an ice axe or a shovel (you don't need to take your skis off to do this) to provide a good solid platform for less confident skiers to use.

Now you have a good platform, position your top pole towards the rear of the top ski and the bottom pole towards the front of the downhill ski. This will give stability and keep your poles out of the way. On a steeper slope having the top pole positioned slightly uphill can give extra stability, but make sure there is enough clearance to get your ski round.

Move your weight so that it is on the downhill ski and lift the uphill ski off the ground. Cock this uphill leg back slightly, then swing it forward up and rotate it so that it lands parallel to the downhill ski but facing in the opposite direction. This feels easiest if done as a single dynamic motion, letting the momentum carry the ski through the turn. The closer and more horizontal your two skis end up (facing opposite directions) the easier the next step will be.

Reposition your downhill pole onto the uphill side, making sure there is enough space to get your second ski round, then transfer your weight to the uphill ski. The most common problem people have is rushing this step, or having their feet too far apart, so reposition your feet if necessary, then transfer the weight.

With your weight on the uphill ski, lift the downhill ski off the ground, let it settle, then hold your leg out slightly to the side, so that the ski is completely clear of the snow. Give a gentle kick with your heel if necessary, just enough to flick the tip of the ski up. As it does this, steer the ski round so it is parallel with the other ski and weight it. If you are struggling with this think about trying to kick your bum with your heel, which should help. Off you go in the new direction. How much kick, or even if you need a kick at all, will depend on your binding. With pin bindings the tip of the ski will generally come up on its own when you lift your leg; if it doesn't a gentle kick is all that's required to get it moving.

Kick turn – key elements

- Good horizontal platform.

- Dynamic change of direction of the top ski.

- Weight transfer to the top ski; don't rush it.

- Lift downhill leg off the snow; don't rush it.

- Soft kick with the heel to lift the tip, steer the ski back in alongside its partner.

Making a track

Now that you have mastered skinning and cornering let's look at making a track. If you are on a popular ski tour there will usually be a track in the snow to follow, so you won't need to worry about where to go. While you are following other people's tracks think, what is good about this track? And what is bad about it? Is it too steep so difficult to skin? Is it too shallow so that it doesn't feel like you are gaining any height? Does the angle allow me a nice, relaxed skinning pace? Or do I have to change my stride length constantly? Are the corners in good places? Do I have to kick turn where a change of direction in a different place would be more comfortable, and hence quicker and safer?

To those questions we have to add safety questions. We will look at avalanche awareness later in the book but, is the track avoiding potential avalanche hazards? Does it keep me away from ice fall or rock fall danger? Am I clear of any crevasse danger (we look at glacier skiing later)? These factors need to be fed into your track planning.

Having analysed other people's tracks you can begin to develop some ideas about what makes a good track yourself. The art of track setting is your opportunity to scribe your mark on the landscape. A good track uses all the subtleties in the landscape to allow you to flow uphill in a safe and efficient way.

A good skinning track using the terrain.

When looking at the landscape to choose where I am going to put a track, I am trying to choose the safest and most efficient route through that piece of ground. If we put safety considerations to one side at the moment and just think about the line of ascent, what are we looking for?

I am looking to try and work the low-angled terrain to give me the easiest skinning track through a piece of ground. It is always quicker choosing a line

A series of kick turns up a slope in the Ötztal.

that keeps you skinning at a smooth consistent pace, rather than setting a steep, direct line where you need to use your heel raisers and work really hard. By choosing the low-angled ground as you work your way through the terrain, you can avoid making too many kick turns and skinning on steep, more awkward ground. By the same token you don't want your route to be too circuitous or you will add too much distance and time.

Look at the terrain ahead and plan your route, look for benches that may lead you through steep ground. If your goal isn't to climb a particular mound or summit, can you contour round it? Imagine you are heading for a col, you want to weave your way through the terrain climbing steadily but never having to lose any height. If you need to make any changes in direction, look for spots where you can step turn instead of kick turn as they use less energy. Looking for the low-angled terrain to skin through doesn't mean skinning on the flat, rather choosing the lowest-angled ground within a piece of terrain so you still may be on what feels like steep ground but with steeper ground around you. The added benefit of this approach is that you are less likely to stray onto avalanche-prone slopes. We will talk more about this later in the book, but you are pretty unlikely to trigger an avalanche on a slope shallower than 30 degrees. It is these slopes that are easiest to skin on. If the slope steepens above 30 degrees make sure all your avalanche antenna are out. I know more guides who been avalanched skinning up than skiing down on this sort of angle.

At times kick turns are unavoidable, and when the terrain dictates you will have to make the classic zigzag track to climb a piece of ground.

If you are forced into this style of track you still need to concentrate on getting the track angle right, to keep that efficient flow and try to minimise the number of kick turns. Think about where you are going to make the kick turns; they will be easier on the lower-angled sections of ground. Be aware of what is underneath you and the consequences of a slip mid-turn for yourself or other members of your team. If the kick turn has to be in an exposed place think about cutting a platform with your ice axe or shovel. When making the track I will make my track horizontal just before the kick turn to give a better platform to turn on.

Skinning track going into the horizontal.

Multi-tasking is the key to an efficient transition.

Transitions

My wife used to adventure race and my brother has competed at World Championship level Iron Man triathlon. They both firmly believe that a race can be won or lost in the transition, and while ski touring is not a race, being efficient in our transitions can save huge amounts of time over the course of a day. Multiply that by time saved over a week and you are looking at quite significant blocks of time.

We have lots of transitions in any ski touring day. If we think about a short ski tour you may start skiing downhill from a lift, stop, put skins on, climb for a bit, stop, put ski crampons on as the snow become icy, then reach a summit. You may then ski down, put skins back on, skin up towards a col, then as the ground becomes steeper you may have to stop, take your skis off, put your crampons on, and attach your skis to your rucksack. At the col you will have to take crampons off and get back into ski mode for the ski home.

If we take the key transitions from the above ski tour we have two skiing to skinning transfers, one basic and one more complicated skin to ski (involving skis on your pack), and one ski to crampon and back with skis onto the pack plus fitting ski crampons. Using that simple ski tour as an example we have seven transitions to be made. If you save five minutes at each transition, that's 35 minutes over the course of a day, which is the difference between getting down in daylight or dark, or having enough time to take some photos or have a second lap on some great powder. Efficient transitions involve multi-tasking; while you are performing the main task you can be chewing on a grain bar or having a drink. As soon as you are done, put some more sun cream on, look at the map and adjust your clothing. Doing all these tasks when you are stopping anyway saves extra stops throughout the day, which again adds efficiency and saves time.

One of the biggest losses of time in any day is when different people in the party decide that they are too hot or too cold at different times. One person is too hot so stops to take a jacket off, by which point the person who has got their clothing just right gets cold waiting for the other person to change their jacket, and so it goes on.

Accepting that at some point in every day there will be times when you are too hot and times when you are too cold will go a long way to mitigating this. Having systems for altering your clothing on the way makes a big difference; heat is lost and gained fastest by adjusting your head and hands. Carrying your woolly hat, or sun hat in a pocket or down your front allows you to swap hats without stopping. Having a hood on your softshell you can pull up if you start getting cold, having somewhere you can easily clip your gloves if you take them off, and so on, all avoid having to stop.

Look ahead to see how far it is to the next transition and decide if you can wait to make any changes. Having an agreed stopping strategy within the team also makes a difference. If the whole team start the day's skinning feeling slightly cold they will warm up as they skin avoiding that first stop 20 minutes into the ascent. In the cold of the morning I will generally go for about an hour and a half without a real break, as you cover more ground in the cool of the morning and lose less fluid. After that I stop for a quick drink and clothing faff approximately every hour, this usually works for most people.

Before we talk about specific transitions let's think about safety aspects. When you are going to perform a transition, look ahead and choose a spot that is going to be easy and comfortable to work on.

Safe transition spot clear of any objective danger marked in green.

A spot where there is some flat ground or a good platform is easiest. If you are concerned about the avalanche conditions then standing together as a group under a steep slope probably isn't ideal. Working in a spot where you may fall off, or where you may drop things, will make things slower and more difficult. If you are on a glacier try and choose a spot without any crevasses and change your skis one at a time, always keeping one ski on to spread your load over the snow, and to reduce the chance of punching through a snow bridge. For the same reason keep a bit of distance between each member of the party.

Only take one ski off at a time when making a transition on a glacier.

If you are going to transition to ski crampons look at the terrain and try to do it ahead of time, before you really need them, it will be easier and you are less likely to put yourself in a position where you may slide off.

Ski to skin transition

We have looked at the basic transitions putting skins off and on but it wouldn't do any harm to run through my system again. If you are in a safe, non-glacial spot, come to a stop and stamp the snow down, pop your skis off, wipe the snow off the bases and arrange them with their bases facing the sun, then get your skins out. I usually have them at the top of the bag, or at least slid down against the back so they are easy to find. It may sound like a minor detail, but having a light-coloured skin bag inside your dark rucksack can make finding your skins much easier. If it isn't super-cold and you are going to skin in thinner gloves, change these first, as it will make you more dextrous. Stick something to eat in your mouth early in the process to start getting the calories into your bloodstream while you are stationary.

When you are ready, lay the skis out on the ground base up and fit the skins. I usually kneel in front working with one skin and having the other one still in the bag under my knee so it won't blow away. Once you have done one, roll up the cheat sheet and put it in the bag, then flip the ski over onto its skin and adjust the binding into walk mode. Some people prefer doing the whole thing standing up so just do whatever works for you. Fit the other skin, flip the ski over and adjust the binding and you are good to go.

Skin to ski

This can be more awkward as you will often be doing this at the top of a col or on a windy summit where the chance of dropping things is much greater, so think about where you are going to put everything. If you are going to put more clothes on for the descent do this first so you don't get cold, but leave your thin gloves on until last, as you will be much faster doing everything in thin gloves. Stick something to eat in your mouth early in the process.

Put the bindings into ski mode, so your skis can't take off down the hill as soon as the skin is removed. One at a time turn the ski skin side up pushing the binding into the snow which will make the ski more stable to work on. Take the skin off as described earlier, then put it in the bag and kneel on the bag while you do the other skin, then stick them both in your rucksack.

If it is just a short ski before the next skin, you can just stick the skins down your jacket (your rucksack waist belt will stop them falling out), so they are warm and good to go at your next transition. You will see some people tucking them under their rucksack waist belt; be careful if you do this as they have a habit of escaping.

Skis on your feet to skis on your pack

If it is just a short, easy boot up I would just put my skis on my shoulders or even carry them in my hands and hike up, if it's longer or more precarious terrain where I need both hands, I will put my skis on my pack. There is a chance that this may include putting on crampons, but we will look at that separately as there are plenty of occasions when you will have your skis on your back and you will just be hiking up in your boots, with no crampons.

This type of transition doesn't always happen where there is plenty of space so you need to look at the terrain and plan the best place to make the change. Usually an ascent on foot to a col or a summit will be followed by a ski on the other side, otherwise you would just depot your skis, climb up then back down to your skis and ski off. If you think there is going to be more room at the top of the climb than at the bottom, you are best to leave the skins on your skis and sort them out at the top. Remember to engage the brakes in either system. If you think space is going to be limited do it before the climb. A classic example of this would be something like the gully you climb to the Col du Passon in Chamonix, where the lower transition is always on a bit of a slope but the top is really spacious and flat.

The way you attach the skis to your pack will depend a bit on your pack; there are two common options.

The first is my favourite as it is the quickest and carries the skis diagonally across the pack so they don't get in the way if you tilt your head back.

The second is to create an A frame using the straps on the side of your pack. Specialist race packs also use a clever system that allows the attachment of skis without removing the pack.

Diagonal loading

Put the two skis together with the bindings locked together, slide the skis into the lower loop until it is tight against the binding then wrap the top strap round the skis securely. If you want your poles in your hand you are good to go. If you only want one pole out, and an ice axe in your other hand, put the strap of one pole over the tip of both skis. Slide it down until it is at the point where the ski tips curve up then twist the pole to shorten the strap. Keep twisting until the strap is really tight round the skis, then clip the pole into a strap on your pack to hold it in place. If you wind the strap nice and tightly the pole won't slide down the skis. If you want to stash both poles do the same thing with the first pole, then loop the strap from the second pole over one ski then slide the strap down between the skis and strap it to the sack in the same place as the first pole. This is faster than twisting again and is secure enough.

Loading skis for a
diagonal carry.

Once you have sorted all this out, put the pack carefully on your back. This is the point when you will be grateful you bought lightweight pin bindings. Your pack will feel very top-heavy at first, until you get used to it, but be very aware when bending over that you have about three foot of ski sticking out above you as you could easily bash someone with it.

A frame

This more traditional method using side straps on the rucksack is the only option on many packs. Slide one ski down each side of the pack, some packs will have a captive loop at the bottom and a quick release buckle at the top making the process really easy. If your sack doesn't have this it's a bit more of a faff; just open the top strap as far as it will go and slide the ski in.

Some people just leave their skis like this, but I always find that they feel really unstable so I tie the tips together. This can be done using a strap, something with a pin works best as Velcro doesn't work when covered in snow. If you want to stash a pole you can just hook the strap over one ski tip and pull it down, so the pole's strap is sitting between the two skis above the strap loop. If you don't have a strap loop, then a pole strap over both tips, a few twists and clipped into the pack, as described above works fine. If you want to stash both poles just loop the second pole strap over one ski and attach it to the pack.

Skis on pack for an
A frame carry.

To take your skis off your pack just reverse the process, being careful not to drop anything or knock your pack off while rearranging your skis.

Putting on crampons

I would generally put crampons on before sorting my skis. There are two reasons for this; it is easier to move around with crampons on than without, and once your skis are attached to your pack it is quite difficult to access your pack to put the crampon bag away and do anything else.

Find a flat bit of snow and lay the crampons out on the ground, with all the straps out of the way. Remember there is a left and right, the buckle always goes on the outside. If there is a wire at the toe of your crampons, hold it up and slide the toe of the boot under the wire, clip the heel into place, and do up the strap around the ankle. If there is a strap arrangement at the toe push the toe of the boot against the front posts, clip the heel into place, then do the strap up threading it through the toe strap and buckle. If you are in an awkward place it's best to fit the downhill crampon first, just as you would when putting skis on.

Fitting boot crampons.

When you go to take your crampons off, do the reverse process, sort skis and clothing etc, then take off your crampons and pack them away in your sack, clip into your skis and you are good to go.

Moving uphill on foot

To many skiers, moving about on a mountain without skis on feels pretty alien if you are used to having the long metal edges to grip with and suddenly they are not there. Don't worry, as touring boots are designed to help and the patterned rubber soles grip really well in snow. You will find it easier to move about if the ankle of the boot is undone and in walk mode; if it is locked solid it is really difficult to keep your weight balanced over your feet.

Moving in ski boots without crampons

If you are in a track just walk normally, look at where you are putting your feet, place them in the biggest footsteps available but keep your stride short, until you feel more comfortable moving around.

Walking in touring boots, Kate Scott approaching the summit of the Similaun, Ötztal.

If the footsteps don't feel that great, kick into them, this will improve the step and help the rubber soles bite into the snow. If there isn't much of a track you will have to kick some footsteps. If you are going straight up the slope you can kick straight in. Keep the sole of your boot horizontal or slightly with the toe down, this will give the best footstep. Pointing the toe slightly down means that those coming behind you are less likely to slip backwards out of the step, and will feel more secure.

Kicking in with the front of the boot.

If you are ascending diagonally then kick the edge of the boot into the snow using a sawing action, this will create a footstep, step your other foot through and kick it in using the same sawing action, this is the most efficient way to move uphill. If you need to change direction kick a platform, turn around carefully and move off.

Kicking steps with the
side of the boot.

To move horizontally use the same action, but you may find you need to work a bit harder to create good footsteps for your team.

In descent if there are no footsteps to follow, go straight downhill plunging your heels into the snow with your toes pointing upwards, this will produce good footsteps that are difficult to fall out of.

Kicking footsteps
in descent.

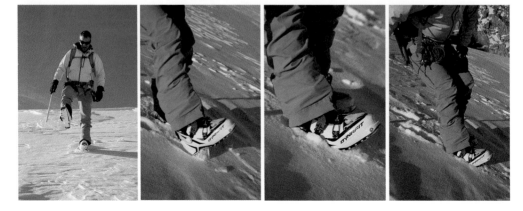

Rolling the ankle
when cramponing
in hard snow.

Stepping through
in crampons.

Moving in ski boots with crampons

If the snow is too hard or icy to provide good footsteps or is steep and you want the extra security, you will need to put your crampons on.

Having put them on as discussed above, you need to remember that you have them on; it's very easy to let your feet drift together allowing you to catch one crampon on the other or on your trousers, and to then trip. While this may just be annoying in certain locations it could be very serious in others.

Crampons have two sets of points, the two at the front and the eight or ten underneath depending on the model. In most situations you will come across you will just need the bottom points to be in contact with the snow. Think about rolling your ankle down the slope to try and engage as many points as you can.

If you edge up the hill like you would with a ski, you will only get the top row of points in the snow, halving your potential security. Rolling the ankle in touring boots does take a conscious effort, so think about how you are placing your feet for maximum security. In hard snow or ice you may need to stamp your crampons into the snow to get the best purchase. When ascending diagonally you would do exactly the same as when moving without crampons, crossing the feet through, but being extra careful not to catch your trouser leg in the process.

If the terrain becomes too steep to ascend using just the base points, you will need to turn your foot around and kick into the hill using the front points. Keep your boot as horizontal as possible and kick with a swing from the knee, push your weight down through the points and step up.

Front pointing.

In descent walk straight down the fall line, keep the ankles, knees and hips flexed to keep the weight over your feet. Plant your heels followed by the rest of your foot, concentrating on getting all the points on the base of the foot into the snow. You can hold the axe in whatever hand is more uphill, if you are in the fall line either hand will work.

Cramponing in descent.

Using an ice axe

The ice axe is a really versatile tool. The most common use for it is to add security when moving around in the mountains, and we have to be careful when ski touring not to end up using ski poles all the time instead of an ice axe. While ski poles are great for balance, they are no real use if you slip and need to arrest a fall.

If the terrain is at all steep, I will use an ice axe, if you want extra support use an axe in one hand and a pole in the other. Don't use the wrist loop on the pole, and then if you do have a slip you can let go of it and it won't get in the way.

Holding an ice axe.

Axe in the uphill hand, pole in the downhill hand.

When touring, if there is any chance I may need to use an axe to chop a section of track or a turning point, I will carry my axe slipped between my rucksack and my back.

Carrying the axe between the shoulder blades.

I will often do this if I am ascending on foot to a summit or col, so it is really easy to grab hold of if I need it. If the axe is stored on or in your pack you are less likely to use it, so decreasing possible security. When I am ready for the ski descent I will pack the axe inside my sack where I am less likely to lose it, and it is less likely to injure me should I have a fall.

When you use the axe, hold it in your uphill hand, there are lots of debates about pick facing forward or backwards; I prefer backwards.

Ice axe held pick
backwards and forwards.

You can then use the axe like a walking stick to give security. If you change direction remember to swap hands so that the axe is always on the uphill side. If you fall over with it on the downhill side you will end up lying on it, and not able to use it to stop yourself. It is worth learning the techniques of self-arrest so you can stop yourself if you have a proper slip, but we are getting to the limit of the scope of this book. You can learn more about this and other mountaineering techniques in *Alpine Mountaineering* by the same author.

Using the rope for security

We are going to look at using a rope in a glacial environment in the glacier skiing chapter of the book, but it is worth considering the use of a rope in a mountaineering context here. The big question for me when I am considering using a rope is, "Will the rope add any real security?" You will often see guides short roping (safeguarding) a client or clients, but this is a technique that requires years of experience to do safely. A guide has the techniques and experience to be able to stop a slip from a client becoming anything more serious, but this technique is not designed to arrest a full-blown fall. If you are taking a less experienced person into the mountains and think you might need to short rope them, you should think very carefully about your own ability and if you could really hold them if they slipped. If you are in any doubt, choose another objective, or make the place where you feel you need the rope your high point or objective for the day.

The message is if you don't have the mountaineering experience to use a rope in a way that adds safety, think about if you should be there, and carefully consider the suitability of your objectives for the day.

Winter Weather

Mike Austin getting the most out of a day of variable winter weather on the Grands Montets, Chamonix.

The weather affects everything we do in the mountains no matter what time of year it is, but in winter it takes on a new significance. Every tiny change in temperature, wind speed, wind direction and precipitation affects not only the snow conditions, but also the avalanche risk. The big weather events have obvious effects, for example lots of cold snow (but not too much) with no wind equals powder heaven, but add a bit of wind or too much snow and suddenly you could have recipe for an avalanche. If we use the scenario of 50cm of fresh snow fallen with a wind, in the trees and sheltered areas we could enjoy some fantastic powder skiing, but on lee slopes we would be looking at the formation of dangerous slab avalanche conditions. Not only is wind slab dangerous, but it would also be hideous to ski. If you choose the altitude and the terrain correctly you could have a fantastic day on the hill, if not, it could be your last day on skis.

Everything about winter weather and its effect on the snowpack is tied to avalanche risk and awareness. It is impossible to separate the two things, but we also need to think about the quality of snow and where will be the most fun places to ski as well as the safest.

Kate Scott enjoying powder in the trees.

Sources of weather information

As skiers and mountaineers we live in very fortunate times, with the advent of the internet it is incredibly easy to get hold of weather and avalanche forecasts. There are many sites that provide weather information and it is worth looking at a few different ones, as some tend to be a bit optimistic and some a bit pessimistic. If you review a spread then you can take a bit of an average. In each area there will generally be only one source of avalanche information. The avalanche forecast will record what was observed on a specific day, and will then predict the evolution of the snowpack and avalanche conditions based on the weather forecast.

You can use this information to check the accuracy of the weather forecast you looked at the previous day.

Weather websites

www.snow-forecast.com – This gives weather forecasts specific to ski resorts around the world, part of the site is free with more detailed information available for a small fee.

www.yr.no – A Norwegian site available in English which gives forecasts around the world in good detail and seems pretty accurate.

www.meteoblue.com – Weather around the world in good detail.

www.meteoswiss.ch – Swiss national weather service.

www.chamonix-meteo.com – Forecasts specific to the Mont Blanc Massif.

www.meteo.fr – French national weather service.

www.meteo.it – Italian national weather service.

Before you go

If you are heading to the mountains for a ski trip, your information gathering on the snow and avalanche conditions should start at least a week before you travel, preferably longer. Look at the weather forecasts and the avalanche forecasts together to build up a picture of what has been happening in an area. Start questioning.

When you are looking at the forecasts don't just look for the quantity of new snow and how sunny it is. Look also at the wind speed and direction, the temperature and how it varies throughout the day, as well has how much new snow has fallen.

If you are interested in the weather, you can have a look at a synoptic chart and start relating it to the forecast and the avalanche forecast. These are easy to find at www.weathercharts.org and www.metoffice.gov.uk

If you aren't interested and are happy to let someone else do the interpretation, just skip the next section and concentrate on what the forecast says. As a geography graduate I find the whole thing fascinating, but I know everyone doesn't.

Remember weather forecasters get it wrong sometimes, and this can impact on your day but it will also mean that the avalanche forecast may be wrong.

Basic synoptic chart interpretation

If you have never looked at a synoptic chart before, the chart is made up of lines joining points of equal air pressure together called isobars. Areas of high pressure indicated by an H usually give good stable weather; areas of low pressure signified by an L usually have poorer weather. Isobars that are well spaced generally have light winds, isobars close together indicate strong wind.

There are then fronts superimposed on the chart. Fronts are the dividing line between areas of warm and cold air. An area of one type of air is being replaced by another resulting in warm, cold or occluded fronts. These affect the mountain weather in different ways.

A synoptic chart with cold and warm fronts. *Contains public sector information licensed under the Open Government Licence.*

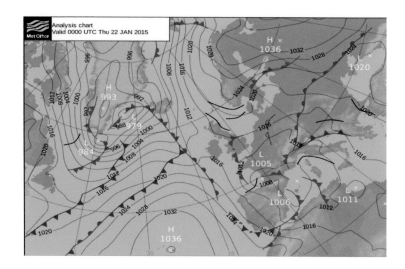

Analysis chart
Valid 0000 UTC Thu 22 JAN 2015
Met Office

Warm front – Indicated by a line with semicircles on it. Warm air is replacing cold air; this usually results in warming temperatures and precipitation. The effect on the snow is that the snow will warm up, making it less fun to ski. The avalanche risk will probably increase as warmer temperatures can weaken bonds within the snowpack. Increased temperature can make the snowpack more dense; new warm snow landing on less dense, cold snow can create a buried weak layer in the snow so increasing the avalanche risk (more of this later). On the flip side if the base is hard, so wet warm snow bonds well; then as the snow gets colder as the front moves through, the snow cools making for a quickly stabilising snowpack with great skiing.

Cold front – A line with triangles on it. Cold air replacing warm air, the temperature will get colder improving the snow quality, you may get fresh snow which can increase the avalanche risk. Generally a cold front will produce less snowfall than a warm front, but of better quality.

Occluded front – Alternating semicircles and triangles on the line. A mix of warm and cold air, which can mean cloudy conditions with precipitation. The type of precipitation will depend upon where the air mass has come from. If it has moved in from the north of the Alps it will be cold, so bringing snow, if it has come from the south it could be warm which could be a disaster for the skiing.

Reading a weather forecast

When I look at a forecast I start by looking at the overview for the next few days. Is it going to be sunny? Is it going to snow? Will there be cloud? Then I start to look at the detail. If it is going to snow, how much? What altitude is the rain/snow limit going to be at (the altitude it is going to snow down to)? How much snow does the forecast predict at different altitudes? If it is going to snow, is there going to be any wind? If so, how much? And in which direction will it blow? What will the strength be at different altitudes? What will the temperature be? And how cold will it feel when we add in the wind; this is called wind chill. If it is going to be warm, how warm? And how quickly is it going to warm up throughout the day?

If there is no fresh snow forecast, again look at the wind; is there enough wind to transport snow? Thirty miles per hour (48km/hr) seems to be the optimum wind speed for maximum wind transportation, but even at lesser wind speeds snow can create wind slab. If there is enough wind, which direction is it moving in? You should know from your research when the last snowfall was and how much snow fell.

Ski touring in Finnmark.

If the weather is going to deteriorate throughout the day, how quickly? And what is it going to do? If bad weather is coming, how long is it going to last?

You now have a good picture in your head of what has happened and what you can expect during the day. You need to have the flexibility in any plan to be able to change it if the weather forecast or the actual weather changes. Gather all the information you can and evaluate it in conjunction with the avalanche forecast, which we will look at shortly. When you have done all of this you can make a reasoned, informed decision about the conditions and how they will affect your ski plans. There will always be occasions when you will get it wrong or the forecasters will get it wrong; that's just the way of the mountains.

How to find the good snow

We will talk in depth about avalanche considerations in the next chapter, but for now we are going to think about snow quality and how the weather will affect it.

If we consider a fresh fall of snow on a cold windless night we are thinking about perfect powder skiing conditions the following morning. Have your avalanche radar on, but make sure you are on the first lift to enjoy the snow before it changes.

Let's think about what can affect the snow so that its quality will change.

Temperature

If the temperature is really cold, the snow will be slow to transform, keeping its quality. If the temperature warms rapidly throughout the day then the snow will become heavy, wet and difficult to ski. This is typical of fresh falls of snow late in the season where you may get fantastic powder skiing in the morning that has turned to porridge by the afternoon.

John McMaster skiing bottomless powder ... by the afternoon it was un-skiable porridge

The change in temperature throughout the day will have an effect on the whole snowpack, but initially it is the surface layers that will be most affected. As the surface layers warm up, the snow will become damp, and as the temperature cools in the evening this moisture can freeze into a layer of ice. This layer is on the surface with soft snow underneath; we call this crust and it is a skier's nightmare. The good news is that this repeated cycle of melting and refreezing is what creates spring snow and thin layers of crust will often break down as the day warms. I was skinning up the Col d'Argentière one spring with breakable crust all around us. We were dreading the descent, but while we were skinning up, the temperature went up, the crust softened and we had a really nice ski down.

This is of course not always the case so be aware of variations in temperature.

Aspect

The direction the slope faces has a big impact on the snow conditions. North facing slopes are colder as they face away from the sun, sometimes there can be an amazing difference in snow quality with northerly aspects holding cold air and hence good snow long after all the other aspects have transformed. I was skiing in the Queyras one February in some really warm conditions; we were skiing spring snow on the south facing slopes and powder on the northerly aspects.

On a trip to the Queyras we were skiing powder on the north aspects and spring snow on the south facing slopes.

This propensity to cold conditions does have a knock-on effect on avalanche conditions, as constant cold weather can encourage the growth of facets within the snow (more later) and prolong any instabilities in the snowpack. It can also keep the good quality snow longer than on any other aspect.

The snow on south facing slopes will transform the fastest as they get the most sun. On the plus side, after a massive snow fall the sun will cause initial instability on these slopes but this will quickly move to a stabilising effect. These slopes will often give the best spring snow skiing as the sun's heat combined with freezing at night combine to give a hard, consistent snowpack, with the surface layers being softened by the sun during the day. With spring snow skiing it is all about timing, so you need to judge the sun's warming effect, so that the surface layers of the snow will be soft and great to ski without melting too deeply into the snowpack and tuning it to soup.

West facing slopes get the afternoon and evening sunshine when the sun has plenty of heat, and can last for a reasonably long period of time especially later in the season when the sun is higher in the sky. The sun will have less of an impact on west facing slopes than on those facing south but the effect is still pretty strong.

East facing slopes are interesting as they do get the morning sun, but in the winter months the sun doesn't have much strength at this time of day, so although the sun will have an effect it will not be as much as west or south facing slopes.

Having thought about the information above, in a fresh snowfall the south will transform first, followed by west, east and finally north facing snow, so I would think about visiting things in that order. Depending on the temperature and time of year those aspects could transform within a day, so I may just do a run on each then move on as the snow changes depending on the terrain.

Wind

You don't need fresh snow to create accumulations of snow. Research has shown that wind speeds of about 10m/s (22mph or 36km/h) can move damp snow and 7m/s (15.6mph or 25.2km/h) can move dry snow (all depending on snow type, humidity etc). These wind speeds occur frequently on the winter hills, so wind transportation of snow is pretty common.

Wind-transported
snow, La Grave.
Photo – Mark Charlton.

The wind can have a number of effects on the snow quality. At its most basic when new snow is falling the wind breaks up the snow crystals so you don't get the light fluffy powder you had hoped for. This can be particularly disappointing when there has been no wind in the valley, you get the first lift all excited about the powder, only to find it has all been wind affected.

The second effect is when the snow is moved, this can happen during a new snow event or to snow already on the ground. Snow blowing across a uniform area of terrain can create a wind crust. This can be every bit as grim to ski on as a sun crust.

The third and most serious effect is when wind carries snow over a ridge line or edge. As the wind decelerates on the lee side of a ridge it is not able to carry so much snow and some of the snow falls out of suspension loading the lee slope. The crystals in the snow have been smashed up by the wind and they bond well to each other creating a slab, but do not bond well to the layer underneath. In addition this layer of wind slab generally forms in a wedge shape with the thick, heavy end of the slab being at the top of the slope, thinning down slope. In summary, the wind has created a top-heavy layer of cohesive snow that is not well anchored to the rest of the snowpack beneath it; this is a perfect avalanche trap for the unsuspecting skier.

This phenomenon is not limited to the lee sides of ridges, it can form on the lee side of any mountain obstacle, it can also form if the snow is blowing across a hillside forming wind slabs on the lee sides of gullies and depressions. We call this cross loading.

Additional weather considerations

There are additional weather considerations that affect many other aspects when planning a day's ski touring. If the weather is really cold you need to think carefully about where you are going and the equipment you take with you. A twisted knee at minus 20 degrees in January can be much more serious than the same injury on a sunny, spring afternoon. If it is really cold I may consider a ski tour that would keep me in the sun rather than looking for the shady, cold snow.

Skiing in poor visibility on the Pointe de la Pierre, Aosta Valley.

Poor visibility is a major consideration on a number of levels. In poor visibility you need to be confident in your navigational skills to avoid hazards, keep yourself on the right track, and not get lost. Time and energy wasted due to navigational deficiencies can have major knock-on effects later in the day. If the visibility is poor and you are skiing on a glacier you will not be able to see the crevasses, irrespective of your navigational skills, so you will need to take measures to protect yourself and the team.

In poor visibility it is much more difficult to choose the safest line to minimise the avalanche risk, and it is easy to stray onto steep slopes where you cannot see and assess what is above you. You may be skiing on a safe angle of slope but if you can't see what's above you, you may propagate an avalanche that can sweep down onto you out of the cloud. In addition you may be making good decisions about safety but have people above you in the cloud who you can't see, and who may trigger something that may land on you.

Avalanches

Mike Austin and Bruce Goodlad

We are not operating in a benign environment where incidents occur as the result of an individual deviance from a prescribed protocol, we must be conscious that we operate in a high-risk environment where hazard is constantly present and conduct ourselves accordingly.

The Big Lie by Mark Smith

Until recently good-quality backcountry ski touring equipment and information was hard to come by; backcountry skiing was generally limited to hut-to-hut touring that occurred in the snow stable months of late spring, when the layers of the snowpack had settled out and the danger of avalanche was significantly reduced. Today's equipment allows us incredible access and freedom in the mountains, opening up large areas of complicated terrain.

We're not as good as we think we are at keeping safe in avalanche terrain. The truth is, we just get lucky a lot of the time. It's a hostile learning environment; we don't get feedback on our poor decisions from the mountain until the point it kills us!

As a species, we're hardwired to have an overinflated opinion of our abilities. Overconfidence bias means it is not in our nature to think we perform poorly at tasks. Hence, we all think we're great at driving a car, singing karaoke, and making good choices while travelling in avalanche terrain.

A comprehensive toolkit of avalanche knowledge isn't within the scope of this book. Avalanche skills and knowledge are like any other craft; they require study and practice. We do not assimilate these skills by osmosis. Because an individual is a highly experienced and skilled skier or rider, it does not follow that they have a strong set of avalanche skills. Knowledge is king in the avalanche world. Nine out of ten people caught in an avalanche will have triggered that avalanche themselves. That's a really important statistic because it means that if we learn about avalanches, we can avoid getting caught in avalanches. Take an accredited course that's run by avalanche professionals and you'll reap the rewards for years to come.

Skier with avalanche debris.

What is the avalanche problem?

Avalanches are not like elasticated pants: one size does not fit all. There are many different types of avalanche and they all have their own triggers and a different toolkit on how to deal with them. The way a wet loose avalanche is triggered and flows down its pathway is very different to the way a soft slab avalanche is triggered and runs. The way we identify and deal with each of them is as different as chalk and cheese.

With their kind permission we have drawn on some of the descriptions of avalanche types from the Aiare Student Manual (American Institute for Avalanche Research and Education).

A classic slab avalanche.

In the search for fresh
tracks successive skiers
moved onto steep ground
until one triggered a slide.

The components
of an avalanche.

Slab avalanches

When snow falls from the sky or is deposited by wind it can form a slab. This slab of snow is a single cohesive unit. It can be known as soft, hard or wind slab depending on the mechanisms of formation, but as a skier the main concept to grasp is the idea of the single cohesive unit layer upon another layer of snow.

A slab avalanche has some key features that can be useful for us to describe; the 'crown wall' is the upper surface fracture of the avalanche, where the slab has pulled away from the 'bed surface' that is the layer that the slab has slid on. The 'flanks' are the side walls, and the 'toe' of the avalanche is where all the snow debris from the slab has piled up when it has stopped moving. The trigger zone of the avalanche can be metres or even tens of metres above the point from where the avalanche is triggered. It could be triggered by a skier halfway down the slab, or even triggered by a skier on low-angled ground some distance away from the slab.

Slabs vary in their degree of stiffness. Soft slabs generally break away at the feet of the skier, whereas the stiffness of hard slabs often transmit their energy to the weakest point of the slab interface with the bed surface, and so often break higher up the slope from the victim. This makes them much more difficult to escape from. Imagine a rug being pulled from underneath your feet. There is no place to step off as all the ground around you in every direction is in motion.

Think about the snow on a powder day when the snow is so deep you have to find steeper slopes to ski in order to get your skis moving. If you then ski the same slope the following day you will find that you don't sink in as deeply and it is possible to have powder skiing on lower-angled slopes. But hey, it's not as light or fluffy as the day before. What's that all about? This is the settlement process, the snow is settling and sintering; the bonding process has started.

This bonding process may take some time. Initially the surface slab may gain strength with the internal bonds remaining weak so there is still instability. Over time this will bond to the existing snow. The rate of bonding will depend on many factors, temperature, solar radiation, the weakness of existing layers etc. The initial bonding process can be relatively fast which is why you may hear people saying they don't ski off-piste for 24 hours after a storm. They are allowing the settlement process to take effect but you must remember that there are more factors than just this in play when deciding where and when to ski.

Settlement cones.

Wind slabs

Many slabs form due to the transportation of snow already on the ground by the wind. When wind moves snow, it breaks up the crystals into smaller forms, and can carry this snow for significant distances. As the wind flows over a ridge crest or any other obstruction it slows down on the leeward side. As this happens the transported snow falls out of suspension and deposits on the ground at that location, creating a layer. This layer quickly bonds to itself forming a cohesive slab. Now imagine this stiff wind slab forming on top of an already existing weak layer or a smooth sliding surface; a loaded gun waiting for a trigger.

Wind slabs can form without any fresh snow falling; all they need is loose surface snow to be present and for the wind to blow. If you look at the snow when you're skiing you can often see signs of wind transportation of snow; wind tails on the lee sides of boulders, ridges and vegetation are all key

A massive skier-triggered
wind slab avalanche,
Riksgränsen, Sweden.
Photo – Bruce Duncan.

signs of recent wind direction. Look for blowing snow; you can often see wind plumes blowing off ridges – that snow is going somewhere – loading up a lee slope and waiting for an unwary skier to trigger it. You will often find wind slabs on the lee sides of ridges, on the steep slope just under a ridge crest, and under cornices. The strength of the wind will have a big effect on how much snow can be moved – a moderate wind blowing for just a few hours can redistribute a vast amount of snow around a mountain, so it's no surprise that this type of avalanche is particularly common in regions with a lot of wind, such as Scotland.

Wet loose avalanches

The analogy we like to describe wet avalanches is that of a big cement truck emptying its load from a single point on the mountain-side and the debris fanning out and entraining more snow as it flows down the mountainside. They occur when the snowpack warms up, and they're frequently seen when the sun has been on a south- or west-facing slope in the springtime. They can entrain a much greater volume of snow than their drier counter-parts – and are much more destructive than their drier counterparts too. Point releases, roller balls (snow balls rolling down the hill), squeezing water out of a snowball in your hand, and punching through to knee level when walking where earlier in the day your feet barely penetrated the same slope are all indications that this process is starting to occur. The snow entrained in wet snow avalanches is very dense and sets like concrete with very few air spaces, so while relatively easy to predict they are incredibly serious to be caught in.

If we know what type of avalanche problem that we are dealing with we can deploy the correct strategies to counter it. So how do we find out what the avalanche problem for each day will be. Perhaps there will be more than one avalanche problem running at the same time. Which one takes priority? We solve the problem by gathering data. We are always in information deficit when it comes to the snowpack beneath our skis. *The more information we have the safer we are.* The terrain and snow interact to give different layers of snow at different elevations and aspects, right down to micro features of a single slope. Our task is to build up a mental image of the entire mountain snowpack, and figure out what the stability in each of those myriad areas is likely to be. That's a pretty daunting task. Luckily there are many tools out there to help as along our way.

An afternoon wet snow avalanche outside the Branca Hut – Ortler Alps. This slope released every afternoon.
Photo – Andy Perkins.

The most important tool in our data gathering process is the avalanche forecast for the area you're planning to ski. It's free and extremely useful, especially in the European Alps and North America where we have detailed avalanche forecasts posted daily by experts. Europe doesn't have an avalanche forecasting problem; it has a public engagement problem. We constantly fail to draw out the vital nuanced information from our bulletins. Avalanche forecasters diligently provide us with a vast array of information in their forecast in the hope that we will break it down and maximise those pearls of wisdom. Snow pit profiles, mountain weather trends and forecasters' blogs are all there for the taking: every day in winter the avalanche forecast gives us high quality, location and time relevant information. Use all of it. If we understand the avalanche problem we're looking for, then the avalanche forecast becomes a super-rich source for what we're seeking: current, localised trustworthy information relating to a specific type of avalanche problem.

Add into the avalanche forecast other quality information that you can find. Locals that you trust, ski guides, even social media posts of who's been doing what and where that day can all be sources of information gathering that can build upon our picture of the snow conditions before we even step onto the mountain, and in so doing help address that information deficit.

Once we're at our starting point of our ski day and clipping into our bindings we can start to add real time information to all that information that we've already gathered from the avalanche forecast. We can make our mental picture of snow stability richer. *What's the weather doing? Is there snow being transported and causing wind loading? What direction is that wind coming from? Is it blowing from the forecasted direction or has it changed? Am I seeing shooting cracks coming from my ski's? Why am I sweating in this light fleece? Wasn't the forecast for it to stay cold today? Is that avalanche debris over there? is that recent?* Regardless of the forecast, the very best information; bulls eye information that relates to us on the mountain, comes from what we're seeing as we travel through the terrain. It doesn't get more relevant and targeted than that. For this reason, it's vital to keep looking and asking stability questions throughout our day as we ski.

Case study

On February 16th 2014, Martin, Maria and I remotely triggered an avalanche in our "home" mountain range in Kittelfjäll, Sweden. The avalanche broke about 100m above us and caught and partly buried us all. The crown was roughly 300m wide and the path was about 400–500m. In some miraculous way, we all survived and got away with minor physical injuries – I broke both of my legs, got a crack in my chin and a hell of a black eye, Maria got a dislocated femur fracture, while Martin strained his groin and got a small bruise. In time, our bodies and minds will heal, but I suspect that the process will be long and winding. There are so many questions banging against my forehead: How could we let this happen? Where did we go wrong? So many emotions swirling around in my chest; guilt, fear, shame, and an immense gratefulness of being alive.　　　　　　　　　　*Andrea Mannberg*

Case studies are a great way to learn from the experience of others. Often these case studies don't have a smoking gun pointing to an obvious error of judgment; these more complex incidents, that involve experienced and skilled parties, are often much more nuanced in their causation and combine a number of factors and small errors of judgment that lead to the incident. The Kittelfjäll case study explained below is one such event. Could you find yourself in a similar situation?

On Sunday 16th February 2014 three close friends made the five-hour drive from their hometown to the Kittelfjäll backcountry in Sweden for a day of backcountry skiing. They were a solid team of friends that skied together frequently, both in the local ski areas and on long haul trips to world-class backcountry ski destinations. They all had good avalanche skills and even some formal training in the form of a three-day avalanche fundamentals course taken the year before in Jackson Hole. As a team they knew each other well, they'd talked through the current snowpack issues together and they carried and knew how to use all the right avalanche equipment: transceiver, shovel and probe, as well as 'Air Bag' packs.

They hadn't really consulted the avalanche forecast for the area, but they knew it was Considerable (3), and had been firmly stuck at that hazard rating for several days. In the words of one of the group:

"The avalanche forecast for the area was always posted a considerable hazard rating, so we never gave it much attention."

If they'd been tracking the forecast from the nearby ski resort posted three days before their ski tour, they'd have been alerted to a persistent weak layer (PWL) some 20cm below the surface that was reactive and providing clean, planer failures with energy when subjected to testing. You can see a video of the avalanche reported posted at this link: https://vimeo.com/86616686

The visibility was poor as the group set off. This isn't uncommon in Scandinavian countries and Scotland where the culture is to get out into the mountains in flat light and high winds, otherwise you could go weeks without skiing anything. In the flat light the team made the obvious decision to stay below the high alpine part of the mountain, in the sparsely spaced birch forests that are endemic in this part of the world in order to provide them with the contrast needed to ski. Visibility is also a key factor in assessing the gradient of a slope, and the birch assisted them in staying on slopes the angle of which didn't go above 30 degrees. Nor was the terrain they had in mind particularly complicated. No glaciers, no overlapping avalanche runout zones, and no obvious terrain traps such as cliffs or river gullies. These felt like safe slopes.

This is how things unfolded in the words of one of the party who wrote candidly about the incident:

It had snowed an additional 10cm, pretty good for Sweden and the snow was colder than the day before. It looked like we were going to have a good day. We easily found the tree'd small and low incline ridge that would safely take us to our run. On the flat ground, we heard several "whumps", some of them big. To get a sense of the instability, we jumped on a test slope on the side of the ridge – about 35 degrees. This produced a settlement but no movement in the snow.

When the slope got a bit steeper the whumps stopped. Since we knew that the snowpack was a bit unstable, and since visibility was poor, we had no intention of skiing the big alpine terrain. However, we also wanted a run of decent length, so we aimed for the tree line. As we approached it, we all agreed that this was not the day when we wanted to have big snow fields above us, as the current snow condition implied that there was a heightened risk to remotely trigger an avalanche. Since we needed to traverse to get to our run, we stopped to discuss the way forward. We had a small open snowfield above and below us that we needed to cross. After a lengthy discussion, where everyone had the right to say "no", we decided to skin one at a time over to the other side. Martin went first.

While we waited, we isolated two columns of snow with our poles and did hand shear tests. It was very, very hard to get the snow to go anywhere. It seemed to have bonded really well with the old snow; however when we put our full weight on the snow and pulled hard it came out with a very clean shear. Martin's traverse went well, and we followed one at a time. Once at our run that we planned we decided that it was too convex and steep, and too uncertain as to where we would end up, so we decided to turn back. One at a time to the place where we had started. All good. We decided that we would try to get to our usual run. It would be a bit of a slog, but we would at least get one good run. We discussed how to get there, if we should try to stay high or go through the trees and skin back up. Since we didn't have that big snow field above us, we choose the latter. Better safe than sorry.

And then we got greedy. Going down the way we got up would basically mean that we would just skin down that seemed a bit boring. Instead we choose to traverse just a little bit to the west, where a sweet little snowfield with a mellow incline opened up and give us a good run. Visibility was relatively poor, so we really couldn't see what we had above us. I saw something that looked like a cornice that worried me, but since we were heading back I didn't really worry about it.

Martin had only gone a few metres in front of us onto the snowfield when we heard the whump. I remember Martin saying, "this is us turning back, this is no place to be," and starting to come back towards me. I did the same. Then I saw him running towards me. "WTF". Then, from the back of my eye, I saw a huge wave if snow charging down the mountain. When I realised what was happening, I tried to grab my ABS, but before I could, I was knocked over by the avalanche. I reached for the trigger again, and this time I managed to pull it. However, the balloons were of little use. The snow threw me right into the trees. I felt it slamming against my head and ripping the skis off my feet. All I could think was "protect your head" as the snow pushed me forward. Then as soon as it had started, everything went still. My back against a mountain birch and my head above the snow facing uphill.

I heard Martin shouting my name, "I'm Ok". I tried to get up but I was buried to my chest, stuck with my butt and back on one side of the mountain birch and my legs folded on the other side. I tried to dig with my hands but I was shaking too hard. Martin was surrealistically fast at digging himself out, he came running asking if I was okay, then ran forward to dig up Maria who was half buried face down. Once he checked that she could breathe he dialed 112 for the police and tried to give directions to our position, then called a group of friends who we knew were skiing nearby. I could hear Maria scream, blood freezing in my veins. "Is she okay?" – "she has a femur fracture – her leg is dislocated. I don't know if I should reposition it or not? Then the fear of a new avalanche. I dug frantically with one hand and it became apparent too that my leg was also broken.

Learning points

Persistent weak layers (PWL) are the monsters that lurk beneath the surface of the snow in the backcountry. These weak layers are often associated with continental climates such as the interior states of the United States or central Asia, but all mountain ranges have the ability to develop these layers and do so – regularly. Through a process known as temperature metamorphism, the snowpack changes over time due to temperature variations. Crystals in the snowpack, called facets, form when the air temperature is particularly cold and the snowpack is thin, to create a weak layer in the snow, setting up an unstable structure in the snowpack.

A large facet. Photo – Miles Perkins.

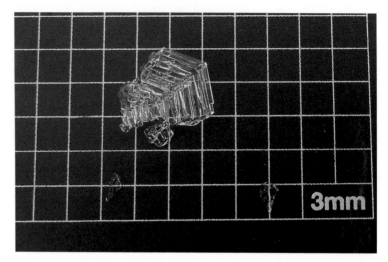

Added to this lurking layer of facets an ever-increasing snow load being deposited onto the lee slope from the alpine winds above them, the slope's strength was stretched to its limit – like an elastic band stretched to breaking point. Martin's weight as he stepped onto the *connected* slope beneath the wind-loaded slope above was literally the straw that broke the camel's back of the slope. Once the fragile weak layer was initiated, it then propagated upslope releasing a large slab avalanche on top of the entire group.

Snowpack and weather

While avalanche aware skiers in continental climates are familiar with PWLs and track them routinely, they often slip past skiers from maritime climates who sometimes fail to appreciate how dangerous they can be.

If the snowpack was so unstable, why was it so difficult for them to trigger the faceted layer during their stability tests? Stability tests are great at telling us when a snowpack is dangerous. They're not so good at telling us when a snowpack is safe. This is because of something called spatial variability. Spatial variability is a key factor in avalanche accidents for skiers who have avalanche skills and training. Although the weak layer was present in their pit, it presented as being very strong when tested. The snowpack is never uniform but changes from place to place due to the effects of wind, angle and aspect. Even very subtle differences on the same slope will often hide a PWL from us, or as in this case disguise its weakness. Basing our decision to ski a slope on the results of just a couple of targeted information points such as a snow pit can lull us into a false sense of security about slope stability. Just because the snow is strong at points A and B, it doesn't necessarily follow that it will be safe at point C. *Use the results of a stability test such as a compression test or an extended compression test (ECT) to say no, never to say go!*

The weather was a significant factor in the accident. It's easy to make good route choices when the sun is shining. Biting cold arctic winds and flat light turn easy decisions into hard decisions. Communication in a team is compromised by poor weather. Route planning the night before is a key way to provide a margin of safety, providing a considered passage through avalanche terrain and pointing us towards the safe aspect and elevation zones away from the current avalanche problem. But often, such as in this case study, the reality is that we don't operate in the mountains like that. On short cold winter days, we often play 'mini golf' in areas that we are vaguely familiar with and chalk up short laps of powder, or we alter our original plans depending on the weather conditions and snow quality we find. Fatmap can help here, the ability to instantly locate ourselves live in a 3D terrain map while in poor visibility by simply pulling out a phone is a great ace to have tucked in your back pocket. In this way we cannot only see the angle of the slope we're on, but equally as important, the scale and angle of the slopes that we're connected to and threatened by.

Human factors

Add to these snowpack and weather influences a few human factors such as confirmation bias – we all want to get a stable snowpack test result, right? So even when the pit gives us a strong clue: *"It seemed to have bonded really well with the old snow; however when we put our full weight on the snow and pulled hard it came out with a very clean shear."* We have a tendency to focus on the hard to release part of the test as opposed the clean shear that's just occurred. Clean shears are a red flag.

Other human factors that would have been pressing on the group that day were both commitment and familiarity. After a five-hour drive, like any of us, they were keen to get a few decent turns from their day. In an area that they knew well and had always felt pretty benign in the past, they felt confident to push their margin of safety – just a little.

Clean shear.

What about the good stuff? What did they do right? They were a team not a group; they knew each other's strong and weak points. They communicated and made decisions together in an open and flat hierarchy. More often than not that kind of facilitated communication will expose a bad idea. They had the right equipment and just as importantly knew how to use it. They carried a mobile phone to contact nearby friends and alert the rescue services, and were able to accurately provide their location. They were all physically strong and capable with a positive mind-set, so when things did go badly wrong that had the capacity to minimise its impact.

There's no such thing as a textbook avalanche accident rescue. We run dozens of rescue scenarios every season on Avalanche Geeks' courses; they all are pretty chaotic. That is the nature of unexpected high-stress situations in hostile environments. What is worth highlighting from this incident is that the rescue isn't over once the digging is finished. In many ways, it's just the beginning. Do you carry appropriate warm clothing, group shelter and first aid kit? Do you have appropriate first aid skills? We often don't think about such things, but this is a great demonstration of how vital these skills are just for a short day's backcountry skiing in an area close to a ski resort.

This case study teaches us to always be vigilant about persistent weak layers in the snowpack and to fully examine the avalanche report for their existence, as opposed to just noting the headline figure of 'category 3'. It teaches us the dangers of placing too much emphasis on our own snowpack tests due to spatial variability. It's also a stark reminder that we should repeatedly practice our rescue skills and carry the right equipment for such a rescue including appropriate spare clothing, group shelter, first aid kit, GPS and a communication device.

Avalanche forecasts

We are fortunate that in many of the areas we choose to ski there will be professional avalanche forecasting services. You can find links to all the European forecasts at www.avalanches.org

Danger level	Icon	Snowpack stability	Avalanche triggering probability
5 - Very High		The snowpack is poorly bonded and largely unstable in general.	Numerous large-sized and often very large-sized natural avalanches can be expected, even in moderately steep terrain.
4 - High		The snowpack is poorly bonded on most steep slopes.	Triggering is likely even from low additional loads** on many steep slopes. In some cases, numerous medium-sized and often large-sized natural avalanches can be expected.
3 - Considerable		The snowpack is moderately to poorly bonded on many steep slopes*.	Triggering is possible, even from low additional loads** particularly on the indicated steep slopes*. In some cases medium-sized, in isolated cases large-sized natural avalanches are possible.
2 - Moderate		The snowpack is moderately well bonded on some steep slopes*, otherwise well bonded in general.	Triggering is possible primarily from high additional loads**, particularly on the indicated steep slopes*. Large-sized natural avalanches are unlikely.
1 - Low		The snowpack is well bonded and stable in general.	Triggering is generally possible only from high additional loads** in isolated areas of very steep, extreme terrain. Only sluffs and small-sized natural avalanches are possible.

European Avalanche Hazard Scale.

These forecasts are not infallible as they are based on a weather forecast; if the weather forecast is wrong, there is a likelihood that the avalanche forecast will also be off. You also have to be aware that the forecasts are often for large geographic areas and local conditions may be very different. The forecast scale is the same Europe-wide, indeed it is virtually the same as the North American scale, but some forecasts are a bit understated and some a bit overstated. It can depend on the region and the individual forecaster.

We have included below the Avalanche Bulletin from the Tyrol in western Austria from the 19th of March 2011. We were planning to start a ski tour in the Ötztal mountains, but when we saw this forecast we chose to delay the start of our tour by 24hrs and went lift-accessed skiing in St Anton. The pictures following the report show what is meant by avalanches triggered by low additional loads. In this case spontaneous releases were triggered by overloading on the snowpack by fresh and wind-transported snow. You can see from the rose (danger aspect) that hazard was forecast on all aspects; if you look at the photographs you can see that both sides of the same ridge have avalanched and many aspects have slid.

Avalanche Bulletin for the Tirol 19/03/11.

Avalanche Bulletin
of the Avalanche Warning Service Tyrol
Saturday, 19.03.2011, at 07:30

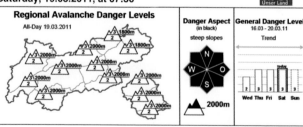

Considerable avalanche danger widespread - Touring possibilities are limited

AVALANCHE DANGER

The avalanche danger level in Tyrol's backcountry touring regions is considerable far and wide. Avalanche prone locations are to be found on steep slopes in all expositions above approximately 2000 m. Freshly formed snowdrift accumulations, in particular, are inadequately bonded with the old snowpack and can be triggered as avalanches even by minimum additional loading. Evaluating the avalanche hazards is more difficult today, since the danger zones are blanketed over by a few centimeters of new fallen snow, making it hard to spot the perilous spots. Backcountry skiing and freeriding tours require experience in assessing avalanche dangers. Below about 2200 m, especially in avalanche starting zones which have not yet discharged, isolated moist sluffs and wet snow avalanches are likely today.

SNOW LAYERING

Over the last 24 hours there has been noteworthy snowfall only along the Main Alpine Ridge and in the Northern Alps. Overall during this last period of precipitation along the Main Stubai and Ötztal Ridges, in the Silvretta, in the western part of the Northern Alps and in the Carnic Alps, there was between 50 and 80 cm of new fallen snow. In the remaining regions of North and East Tyrol there was usually 20 to 40 cm of fresh fallen snow, least of all in the Lower Inn Valley. Brisk to strong velocity northwesterly winds gave rise to new snowdrift accumulations, particularly in high alpine regions. The snow layering is least favourable between 2200 and 2800 m, where there are some weak layers interspersed in the old snowpack which can serve as bed surfaces for avalanches. The old snowpack surface in shady zones is also quite loosely packed; thus, the latest snowfall and snowdrift masses are poorly bonded with it. Below about 2200 m, the snowpack is thoroughly wet, which has caused it to forfeit its stability.

ALPINE WEATHER FORECAST (ZAMG-WEATHER SERVICE INNSBRUCK)

Weather in general: A disturbance which is embedded in a northerly air current will sweep across Tyrol today, bringing some precipitation and a drop in temperatures in the mountains. Tomorrow, Sunday, a high pressure system will regain dominance for a few days. Mountain weather today: North Tyrol's peaks are shrouded in cloud and fog, accompanied by intermittent snowfall. By tomorrow morning, about 5 cm of fresh fallen snow is anticipated, from place to place as much as 10 cm. Temperatures will drop somewhat. The Southern Alps are free of cloud, except for occasional summits, the visibility is diffuse, occasional snow flurries are possible. Temperature at 2000 m: minus 5 degrees; at 3000 m: minus 10 degrees. Moderate to brisk northwesterly winds, shifting increasingly to northeasterly this afternoon.

SHORT TERM DEVELOPMENT

On Sunday, the avalanche danger is still considerable, thereafter it will recede.

Photos from this forecast day illustrate how this forecast manifests itself on the mountain.

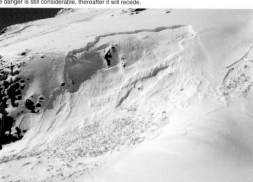

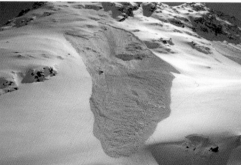

How to interpret an avalanche forecast

Unfortunately, there isn't a standard format for avalanche forecasts. As you travel from country to country the forecast is presented in a slightly different way. Having said that the basic format is pretty similar and the concepts are the same. Some countries provide a descriptive forecast in multiple languages, others don't, so it is worth having a dictionary or translation software handy. The information contained in most forecasts uses similar language and vocabulary, so if you don't speak the language in question you will soon pick up the key words and phrases.

If we look at our Tyrol forecast it starts with the date and time of issue, we obviously want to check the date to make sure it is the latest information, but it is also worth checking the time. In the main ski season some forecast centres provide two forecasts a day; one in the morning and one in the evening.

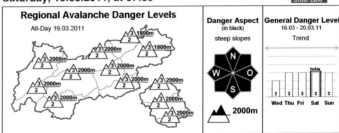

Avalanche Bulletin
of the Avalanche Warning Service Tyrol
Saturday, 19.03.2011, at 07:30

Considerable avalanche danger widespread - Touring possibilities are limited

AVALANCHE DANGER

The avalanche danger level in Tyrol's backcountry touring regions is considerable far and wide. Avalanche prone locations are to be found on steep slopes in all expositions above approximately 2000 m. Freshly formed snowdrift accumulations, in particular, are inadequately bonded with the old snowpack and can be triggered as avalanches even by minimum additional loading. Evaluating the avalanche hazards is more difficult today, since the danger zones are blanketed over by a few centimeters of new fallen snow, making it hard to spot the perilous spots. Backcountry skiing and freeriding tours require experience in assessing avalanche dangers. Below about 2200 m, especially in avalanche starting zones which have not yet discharged, isolated moist sluffs and wet snow avalanches are likely today.

SNOW LAYERING

Over the last 24 hours there has been noteworthy snowfall only along the Main Alpine Ridge and in the Northern Alps. Overall during this last period of precipitation along the Main Stubai and Ötztal Ridges, in the Silvretta, in the western part of the Northern Alps and in the Carnic Alps, there was between 50 and 80 cm of new fallen snow. In the remaining regions of North and East Tyrol there was usually 20 to 40 cm of fresh fallen snow, least of all in the Lower Inn Valley. Brisk to strong velocity northwesterly winds gave rise to new snowdrift accumulations, particularly in high alpine regions. The snow layering is least favourable between 2200 and 2800 m, where there are some weak layers interspersed in the old snowpack which can serve as bed surfaces for avalanches. The old snowpack surface in shady zones is also quite loosely packed; thus, the latest snowfall and snowdrift masses are poorly bonded with it. Below about 2200 m, the snowpack is thoroughly wet, which has caused it to forfeit its stability.

ALPINE WEATHER FORECAST (ZAMG-WEATHER SERVICE INNSBRUCK)

Weather in general: A disturbance which is embedded in a northerly air current will sweep across Tyrol today, bringing some precipitation and a drop in temperatures in the mountains. Tomorrow, Sunday, a high pressure system will regain dominance for a few days. Mountain weather today: North Tyrol's peaks are shrouded in cloud and fog, accompanied by intermittent snowfall. By tomorrow morning, about 5 cm of fresh fallen snow is anticipated, from place to place as much as 10 cm. Temperatures will drop somewhat. The Southern Alps are free of cloud, except for occasional summits, the visibility is diffuse, occasional snow flurries are possible. Temperature at 2000 m: minus 5 degrees; at 3000 m: minus 10 degrees. Moderate to brisk northwesterly winds, shifting increasingly to northeasterly this afternoon.

SHORT TERM DEVELOPMENT

On Sunday, the avalanche danger is still considerable, thereafter it will recede.

The map shows the area covered by the forecast and outlines the hazard across the area. This may vary in different locations depending on wind direction, snowfall etc. In the example forecast there are small mountain symbols that are split with an altitude reading at their right-hand side. This indicates that the forecast hazard is at one level above the line and a different level below. The altitude can affect how much wind there will be, and any instabilities within the snowpack will not change so quickly due to the colder temperatures. In the forecast example shown, above 2000m the forecast hazard is 3 – Considerable, and below 2000m it is 2 – Moderate.

The next piece of information is the danger aspect or danger rose, this indicates which aspects are the most dangerous by shading the rose. In this case the danger is on all aspects so the whole rose is shaded. Under the rose is an altitude indicator, which shows above what altitude is the greatest risk. This is followed by a graph showing the trend in avalanche hazard. In this case the hazard has increased and then stayed constant, and it is expected to remain at the same level for the following day.

This initial visual indicator provides a lot of information in a simple, easy to understand way. You now have the hazard level, the altitudes where the hazards are to be found, and the aspect where the hazard is greatest (though this does not mean that hazard does not exist on other aspects). You also have the trend of stability. By studying the forecasts and the weather you will be able to spot the trend yourself, but it helps to have it visually represented in front of you.

The next section in the avalanche forecast is where the forecaster discusses different aspects of the snowpack, hazard, weather and stability development. The avalanche danger comes first; in this section the forecaster discusses the current danger and will highlight key pieces of information. In this forecast the chance of spontaneous and skier-triggered avalanches has been highlighted.

The following section discusses snow layering; this is where any weak layers will be identified and any new snow will be discussed. The distribution of new snow is highlighted, and also the fact that the wind will be strong enough to move the snow creating possible slab. The forecast also discusses any known weak layers within the snowpack.

The weather forecast comes next; you need to remember that this is just a forecast, if the weather forecast is wrong then everything else will be affected. If you have been watching the forecast and the avalanche forecast you should be able to come up with some ideas about the evolution of the snowpack and stability yourself, before moving onto the final section which deals with the short-term development. This will discuss how the pack is expected to develop over the next few days, taking into account the snowpack history, what the forecasters have observed, and what the weather forecast says is about to happen.

This will all help to build a picture in your mind of the snowpack, and you can now feed that information into your tour plan and so avoid areas of instability that have been highlighted in the forecast. With good judgment and appropriate choice of venue, terrain and route it is possible to ski on days with a high avalanche hazard forecast (not that I would recommend this for anyone other than an expert). It is important to remember that you can also get avalanched on slopes that aren't mentioned in the forecast, even on days with a moderate avalanche forecast.

How do we create an avalanche?

We have talked about some of the common types of avalanche that we may encounter. We now need to think about what it takes to actually create an avalanche. There are three factors required for an avalanche: *terrain*, *snow* and a *trigger*. It is our interaction with these factors that can lead to us to be involved in an avalanche. If the *trigger* is occurring naturally but we are safely drinking cocoa in the ski lodge then the avalanche is irrelevant! It is the interaction of *people* with *terrain* and *snowpack* this is our concern in this chapter. More often than not it is us who are the *trigger*! Let's look at each element in turn.

Terrain

If your snowpack is the question, then terrain is your answer – always.

Drew Hardesty. Utah Avalanche Centre

Simple, Challenging and Complex terrain

If we use the Parks Canada Terrain Exposure Scale as a starting point, this can help us decide if the terrain we are planning to ski through is appropriate, when compared to the avalanche forecast and our experience of managing and dealing with the avalanche hazard.

Simple avalanche terrain in Les Contamines.

Simple Terrain – low-angled terrain, there may be some skiing in trees but generally not through obvious avalanche paths. There is lots of low angle terrain available without any overlapping pathways. No glaciers to think about. The Kittelfjäll avalanche was in simple terrain with elements of challenging terrain thrown in.

Challenging Terrain – This is classic alpine ski touring terrain; the mountains are steep enough for avalanches to occur and you will have to pass through terrain where it would be possible to trigger an avalanche in certain conditions. There will almost certainly be terrain traps. You will need to route-find carefully to minimise the risk. There may be glacial skiing with crevasse hazard.

Left: challenging avalanche terrain in the Ortler.

Right: complex avalanche terrain in the Ötztal.

Complex Terrain – The terrain is generally much bigger, where lots of steep slopes may be encountered; in high avalanche risk the skier may be threatened from a number of sides. Avalanche-prone slopes will often have terrain traps (see below) and there are minimal options to minimise the risk. Glacial sections may be complicated with crevasses and icefalls to navigate round.

An Avaluator risk reduction tool.

When planning your ski tour look at the map and consider the terrain. If you think about it in these broad categories it can help you decide whether it is appropriate for the conditions. Check out the Canadian Avalanche Centre's website to learn more about how they can help you reduce your risk in relation to terrain. In particular their Avaluator card is our favourite risk reduction tool. www.avalanche.ca/

Terrain management

Always follow basic travel protocols that limit exposure of you and your group to the avalanche hazard. Avoid skiing above or into terrain traps, don't loiter on or beneath avalanche pathways, and negotiate risky terrain one at a time. Always favour the lower consequence option if it exists. Think about when it's appropriate to ski a line one at a time as opposed to as a group and ski between islands of safety such as tucking beneath cliffs or very large rock features. Be sure that your island of safety is just that and not just a psychological island. If an island isn't present consider skiing the entire slope right out of the runout zone one at a time. If that's the safest option then it's much better than placing the group together on an exposed slope. It can feel alien to ski 300–400 metres away from your group – safer to all stick together right? Wrong! That's a false sense of

Mark Charlton watches the author as he skis into steeper avalanche terrain in Arctic Norway. Photo – Neil Stevenson.

security on an avalanche slope. To put it bluntly, if you follow these terrain management techniques and you screw up, only one member of your party will be avalanched leaving the rest of the party to conduct a rescue.

Terrain traps

Terrain traps are features in the landscape that result in an avalanche being much more serious than its size would suggest. A classic example would be if an avalanche swept a victim into a gully, and then the rest of the avalanche debris piled in on top. The victim would be buried to a significantly greater depth than if they had been avalanched onto a gentle low angle run-out zone. On steep glaciers crevasses are the obvious trap, with the possibility of being swept into a crevasse and it being back-filled. Other obvious terrain features that have serious consequences are: being swept into rocks, over cliffs, into trees or even into a lake. The consequences of being avalanched in trees should not be underestimated. Recall the case study. Twenty-six per cent of all deaths from avalanches are as a result of trauma (Boyd et al. 2009) – being swept through trees by avalanches contributing significantly to this statistic. A further possibility often missed is where a slide path abruptly changes angle, say at a snow cat track, the end of a Scottish gully on a corrie floor, or the bottom of a valley, which causes the debris to slow down and pile up, instead of fanning out and dispersing evenly.

A series of terrain traps.

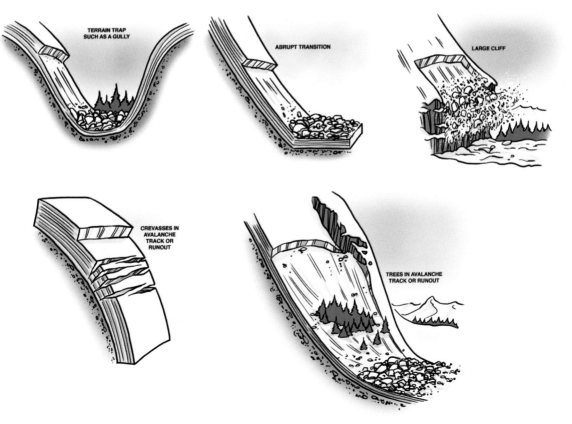

Snow

Snow on the ground is made up of layers. If you like it is the historical record of snowfall for that season. Each new snow event will add a layer. All of these layers interact with each other. It is the bonding between these layers that interests us as skiers because it is at these interfaces that avalanches occur. As a generalisation, over time the snow at these interfaces becomes more stable, but in a cold and thin snowpack facets can grow making the snowpack less stable.

In the long term the snowpack will trend towards stability, but in the short to medium term it could get stronger or weaker depending on a number of factors. Each climatic zone that we choose to ski in will have different characteristics in its snowpack. The snowpack in the Alps tends to stabilise fairly quickly after snowfall as the temperatures are generally quite warm, but the snowpack in a more continental climate is colder and receives less precipitation. In somewhere like Colorado, with its shallow, very cold snowpack, the snow is much slower to stabilise, and weak layers may persist for significant periods of time – sometimes for an entire season. You need to be mindful of this when you move from one mountain region to another in the world.

Andy Helm enjoys some great skiing in Japan. With modern air travel it is so easy to jump continents and snowpacks, and you can spend a lot of time in information deficit.

There used to be a fashion of digging snow pits to make decisions on snow stability. The problem with using this as a single decision-making tool is that the stability information is only representative for that one location. A snow pit can still be a good source of information on the structure of the snowpack, but they do not offer an answer to the stability question over a larger area. Nonetheless, we would encourage you to dig pits in the snow to see what is down there. Looking at the snow in a pit will help you to understand the structure of the snowpack. We always suffer from a lack of snowpack information when travelling through the mountains, and regularly digging around will improve your big picture of what's going on around you on that day.

If you have read the avalanche forecast before you go out you may be able to identify the layers and relate them to what you intend to ski or travel through. The pit dug quickly on the move (just dig down with your hands – no need to bust out your shovel) adds to your information about the snowpack and avalanche hazard. It feeds into the bigger picture, but remember it doesn't offer the answer on its own. It's just another piece of your information-gathering jigsaw. The most useful exercise is to identify any differences in hardness, running a finger down through the wall of your pit can help you feel for these differences.

Snowpack red flags

We could make a huge list of red flags but we have distilled down to the four key red flags relating to snowpack. Alain Duclos, the French avalanche expert, identifies:

- New snow in the last 24 hours. Ninety percent of avalanches happen within 24hrs of fresh snow. We all love skiing fresh snow, so it's a time to be extra aware. The new snow can also arrive by wind transportation.

- Avalanche activity, current and recent. Seeing evidence of a very recent avalanche is nature's biggest clue. If I see an avalanche I am looking at its size – both its width in relation to the slope, and also the size of its crown wall, the aspect of slope it is on. Recent avalanche activity is a **massive indicator of on-going avalanche activity**, but you need to try and work out when the avalanche occurred. If you are in an area and debris wasn't there yesterday and is there today, it is easy. If you are new to the area it can be really useful to have a look at the debris. New debris will look fresh, the edges of the blocks in the debris field will still be angular and appear clean. Over time the edges round off and the surface can become glazed by the sun.

- Weak layers. The presence of weak layers within the snowpack is a red flag.

- Rapid warming. If the air temperature is rising suddenly this can 'activate' instabilities within the snowpack and avalanches may occur. This can lead to long-term stability, especially if there is a cycle of overnight freezing like we often get in the spring, but in the short term it will cause instability. Rapid temperature spikes are a red flag.

Having these four red flags in your mind when you ski is vital to good decision-making. Print them on a card at the start of the season to carry in your pocket to help lodge the key points in mind.

A shooting crack.

There are a couple of other red flag clues that you need to be aware of and which usually indicate significant instability:

• Shooting cracks emanating from your skis for several feet. This often means that you are on a slab that is unstable, containing a lot of energy, but there isn't enough angle or tension in the snow to slide and create an avalanche. If you find this be super-careful about moving onto steeper ground; your head is in the lion's mouth.

• Whumping sounds coming from the snowpack on easy-angled ground. This is the sound of the snowpack collapsing, the noise being a buried, a weak layer collapsing. An indication of poor strength within the snowpack. If you are hearing this on the flat there is a good chance of an unstable layer on steeper slopes. If you are in a safe place this is a great opportunity to dig a pit and have a look at this layer.

People

How we as *people* choose to interact with the *terrain* and the *snowpack* is the key to staying safe in avalanche terrain. We've previously noted that 90% of human involved avalanches are set off by the victims themselves. It's such a powerful statistic because it shows we decide the risk we are willing to expose ourselves to of being avalanched. We can literally choose if we're going to get avalanched or not.

Hazard and risk

If we're going to interact with avalanche terrain by skiing the backcountry we need a toolkit of skills that includes a systematic process of making an assessment of the avalanche hazard before going into the mountains each day, and once in the mountains the ability to re-evaluate the hazard:

What is the relevant avalanche hazard today?

Where will this hazard be present on the mountain?

How serious a hazard is it?

How will we mitigate the risk it imposes?

The avalanche hazard on any given day on the mountain that we choose to ski will be constant. Be it a Low hazard (1), a Moderate hazard (2) a Considerable hazard (3) or a High hazard (4). We should not confuse hazard with risk. We cannot control the hazard, but we most certainly can control our risk when skiing. Risk is how we choose to interact with the hazard. Risk breaks down like this:

What is the **probability** of us being avalanched here?

What are the **consequences** of us being avalanched here?

Probability x consequence (size of avalanche + our vulnerability and exposure) = **risk**

Predicting the **probability** of where and when avalanches will occur is an uncertain business. Throughout the winter, skilled and experienced forecasters have a daily inner struggle to prescribe the correct hazard rating for their forecast area. If the pro's struggle, then in order for us to address that uncertainty, even when we've taken on board all the key points of the avalanche forecast, it's important that we add a margin of safety to our uncertainty. Fortunately, we can add margins in all sorts of ways. Carrying rescue equipment and being well practiced with it adds a margin to our safety, as does skiing one at a time and minimizing our exposure to avalanche slopes. The margin of starting early, the margin of not constantly operating at the edge of our skill ability, the margin of being with an experienced strong team that communicates together well ... there are dozens of margins we can add every day. It's all these small margins that when put together allow us to operate safely in Smith's high-risk environment such as the winter mountains.

Iain Muir skiing low consequence terrain in the Val Claree.

Mike Austin skiing high consequence terrain in Finnmark, Norway.

Predicting **consequence** is much easier. *If I get avalanched on this slope I'm about to ski, what's the likely outcome for me going to be?* Is this a question we should be constantly asking ourselves when skiing in the mountains? For example:

If we drop into a narrow 45-degree rock-lined couloir that funnels out into trees and then a cliff, then we need to be very sure indeed that the probability of the slope avalanching is extremely low, because the consequences of being caught in an avalanche in such terrain would be extreme.

Risk tolerance

Risk is a personal matter. Our risk tolerance is as individual as ourselves. Even within ourselves our risk will vary and change over time. Experience has a direct influence on our risk taking, as friends are lost in the mountains or we suffer the personal consequences of a serious injury, then we tend to dial things back. In our personal risk equation, we judge that the reward doesn't always warrant the risk. Experience is the result of going nose to nose with consequence. We move to operating within the 'green' zone of the various avalanche risk assessment tools such as the Canadian Avalulator where both the probability and consequence are both low and come together to give a 'green' light.

Repeated exposure

But as Manuel Genswein, the Swiss Avalanche expert, critically points out, we forget the crucial element of *repeated* exposure. Yes, by operating in a safe consistent manner we can pull the risk back to a 1:100,000 risk of death every time we go ski touring (*source: based on British Health & Safety Executive*) – not dissimilar to driving a car, but we must factor in *repeated* exposure.

"Because you obviously accumulate exposure over your life." The more frequently you go out, and the greater the level of hazard you expose yourself to each time, the greater your likelihood of dying through *repeated* exposure to the same risk. (The risk remains 1 in 100,000 even on your 100,000th ski tour.)

Risk acceptance

So here is the reality of the 'Big Lie' that Mark Smith, who is quoted at the beginning of this chapter, refers to within the context of backcountry skiing. As a result of repeated exposure, a very frequent backcountry skier – say a sponsored skier or ski guide, one who routinely follows safety protocols all the time, and generally favours the conservative line when available, still has a 1 in 50 chance of death by avalanche over their lifetime. If their risk acceptance finds them constantly riding high consequence aggressive lines repeatedly over their lifetime it drops to 1 in 12.

What is your risk acceptance? It doesn't matter if it is much greater or much less than ours; but it does matter that you know what it is for yourself. Constantly ask yourself the key questions: What's the probability of this slope avalanching? What are the consequences if this slope avalanches? Each of us should be comfortable where we stand in our personal risk verses reward equation.

When thinking about your behaviour consider Alain Duclos' four risk management modes:

- Relaxed – no major concerns of avalanche, but the team stays attentive to any signs of avalanche.

- Concerned – signs of avalanche; new snow, wind, warming. Route choice is important, team will make defensive group management decisions, skiers move spread out. Maybe anticipating moving to alert mode.

- Alert – reactive, group management and route choice very important. Moving from islands of safety to islands of safety, skiing one at a time very defensively.

- Hazardous – strong chance of being avalanched. Choose another tour, objective or do something else that day.

Decision-making, communication, and creating margins

The way we behave in the mountains has become an ever-increasing component of what the avalanche education community focuses on. Educators now recognise that it is our own poor decision-making that invariably results in avalanche incidents, not the 'bad luck' that the media would have the uneducated public believe. The poor decisions we make are often a result of poor communication within the group, while creating margins helps us address these human errors.

Decision-making

Good decision-making is reliant on good quality information. We've already noted that avalanche forecasts, a friendly ski patroller in a bar, and an accurate weather forecast are all very useful planning tools. Conventional maps are an obvious basis of planning our route and afford us the possibility of looking at the terrain we intend to ski and making alternative easier get out of jail options – a plan B should the conditions not be what we expect. Digital mapping is quickly becoming an essential planning tool. The ability to fly over our intended route from the comfort of your sofa the evening before a ski adventure is an incredibly powerful tool. Ski guides have been using this technique in a limited fashion with Google Earth for years. But with new products coming onto the market such as Fatmap and Avanet we can activate a gradient colour overlay that allows us to see exactly if the angle of the wind-loaded bowl we're hoping to drop into is under 30 degrees.

Tour planning is an essential part of any risk mitigation strategy and tools such as Fatmap help greatly in this process.

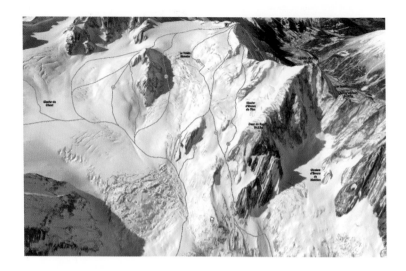

By using digital mapping to plan and then create a route through the mountains that can be transferred onto a mobile device that we can take with us onto the mountain, we now don't have to spend our time in the mountains focused on navigation. That's important too; if 80% of our focus in a whiteout is on navigation, there's very little mental bandwidth left for us to give to the avalanche hazard or to communicating our thoughts and concerns within our companions. Advance planning frees up extra time on our route and gives us a margin of both safety and fun.

Communication

Silence is *not* golden. Not in the backcountry at any rate. There are many impediments to communication in the backcountry ... excitement, fatigue, stress, weather, task overload. That's a problem, because we operate much stronger as a team in avalanche terrain than as a group of individuals. More eyes looking for warning signs that the mountain is trying to give us; signs of recent avalanche activity, changing weather, wind loading. Together we can confirm or challenge our thoughts on stability as the day unfolds, and provide a sounding board for our concerns.

At this point we should differentiate between talking and communication. People have a tendency, when excited about skiing fresh powder, to talk a lot without communicating anything of relevance. When it comes to talking through our avalanche concerns within our team we need to be able to express ourselves clearly and precisely. The ability to eliminate the white noise of chatter while negotiating complex avalanche terrain is a fundamental avalanche skill.

There is in zero room for miscommunication in the backcountry. *Which rock outcrop does she mean we should ski to? Who did we decide was skiing this line last?* Active listening is a huge part of communication. It's a skill to be practised, because when we're stepping into our skis on the summit of a mountain the 'stoke' is high, and more often than not our ears are turned off. Take a minute. Talk it out. Pause. Repeat your thought process and get verbal confirmation: *Does that plan sound good to you? Yes? Ok?*

My regular ski partner is naturally quiet and reserved whilst I am naturally grumpy and always think I know best. This is not a good recipe for effective communication in the backcountry. Fortunately, we have recognized these biases within our team of two and we make time to counter them by having a rule to have an avalanche conversation at natural transition points in our ski day; such as stripping skins or taking a water break. We create a space during a natural break in the day to ask each other the questions that we have been mulling over in our heads. Have you seen anything weird with the snow? ... how do you feel about the stability today? Is our plan for the day still a good idea now we're in the terrain or should we go for the low angle option? Incorporating these discussions into our day helps counteract our biases. It's a simple and effective way to confirm or deny observations and by so doing increases our margin of safety. Mike Austin – Avalanche Geeks

The best backcountry ski teams are a democracy. Everyone is working to the same goal and discussing their snow, weather and terrain concerns as the day unfolds. For this reason, we don't like skiing with strangers. We don't like skiing with friends of friends who have asked to tag along for the afternoon. You don't know their avalanche skills should things go wrong nor their tolerance to risk, and skiing in the backcountry isn't the place to find out. The inclusion of strangers turns your team back into a group. By skiing with people we know and trust we facilitate effective communication. Either way it's hard to ignore key words and phrases:

This isn't safe.

I'm not happy with this decision.

We need to stop.

Why is this a good idea?

This feels dangerous.

These phrases are actually hard to say, that's because they're extremely powerful. They are almost impossible to ignore regardless of the group dynamics or the level of excitement about the skiing that's about to unfold. Keep these phrases tucked away in your avalanche toolbox and be brave enough to pull them out if you need them.

The mountains will always be there; the trick is to make sure you are too.
Hervey Voge

Further reading

Allen & Mike's Avalanche Book by Allen O'Bannon

Staying Alive in Avalanche Terrain by Bruce Tremper, Baton Wicks Publications, 2nd edition, 2008, 978–1898573753.

References

Yin, Yang and You – Roger Atkins ISSW Banff 2014

Conceptual Model of Avalanche Risk – Parks Canada & Canadian Avalanche Assoc.

Grant Statham – TedX Canmore

Grant Statham – SAFOS Edinburgh 2014

Slide – The Avalanche Podcast – Doug Krause

The Big Lie – Mark Smith, Wildland Fire Leadership

Patterns of death among avalanche fatalities: a 21-year review, Boyd et al, CMAJ Mar 2009, 180 (5) 507-512

Avalanche Rescue

The aftermath of an avalanche – no one was injured.

Being avalanched is a bad thing – at best it's scary, at worst fatal. As skiers and ski tourers we have a responsibility to those with whom we ski to know how to search for and rescue someone buried in an avalanche. They have the same responsibility to you, so I would suggest not skiing with people who do not take the need for avalanche rescue techniques seriously and practice it on a regular basis.

If you are not killed by the trauma of an avalanche you have a 92% chance of being dug out alive, if you are rescued in the first 15 minutes of burial. This drops steeply after 15 minutes, to a 37% chance at 35 minutes, and continues to drop after that. Statistics from the American Avalanche Association.

It is the party who you are skiing with who **must perform the rescue;** if you rely on outside assistance you will be looking for dead bodies. We are going to look at a standard method for searching and recovering an avalanche victim, using some standard terms to refer to the different phases of a rescue. They may sound a bit North American, because they are! North America leads the way in considering avalanche education a necessary and integral part of ski touring. In Europe, we could do with accepting that we don't know as much as we should, and invest in some avalanche education. This chapter will provide you with the basic information you need, but it is no substitute for on snow training and practice. Don't assume that just because the people you're with ski a lot they know how to use all of their equipment or make good decisions, and even if they do it's essential that you all practise together throughout the season.

What we are going to talk about in this chapter is a system for rescue that will work with any avalanche transceiver. The principles can be applied to any rescue scenario; it is commonly referred to as 'companion rescue'. Once you have mastered the techniques here, it may not be long before you are teaching them to other people.

Top Tip

Swiss avalanche educator and researcher, Manuel Genswein, has worked out an efficient step-by-step way of teaching a new user the basics of companion rescue in about 15 minutes. This was designed so that guides could pass on the basics to their clients in a clear, structured way to give them some chance of digging out a guide should he be avalanched. I have outlined this method in the Appendices. I would suggest using it as a basis for training friends who have not done any rescue training before you ski off-piste with them.

Transceivers

The transceiver should be worn under a layer of clothing; this allows quick access but reduces the chance of the unit being ripped off the body in an avalanche. Each unit has a different harness system so follow the manufacturer's instructions. An accepted alternative is to carry the unit in a zipped pocket with the retaining strap clipped to something and the screen facing the body for protection.

There is considerable evidence that the effectiveness of your transceiver can be significantly reduced (potentially fatally) by electronic interference. This can be from any electronic device: mobile phones, Go Pros, GPS units, etc. The recommendation is that the electronic device should be at least 40cm away from your transceiver. Smartphones are particularly guilty of causing interference.

Transceiver check

Transceiver worn under a layer of clothing.

When you head out every morning make sure you check your transceiver's battery power before you leave the house. If you don't manage this, at least check it before you leave the car. I always have spare batteries and usually a spare transceiver in the car.

Start of tour transceiver check

It is essential to check at the start of each tour that everyone's transceivers are working and that everyone can hear everyone else's. This is especially the case if you have any people in the group with older analogue transceivers, which may have drifted off signal and not be detected or not be able to detect modern digital units. Both situations have happened to me at the start of tours. Now I won't ski with clients who have analogue transceivers and am reluctant to ski with anyone who is not using a three-antenna transceiver.

I will perform this check once at the start of a tour, or if I am skiing with people where I do not know if their transceivers work or not.

The easiest way to check that everyone's transceivers is working is to stand the team in a line with their units on 'receive' mode; one person walks away with their unit switched off until they are over 50m away. That person stops, turns their unit to send and slowly walks back towards the line, as the unit is detected the detector puts their hand up. This gives a visual indicator of the range of a unit. Walk in until the units all read ten metres, this is a further check that all the units are working the same.

To check that units are sending, everyone turns their unit to send, the same person who walked away last time walks 50m away and turns their unit to receive. The team walk towards them one at a time, the receiver can note when they first picked up the unit. Make sure there is at least a 50m gap between each person to ensure the correct units are being detected. The person can walk on by and get ready to go skiing.

This way the send and receive function on everyone's unit is checked.

If you are skiing with the same team regularly or for a week I will only perform this at the start of skiing time together.

Daily transceiver check

I do this **every day** before skiing. If leaving from the car with or without a lift, it is best done in the car park so something can be done if you discover a faulty transceiver.

The test is a simplified version of the previous test. One person is chosen to perform the test. They stand about 50m from the group and turn their unit to receive. The group then turn their units to send and come past one at a time; this can be performed on foot, skin or ski. If on ski just make sure the group come past slowly enough to confirm the test for each person, and keep far enough apart to check one person at a time.

Some transceivers have a group check function which reduces the range to one metre, so that the checker can go round the group, and easily check one transceiver at a time.

Daily transceiver check best done next to the car or hut where you can sort a problem if you discover one.

Most modern transceivers have a group check function; this reduces the range to 1m, which makes it much easier to check that everyone is in send mode. The checker can stand still and get his group to come past one at a time; the sending unit should be picked up at 1m distance. When all is done the checker turns his unit to send and shows it to one of their team as confirmation.

Companion rescue

The exact organisation of a rescue will depend on the number of victims, rescuers and the situation. We will start with the most basic, one-to-one rescue and build from there. We will look at managing a rescue once we are comfortable with the techniques. You will hear this referred to as 'companion rescue', and if you read more into the subject you will hear the actual search referred to as the 'induction method'.

There are two possible scenarios; the first, where you witness someone being avalanched, the second, where you come across a situation where someone has been avalanched.

Let's start with the first. If you see someone being avalanched watch where they go, if they vanish under the snow mark in your mind the last point where you saw them. If you deem it safe to enter the area, ski in and mark that point; a vertical ski pole is ideal. Now you do not need to search the area above that point. Look for visual clues; it is easy to get focused on your transceiver and miss the foot, glove or hand sticking out.

Avalanche search pattern showing the different search phases. This diagram has been reproduced with kind permission from Backcountry Access Copyright © Backcountry Access Inc 2014.

(1) **Signal Search**

20m | 40m | 40m | 20m

(2) **Coarse Search**

Fine Search

(3)

| single searcher search path | multiple searchers search path |

If you come across an avalanche incident, hopefully a search will already be under way. If not, find out **how many** people are buried, and ask the witnesses to turn their transceivers off and get out their shovels and probes. If they haven't already started searching they probably don't know how to, so don't waste time finding out.

Make sure all the other transceivers on site are switched off, and ask someone to make a manual visual check so you don't waste time following a false signal.

Avalanche on Mont
Blanc du Tacul with
searchers choosing to
accept the risks involved
in being in the line of
any debris falling from
seracs above. They have
made the decision to get
involved in the rescue.

Take care!

Only perform a search if you
feel it is safe to do so; do not
put yourself or your team in
danger. Adding more victims
is bad. In most scenarios once
an avalanche has occurred the
slope is stable, but there are
occasions when this may not
be the case. The most common
situation where you may choose
not to perform a rescue is if
there is a risk of a secondary
avalanche, or you have to go
under a serac (unstable ice cliff)
to perform a rescue.

Signal search

This is the first phase of the search, and you need to make sure you cover
all the debris (if you have marked the last seen point you can start there).
Traverse the slope on foot or ski depending on whichever is easiest. Move
horizontally across the top of the search area 20m in from the edge, drop
down 40m then traverse again until you are 20m from the other side. You
have to assume that the victim is buried deeply, is lying on top of their
transceiver, and has weak batteries; all of these factors will reduce the
signal strength. This search pattern will ensure that the victim is not missed
on the first pass. Move quickly looking for visual clues. You may pick up an
intermittent signal at extreme range which can be confusing. Keep going
with your signal search until you have a solid lock – you are unlikely to get
this until you are within 40m of the victim. Keep moving until the unit reads
less than 40 metres.

Coarse search

Once you have detected the signal follow the direction and distance indicator on your transceiver. Keep moving quickly.

The coarse search done is on skis if the terrain allows.

Mammut Barryvox S showing distance and direction.

Fine search

As you reach 3m from the victim, move your transceiver down next to the snow and use the distance display to find the minimum reading. Mark the minimum point on the snow. Keep your unit in the *same orientation* (i.e. always pointing the same direction) during this phase. When you get close the easiest way to get the minimum reading is to use a system referred to as 'bracketing'. Get as low a reading as possible on your unit as you come in – you may go past the victim and the numbers will increase. If this happens go back to the minimum and, keeping your unit in the same orientation, move the unit from side to side again looking for the minimum. You may have to repeat this procedure a couple of times to reach the minimum. When you have found it mark the point with a hat or glove so you don't lose it while you are getting your probe ready.

Fine search with transceiver close to the snow and always in same orientation.

Pinpoint search

Get your probe out and probe *perpendicular to the surface of the snow*. Start at the lowest reading you got from your transceiver, then if you don't get a positive strike move out 25cm and probe in concentric circles. Each new circle should be 25cm out from the last one.

When you probe, stand with your legs apart and probe vertically between your feet at right angles to the surface of the snow, Always use gloves to protect your hands from a cold injury, and to avoid the probe warming up and getting snow stuck to it which will reduce its efficiency.

Once you have got the lowest reading deploy your probe.

Probing using a hat
to mark the lowest
transceiver reading.
This avoids confusion
in the debris.

When you get a positive probe strike (it will feel like a body, not a rock or snow – practise on a buried rucksack to get the feel) **leave the probe in place.** This does two things; it reassures the victim that you have not missed them and that you are starting to dig, and the probe also gives a visual reference. Once you start digging the snow all looks the same so you need a reference point.

Shovelling

With modern transceivers and practice the search phase of any companion rescue should be fast; digging the victim out is what takes time and is really hard work.

A lot of research has been done in this area to find the most efficient way to dig a victim out of an avalanche. As a general principle you want to avoid moving snow more than once, so efficiency is everything. Start by 'paddling' the snow to the side, this is best done from a kneeling position, once you can't effectively move any more snow this way change to classic digging.

Avalanche debris is usually pretty solid so you may find the best way to move snow is to block it using your shovel then move it. Even dry snow compresses into a solid, hard-to-dig mass, and wet snow sets like concrete. Effective digging in avalanche debris requires a metal-bladed shovel. Plastic shovels flex and bend, they do not cut into the debris and are ineffective in digging. If someone comes skiing with me with a plastic shovel I will swap it with my metal shovel, that way at least they will have the best tools to dig me out.

If the probe strike is less than 1m deep (markings on the probe) start digging one pace downhill from the probe. If the victim is deeper, move 1.5 times the burial depth downhill, and start digging into the hillside towards the victim. Think about digging a ramp down towards the victim, this is the most efficient way to move snow. The advantages of starting downhill are that there is less snow to move and you won't compact the snow on top of the victim so compressing their airspace.

There have also been lots of tests done as to the most efficient use of manpower if there is more than one rescuer. The consensus seems to be:

One rescuer. As above.

Two rescuers:

< 1m burial, start just below the probe then work side by side.

>1m burial, one rescuer just downhill of the probe, the second downhill 1.5x the burial depth.

Three rescuers:

<1m burial, one rescuer digs down just below the probe and the other 2 rescuers dig in from 1.5x burial depth downhill.

Paddling snow to the side, then blocking snow and rolling it out of the way.

>1m burial, two rescuers 1.5x burial depth downhill and the third rescuer clearing snow below them.

Four rescuers:

<1m burial, two rescuers work downhill of the probe then the second two work 1.5x the burial depth.

>1m burial, start as above, as the hole gets deep you may want to pull one person out of the hole to create space to work, they can then rotate back into the team as people tire.

Five rescuers:

<1m burial as with four, but the extra person prepares for the victim and rotates in as the shovellers get tired.

>1m as with <1m.

If you have more rescuers they can rotate in as the team tire, rotating every minute seems the most efficient. When digging there is no point in making the front any wider than 2m; when you find the victim work out which way round they are facing and dig towards the head.

Once you have got to the head, clear the airway (this may involve scooping snow from their mouth), reassure them, and dig the rest of their body out as quickly as possible as it is common for people to be in a panicked state. Turn off their avalanche transceiver as soon as possible, so it doesn't interfere with the search for any other victims. If they are unconscious you will have to go through your standard first aid and look after their airway. You can assume a degree of hypothermia as well.

You must practice this regularly; by practice I mean realistic scenarios on difficult ground with deep burials. Burying transceivers under leaves in the park is no substitute for avalanche education and regular practice.

Managing a rescue

If there is more than just you to perform a rescue then there is a degree of management and teamwork required to carry out an efficient rescue.

We will consider one buried victim and multiple rescuers to begin with, then we will move onto multiple burials.

Whether you arrive on scene or if it is one of your party who has been avalanched, the most important thing is the safety of the whole party; there is no point adding to the victim list. If you don't feel it is safe to enter the area of the avalanche you will have to make that horrific decision.

Managing a rescue –
teamwork is the key.

Start by appointing a leader. This person needs to manage those on the surface to ensure efficient use of manpower, and keep track of victims as they are dug out. This may not be the most experienced person, whose expertise in the use of a transceiver may be best used in the actual search.

Identify your searchers and manually check that everyone else has turned off their transceivers. Less is often more here as too many people with beeping transceivers will confuse the search. If you have enough people, you could send someone down straight away to ski across the debris looking for visual clues. They can have their transceiver on receive while they do this, but their focus should be on the visual.

Depending on the size of the debris and the number of people you have available, you should have two people splitting the search pattern described earlier, or have people spread at 40m intervals across the debris starting and finishing 20m in from the edge.

Once a signal is detected, it is the leader's role to ensure that the search pattern is reorganised to make sure the whole debris is checked on the first pass.

While the searchers are getting to work, the rest of the team can be assembling shovels and probes ready for the pinpoint search and the recovery. If you have multiple victims it is the leader's job to keep track of the number of people rescued.

It is normal practice to perform the companion rescue, then call for outside help when everyone has been accounted for. In the case of a big team someone could be doing this while the team search and begin the recovery phase. If you don't have the manpower, focus on the rescue first, remember the victims have 15 minutes.

Multiple burials

This is the worst-case scenario when you end up with a number of people buried under the snow. The search is set up as described above. Once the first victim is discovered the people not searching can be straight in with a probe and shovels while the rescuer(s) search for the next victim. You should know there are multiple burials from witnessing the avalanche or interviewing a survivor. If you have arrived on scene and your transceiver is detecting multiple burials then you know to continue the search after the first victim has been found. If you suspect a multiple burial but don't know for definite if this is the case, find the first victim, then once recovery of the first victim is underway search the rest of the debris using the signal search method described earlier.

Research has shown that the best way to ensure the maximum number of survivors is to practice what is known as reverse triage. In a normal first aid situation you go to the quiet unconscious people first. In an avalanche rescue situation you check those on the surface first, they may have a serious bleed that can be easily treated where as those buried under the snow are an unknown quantity until they have been found and dug out. If everyone is buried then digging the shallower burials out first will increase the chance of rescuing some people, whereas if you commit to a deep burial then you will easily use up your 15 minute rescue window before you get to the first victim. If you dig out any shallow burials first you may end up with another digger to help with any deeper burials.

There are a number of possible techniques to deal with a multiple burial situation depending on the type of transceiver you have. We have outlined the two most common multiple burial features, then described two methods that do not rely on any specific transceiver feature.

Mammut Barryvox S transceiver showing the mark function.

Multiple with mark function

The 'mark function' on a transceiver has been a big step forward in effective searching for multiple avalanche victims; however it doesn't always work. Make sure you read and practise the 'micro search strip' and 'three circle' methods outlined below.

If your avalanche transceiver has a mark function, once you have a probe strike on the first victim, hold the unit about 1m above the snow and press the mark button. The unit will then ignore that signal and immediately begin to search for the next unit. When it has found it, follow the unit as per the first victim. If no signal is detected then return to the signal search phase.

Three circle method

If during the coarse search you detected more than one buried victim and don't have, or are struggling with, the Mark Function, then the 'three circle method' may help find a second victim. Find the first victim as normal, then using the probe on the first victim as a central point move out 10m and walk in a circle with a 10m radius. You are looking for a signal on your unit that is not the person currently being dug out. If you don't detect a second signal move out a further 5m and repeat, then a further 5m. If you haven't detected a second signal at this stage return to your signal search at 40m spacing. You may find that certain transceivers won't let you do this so it is worth making sure you have practised and are very comfortable with the nuances of your particular device.

Any avalanche situation is going to be incredibly stressful, so make sure you have practised it thoroughly so all the elements discussed here become second nature.

Three circle method.

Micro search strip

An alternative technique to the three circle method, which also works really well if you have multiple burials in a small area, is the 'micro search strip'. This is effectively a scaled-down version of the signal search with two main differences – the size of the pattern, and the function of the transceivers you are going to use. To make sure the second victim is not going to be missed we use a spacing of 3 to 4m, about the length of two skis end to end. Start about this distance uphill from the first victim. When using the transceiver you are now going to ignore the direction arrow and concentrate on the distance and audible signal.

Move horizontally across the slope until you are 3m in from the edge of the debris, then up or down the debris depending on which direction you have already searched (down if you have already searched the debris above the victim). Move down 3m, then across the slope until you are 3m in from the edge, then down again. It is important to keep the search pattern as rigid as possible and keep the search lines straight. You are looking for a change in the distance reading that will indicate the proximity of a new transceiver. Once this is detected, use the induction method to find the victim. If there are further victims, return to the point where you deviated from the micro search strip pattern and continue with the search pattern.

What to do if you are the victim

Being avalanched is one of the most stressful things that can happen in the mountains. It has happened to me once, I was buried to my waist and don't want to go through that again.

If you are caught, give a big shout so people know you have been caught and they can watch where you go. Try to hold onto anything, or if there is nothing you can claw at the bed surface, or try to dig your ski poles in. Any delay you can make before being swept off will allow snow to move past you. The closer you are to the top of the avalanche the more likely you will be on the surface.

If you have an airbag, deploy it. If you have an Avalung, fight to get the tube in your mouth.

Get rid of your poles, and if possible your skis, as quickly as possible as they will drag you down (I don't use the wrist loops on my poles for this reason). Fight to stay on the surface. As you feel the avalanche slowing down, make a huge effort to get clear. If you can move your arms, try to get them in front of your face to create an air pocket. If you are buried, try not to panic. Easy to say I know, but panicking will use up your oxygen supply more quickly. Finally, hope that your team's avalanche rescue training has been effective and worthwhile.

First Aid

Using tactical digging you are digging a trench towards the victim. When you arrive at the victim slow down and work out where the head is. Clear the head as quickly as possible. Your priority is to clear the airway as quickly as possible. If you can't get to it do not try and pull them out of the snow – clear the snow around them and roll them out of the snow into the trench.

If they are not breathing then you need to consider the following:

- Obvious lethal trauma or body completely frozen; do nothing and look after your team.

- If clear airway but not breathing commence CPR but consider reverse triage. At some point you may not be able to continue and need to look after yourself and your team.

- No pulse AND airway packed with snow and burial time of 35 minutes you need to consider whether it is realistic to start CPR. If you do how long can you continue before effecting you and your teams well being?

Some final thoughts

Now think back to the Kittelfjäll case study in the previous chapter. What about first aid, and what will you do to stop your casualty becoming hypothermic? Are you able to contact the emergency services in a foreign country and guide them precisely to your location? Is there a suitable place to land a helicopter at the accident site? How do you prepare an appropriate landing zone for a rescue helicopter?

Now with all that in mind, doesn't looking for your friends' beacon under some leaves in the park seems pretty inadequate? We recommend that you take a one-day avalanche rescue course where all of these skills get taught and you'll practise complex in-depth staged rescue scenarios. Having the right equipment alone is simply not enough if you're going to give yourselves a fighting chance of a successful rescue. Having the right equipment and these skills honed gives us an important margin of safety in the mountains.

Glacier Skiing

Kate Scott with
John and Fiona Fells
skinning to the Italian
side of the Vallée
Blanche – a spectacular
route through some
large crevasses.

Skiing on a glacier is one of the most exciting elements of ski touring. The fact that you are on a glacier means that you are in the high mountains, which is pretty exciting already, then add in the extra elements of glacier skiing and you have a very special experience. With the grandeur and splendour of skiing on a glacier there is an increased risk, as glaciers are dynamic high mountain environments. A glacier is a body of ice that is flowing down the mountain powered by gravity. The speed and nature of a glacier are a function of the steepness, average annual temperature, amount of snowfall, and the shape of the bedrock. All these factors will affect the hazards we have to deal with when on skis; these hazards include crevasses, serac fall, avalanches and steep ground.

On average glaciers are not particularly steep, and glaciers steeper than 30 degrees where there is regular avalanche risk are rare, but you must be aware of it. The other common thing that people miss when skiing on a glacier is to look at what is above them. You may be skiing on an easy-angled glacier, but the mountains above and around you may be much steeper, so you need to constantly be looking up as well as around. If there is fresh snow or a high avalanche risk, an avalanche may release from a long way above you and land on you, even though you are on low angled terrain.

Some glaciers can be quite steep, especially towards the end (snout) of the glacier. This can add to the risk of slipping or falling, and careful assessment of the conditions and route is essential.

Rob Jarvis fell into this crevasse when a snow bridge broke; there was no sign of the crevasse on the surface. Photo – Rob Jarvis.

The final and biggest danger on a glacier is crevasses. As a glacier flows down the mountain it moves by a number of processes. If the changes of angle and speed are not too great, a glacier can flow by internal deformation of its ice crystals and by the lubrication provided by free water at its base. If the glacier is moving more quickly, the ice fractures creating crevasses. These crevasses can be incredibly deep with obvious consequences if a skier should fall into one. When looking at a glacier try to visualise how it is moving, with the ice behaving as a flowing liquid. Imagine melted toffee flowing through the mountains. Now think how it would flow around corners, and how it will tear at the outside edges forming crevasses. On the insides of the corner the toffee will pile up; these zones of compression are free of crevasses. When skiing we look at the glacier and try to visualise where the zones of compression will be, and plan our route along the glacier linking these safe compression zones. If you look at a glacier in summer, the winter snows have melted and many of the crevasses are visible, this is especially the case on lower altitude glaciers where the snow may melt completely to leave bare blue ice (known as a dry glacier). When the first snows of winter arrive and the wind blows, these crevasses start to cover over, they don't fill in as we might hope, but the snow drifts across the surface creating a hard layer. This layer is known as a crevasse bridge, which can be so big that it covers a crevasse completely, or it can be narrow enough to only allow one skier to cross at a time. If the bridge is thick and well frozen it will be strong enough for a skier to cross without any real danger, but if it is thin or not frozen (as you may find in the late spring) then there can be a real chance of the bridge collapsing and you falling into a crevasse. These bridges take time to form, so if you are skiing on a glacier early in the season you need to be extra vigilant; you can check the depth of snow on the glacier with your avalanche probe. With a snow depth of two metres (i.e. at two metres you don't feel ice), the glacier can be considered well covered with strong bridges, However, even with that amount of snow you can't let your guard down.

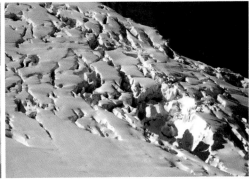

Two shots of the Vallée Blanche, one in winter when all the crevasses are covered and one in summer when they are all revealed.

Luckily travelling on skis our weight is spread out over the surface of the snow, which allows us to travel unroped much of the time, unlike mountaineering in the summer where your weight is only spread across the length of your foot. This is why mountaineers always travel roped-up on a glacier.

With a bit of knowledge and care you can minimise the risk of falling into a crevasse, but it is essential that you have the equipment and know-how to deal with a crevasse incident should one occur.

As we discussed above, crevasses occur where the ice can no longer flow smoothly and so it fractures. This happens when the glacier goes round a bend, over a steep piece of rock, or at the sides where the centre of the glacier is flowing quickly but the edges are flowing more slowly due to friction. If the glacier goes over a big drop then you may get an icefall, where the ice cascades down in a series of crevasses, blocks and towers of ice. One of the most famous of these in the skiing world is the Geant Icefall on the classic Vallée Blanche in Chamonix.

The Geant Icefall.

Icefalls can create significant obstacles to the skier, and they vary from year to year depending on the movement of the glacier and amount of snow. One year an icefall may be easy to negotiate, and another there may be big crevasses and ice cliffs that make passage impossible.

When you are skiing on a glacier you need to look at the terrain, but it doesn't take that long to work out, on a large scale, where the crevasses are likely to be and you can choose your route accordingly. On a smaller scale it isn't as simple as that. Once a glacier moves past an area of crevasse generation, it takes a while for the crevasses to close up again. This is especially the case in cold, slow-moving glaciers where crevasses appear in seemingly bizarre places. An extreme example would be in Antarctica where the temperature is so cold that the glaciers are generally very slow moving, hence you can find large crevasses in the middle of large, flat areas of glacier. You always have to be on the lookout.

The key pieces of kit for glacier skiing are your eyes in ascent or descent. I will be looking for the obvious signs of crevassing, but I will also be looking for the subtle things as well. Dips in the surface of the snow, especially ones that run across the glacier or that look slightly linear, can often signal the presence of a hidden crevasse.

Dip in the glacier indicating a crevasse.

Skiing downhill on a glacier

In descent keep your speed under control so you can react quickly to clues that you spot. When skiing downhill you should be particularly wary at the bottom of a dip or a roll over, as this is the classic place for crevasses to hide. Spread the team out so that the weight is not concentrated in one place. A friend of mine was skiing on a glacier and had just told his client not to stop next to him, so that the weight was not concentrated in one place. He stopped, the client skied in next to him, against instructions. Their combined weight was enough to break the crevasse bridge and they both fell in the crevasse. Andy was carrying an ice axe and crampons and climbed out, then pulled the client out – luckily there were just some cuts and bruises.

You need to discuss how you are going to ski and how you are going to manage your communication before heading onto a glacier. I would suggest skiing about 10m apart as a minimum spacing, and do not all stop in the same place.

Skiing in ascent on a glacier

The same guidelines apply as above, keep spread out, with your most experienced crevasse hound out in front. Look for the big and the small signs of crevassing. The big ones are easier to spot, so concentrate hard on reading the undulations in the terrain. Shadows and small dips in the surface can often indicate a crevasse. When setting a track I will detour around anything suspicious – why take the risk? The rest of the team should follow in the track, as that is known to be a safe line.

Probing for crevasses while skiing on a rope.

If there is a track in place don't assume that it is safe, people do fall into crevasses on skinning tracks so look at the terrain ahead and around you. If you have to head through a particularly complicated piece of glacial terrain, consider putting the rope on (we will look at this shortly). Get an avalanche probe out and use it to probe the terrain ahead. When you push the probe into the snow you should feel constant resistance, indicating that the snow has no big holes in it. If you hit something hard this is probably ice, which is even better. If you push the probe in and you suddenly get no resistance, you are almost certainly probing a crevasse. Hold onto the probe if this happens, if you let go the probe may slide all the way through and you will lose it.

If I am probing, I will generally be on a rope as I am concerned about the risk of falling into a crevasse. If you aren't actually probing but you are in an area where you feel you might need to probe, you can clip the probe onto your harness and let it drag behind. When you are probing in this manner, you will be grateful to have a proper probe instead of some ridiculous lightweight model.

Using a rope on a glacier

I will use a rope on a glacier if I think there is a real chance of falling into a crevasse. Skiing roped up can be difficult to manage, and skiing uphill on a rope is much easier than skiing downhill roped up. The most common reason to use a rope is in poor visibility when, no matter how good your navigation or how good you think a GPS is, neither will help you find crevasses in a whiteout. My personal recommendation is to avoid skiing on a glacier in really bad visibility, unless you absolutely have to. This might happen if the weather changes, and you are faced with a horrendous forecast with an increasing avalanche risk, so you have to escape. I would think very carefully about setting out with the rope on – if the weather is that bad I would sit tight until it is safe to leave. It is a different thing to be out and then decide that the rope is necessary. Setting out with a rope on pushes you into a safety corner, whereby you have deployed all your tools at the start of the day. If one of your team twists a knee or you have some other problem and the visibility/weather is so bad you need a rope, no one will be able to come to help and you are now in an extremely serious situation.

Skiing roped up in ascent and descent.

It is impractical to have every member of the party on the same rope. I would suggest having the three strongest skiers on the rope, then the other members of the team following in their tracks. They should be spaced out, as we discussed earlier. In ascent this is pretty simple as the team can stay in the skinning track. In descent this is much more difficult. The team on the rope won't be able to do much beyond a glorified snowplough, and those following unroped need to stay in their track so won't be able to do much more.

Tying into the end of a rope with a figure of eight knot.

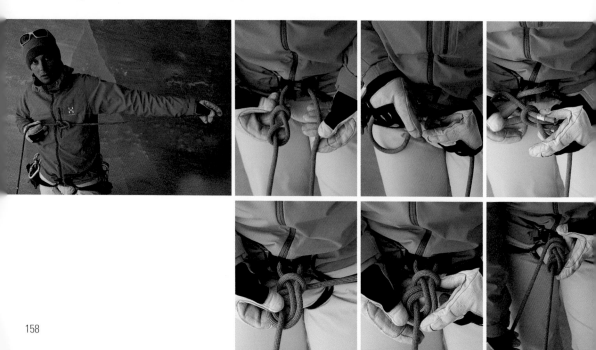

Roping up

When travelling on a glacier always wear a harness. Put it on when you set out in the morning and leave it on, it isn't practical or sensible to put it on when you think you are in crevassed terrain. Your harness should have the kit discussed in the equipment chapter on it. Make sure you know who in your party has the ropes, and ensure they don't ski close together in case they both fall down a crevasse together.

If you decide to rope up I would suggest you start with someone tied to each end of the rope and one person in the middle. The people at the ends then take coils across their body to shorten the rope to the required length. Having about twelve arm spans between each person seems to work pretty well. If the crevasses are really big you may need a lot more rope out between you, to make sure you don't end up with more than one person on a bridge at any one time. Descending a really complicated glacier in Greenland, after a first ascent, we had five people and 75m of rope out as the crevasses were so big. Communication is more difficult with lots of rope out and the rope can be difficult to manage, but you need to adapt to the situation. With three people on the rope, if one person falls in a crevasse then the other two are there to hold the fall, then pull them out.

Tying on to the rope

At each end

To tie onto the end of the rope the best knot is a rethreaded figure of eight. Tie a single figure of eight as demonstrated in the picture, leaving a tail of about 60cm. This is approx the distance from your left shoulder to the end

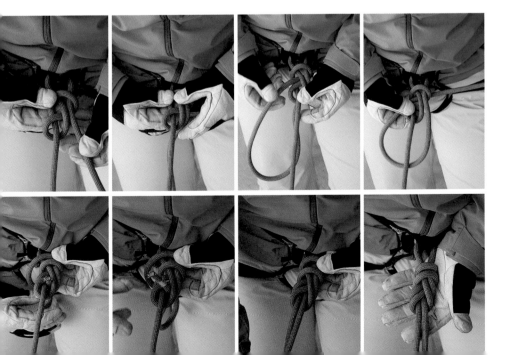

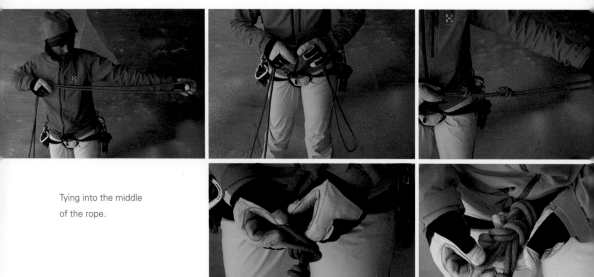

Tying into the middle
of the rope.

of your right arm. Thread the end of the rope through your harness as per
the manufacturer's instructions. Now rethread the figure of eight following
it exactly as shown in the photograph. A loop has now been created through
your harness with about 15cm of tail.

In the middle

Find the middle of the rope; it is useful to have marked this previously, if it
isn't marked take the two ends and flake the rope doubled, until you find
the middle.

Top Tip

Mark the middle using a specialist rope marker designed not to
damage the rope or wrap it with a piece of tape.

Take a loop of rope at the midpoint of the rope (the distance from your
left shoulder to the end of your right hand should be long enough). Tie an
overhand knot in the rope, then tie a second overhand about 10cm out
(towards the loop) from the first, and thread the end of the loop through
your harnesses as per the manufacturer's instructions. Poke the end of
the loop through the middle of the knot closest to your body, then tie an
overhand knot round the rope between the two knots. You should have a
small tail left, which you need to clip back into the loop created by the rope
running through your harness with a screwgate karabiner.

Taking coils

Once the middle person has tied into the rope, as detailed above, measure out the twelve arm spans from them towards each end, and tie a little thumb knot in the rope as a marker. Now take coils from each end; this is the easiest way of dealing with the extra rope. Start by putting your hood up and your rucksack on; it is much more comfortable having the rope outside your hood. It is easier to adjust the coils if they are on top of your rucksack straps.

Start by running the rope up the front of your body round your neck and under the opposite arm, then back up the front to make a loop. My preference is up my left side and under my right arm but this method works either way round, (I will refer to hands in this orientation). The bottom of the loop should be mid way between your waist and your armpit. If the loops are longer the coils will fall off your shoulder, if they're shorter they will feel restrictive. Once you have the length correct, flick the rope over your head and under your right arm – putting a small twist in the rope as you do this will make the coils sit better.

Taking coils – loop method.

Taking coils – hand method.

An alternative method is to choose the correct length of coil, and then use your other hand as a spacer and wrap the coil between your hand and your neck in front of your torso, and then slide your arm through once the coils are done. I don't think this makes for such a neat set of coils but it is easier to learn.

Locking off coils.

Once you have your coils, you will need to lock them off. If you don't and someone falls in a crevasse you will be strangled by the rope. There are a number of methods for locking off coils, this is just one that works for me.

When you have an appropriate amount of coils around your body, put your right hand across your body behind all the coils, between your torso and the rope. Take hold of a loop of rope, about 30cm long, from the tail of the rope and pull it through, across your chest, so it is now in the centre of the coils. Tie a hitch around the rope leading to the next person. Clip this into the rope knot loop on your harness with a screwgate karabiner.

When practising this, get someone to pull on the rope as if they were falling into a crevasse, you will feel that the pull point is quite high and it is easy to be pulled off your feet. You can lower the pull point by tying an overhand knot in the rope leading towards them and clipping this into your rope knot loop. Alternatively you can create the same effect using a prusik knot (see tying prusik knots later in the book).

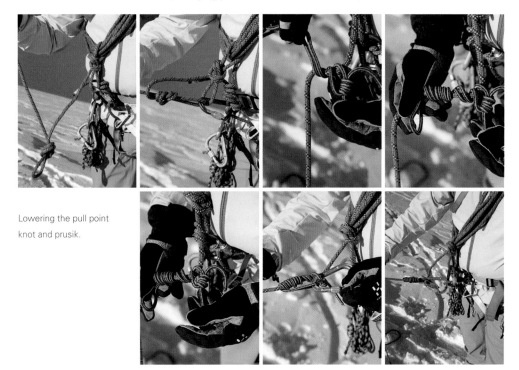

Lowering the pull point knot and prusik.

Crevasse rescue

There are two possible scenarios; falling into a crevasse unroped and falling into a crevasse roped-up. The former is probably the most likely when skiing, but the latter is the preferable.

I cannot suggest strongly enough practising all this stuff before you go on the hill. You can practise all the rope work and techniques at home, in a park or your garden, or in a climbing wall. On the hill, find a drop-off or a small edge on a non-glaciated piece of ground to practise, if you do need to do any of the following techniques in anger they will come much more easily if you are well practised. A French guide friend of mine died while teaching this on a glacier, when he discovered a huge crevasse under the place he was digging an anchor, so be sure to practise where it is safe. I will rarely teach or practise this on a glacier. Like avalanche rescue these situations are always extremely stressful, so the more you have practised, the easier the real thing will be. This is especially important when skiing with new ski partners, as you cannot assume they know how to perform a rescue. It is no use being the expert if you are in the bottom of the crevasse and you haven't taught your team how to rescue you.

Unroped crevasse fall – person in the crevasse

If someone falls into a crevasse, unroped, they are probably going to need medical attention, so if there are enough people in the party, it is worth getting someone to call for assistance straight away while everyone else gets on with the rescue. Make sure you have the rescue numbers pre-programmed into your phone and know what information will be required when reporting an incident. See chapter 'When It All Goes Wrong'.

In a crevasse there may be a number of snow bridges at different levels. If you fall through one bridge, you may be lucky enough to land on another bridge and not go all the way to the bottom, which is usually fatal. Research by the Chamonix rescue services (PGHM – Peleton Gendarmerie du Haute Montagne) has found that most unroped crevasse fall fatalities occur during a fall through a secondary snow bridge.

Screwing an ice screw into the wall of a crevasse and clipping in.

Cord loops can help secure skis when taking them off in a crevasse.

If you do fall into a crevasse, once you have landed don't stand up or move about, look around you. If you can reach the crevasse wall, carefully and gently, take your ice screw and screw it into the ice wall. If possible place the screw at shoulder height, that way when your team start to rescue you, it is easy to unclip. Once you have placed the ice screw, clip your long sling into it and into your harness. Even if the bridge you have landed on collapses, you are now safe and you can get organised to be rescued.

If you can't reach the wall, you will have to decide if it is best to stay still or gently move towards a side wall where you can place an ice screw and clip in.

Once you have clipped in, you need to organise yourself to make it easier for the team on the surface to pull you out. You will see lots of texts covering climbing up the rope out of the crevasse, usually referred to as prusiking. In 20 years of ski touring I have never heard of anyone doing this. It is a useful technique to know and there may be an occasion to use it; for example, if you fall into a crevasse and the team you are with can't do anything more than create an anchor and throw you a rope. This should be the minimum competence of the people in your team.

Mike Austin takes skis off hanging in a crevasse; James Thacker is hauled out of a crevasse with skis below him.

To be pulled out, or if you have to climb out of a crevasse, you will need to take your skis off, but there is a real danger of dropping them into the crevasse, where they may never be seen again. Prepare your skis before you go into the mountains with small loops of cord in an accessible place on the bindings, so they can be clipped with a karabiner before you take them off.

You can then clip the skis into your harness or rucksack so they will hang below you out of the way. If you are going to climb out on the rope or be pulled out they should hang nicely below you.

Prusiking out of a crevasse

If you are lowered a rope and have to climb out, rather than have your team mates pull you out, you will need two prusiks, as discussed in the kit section. One at a time, wrap the prusik around the rope leaving a small loop at the top, pass the knot through the loop and pull down, this will cause the knot to bite on the rope. This is known as a Klemheist knot.

Tying a Klemheist knot.

When you have attached both prusiks like this, clip the top one into your harness with a screwgate karabiner. Slide it as far up the rope as you can then sit down; you will probably sink back down as the rope stretches. Now make a foot loop.

Attaching a prusik
to the waist and
making foot loop.

Take an 8ft (120cm) sling and attach it to your foot. If you wrap the sling round your boot it is less likely to slip off; this stops the sling from continuously falling off your foot. Attach this to the lower prusik with a karabiner. You may need to adjust the length of the sling, which you can do by tying an overhand knot in the sling. Slide the lower prusik up until it is just below the top prusik, then stand up in the sling. Hold yourself in balance with one hand then loosen the top prusik and slide it up as far as it will go, then sit down into your harness, weighting the prusik. You can now loosen the bottom prusik and slide it up, stand up, move the top one again and repeat.

Prusiking up a rope.

As you get higher, it is worth tying an overhand knot in the rope, below the lower prusik, and clipping it into your harness in case either of the prusiks fails. As you get to the lip of the crevasse you may have a bit of a battle to get over it, but that will depend if your team have prepared the lip or not.

Unroped crevasse fall – people on the surface

Lots of people

If you have enough people and the victim is conscious, pulling someone out of a crevasse is relatively straightforward as long as you can get a rope to them. If the person is unconscious you will need to go into the crevasse to attach the rope. You will also need to create a chest harness to keep them upright, as they will quickly suffocate if they are hanging in a harness unconscious.

The key thing, like avalanche rescue, is not to become a victim or make the situation any worse yourself. Hopefully the person in the crevasse will have made themselves secure to the side, you then need to probe the area to make sure there aren't any hidden crevasses. If you have enough people you just need to get a rope to them then pull them out. The best way to do this is to get four of your team to clip into the rope at one end and sit down. This is as good an anchor as you will create. Keep everyone spaced out, attaching themselves to the rope by tying an overhand knot in the rope then clipping this into their harness with a screwgate karabiner, then spreading out so there is light tension in the rope and sitting down.

You now have an anchor and the next step is to get the rope to the victim, so someone needs to approach the edge of the crevasse. Use a Klemheist knot, as described earlier, wrap it around the rope, then clip it into your harness; this will protect you as you move towards the crevasse lip.

Using a Klemheist knot to protect while probing the edge.

Preparing the edge of the crevasse.

It is a good idea to use a ski pole or an avalanche probe to feel for the edge, as it may be sooner than you think. Approach the edge from an angle so that you don't knock snow or collapse the lip onto the victim. As you approach the edge, shout to try and establish communication with the victim. At the edge you should be able to see them – if the edge feels unstable you may want to lie down. Throw the end of the rope to the victim with an overhand knot in it. They can then clip this into their harness and your team can now back up, to take the slack out of the rope. You can now prepare the edge. If it is very overhung you will need to cut away the snow to make it easy for the victim to climb out. Pad the edge or lip with a ski pole, ice axe or rucksack to stop the rope from cutting in.

Klemheist with a sling.

Top Tip

You can tie a Klemheist knot using a sling, this is the only prusik knot that can be tied with a sling.

Once you have prepared the edge, everyone can stand up and walk backwards away from the crevasse pulling the victim out. Someone should stay at the edge to communicate and monitor.

Top Tip

> There have been some nasty accidents with victims being pulled into the underside of crevasse lips by over enthusiastic rescuers, so it is vital, no matter what the situation, that the victim is monitored as they approach the crevasse lip.

Fewer people

If you are a typical, small ski touring party, you aren't going to have enough manpower to use the system described above, so you will need to create an anchor in the snow then set up a hauling system. There are a number of different hauling systems, but we will look at the two most common ones here.

There are two options when building an anchor; you can place an ice screw, or bury something in the snow. If the snowpack is thin you may be able to dig down in the snow to the ice and place an ice screw.

Building an anchor in ice

An ice screw is the most solid anchor you will get on a glacier but it isn't usually possible to be able to dig down to the ice, due to the volume of snow. If you can reach the ice, clean the surface of the ice to get to the best quality ice, place two ice screws 30cm apart, preferably offset. Take a long sling and clip an end into each ice screw, using your finger to find the pull point, tie an overhand knot in the doubled sling. The knot splits the load between the ice screws and ensures that should one fail then the other isn't shock loaded. The knot also creates a central loop where the rope and haul system can be attached.

Building an ice screw belay.

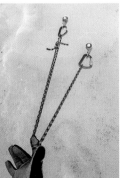

Building an anchor in the snow

If you have to bury something in the snow your skis are probably the best thing to use as they have a large surface area that can create a solid anchor. In some snow conditions you may need to bury your rucksack or in really soft snow you may need to use a person as an anchor. The latter would be particularly hard work but you have to be able to improvise. A classic situation for a human anchor would be glacier skiing on a big powder day, where the snow is too soft and too deep to reach consolidated snow in order to create an anchor.

Human anchor in the snow.

The easiest anchor to create is a buried horizontal ski. Be sure to have a good probe around the area to make sure you are not on a crevasse, before you take your skis off and get your shovel out. Dig a horizontal trench, just longer than your skis, perpendicular to the direction of pull. The exact depth will depend on the quality of the snow. In consolidated snow, going down about a foot would be fine, in softer snow you will need to go deeper. The anchor should be dug about 5m back from the edge of the crevasse. Further back and you will use up too much rope getting from the anchor to the victim to create a haul system, too close and you will be operating dangerously close to the edge.

When you are digging the horizontal slot try not to disturb the snow in front of the anchor, as this is what gives the anchor strength. Dig the slot with the front face as smooth as possible and angle it backwards slightly to help keep the ski in place when it is loaded.

Once you are happy with the back slot you will need to dig a front slot, where the attachment point for the haul system will go. This should be dug in the direction of pull, the slot needs to be as deep as the ski slot and should be as narrow as possible. If you cut it with your shovel handle or an ice axe you should be able to keep it really narrow.

Tie a long sling, or the 5m of cord mentioned in the kit section, around the waist of the skis, the best knot to use is a clove hitch as it tightens round the skis, but if you can't remember how to do one anything solid will work.

Building a horizontal
ski anchor.

You need to be careful that the edges of the skis can't cut the sling/rope. If you are using two skis face to face this isn't such an issue, but if you are using just one ski I would wrap a glove or something around the ski, under the cord or sling, at the attachment point. If you are using a frame binding, especially a model with a raised bar like a Fritschi, it is worth feeding the rope or sling under the bar to avoid the risk of damaging the binding.

Tying into a horizontal
ski belay with a
sling or cord.

You can back-fill the ski slot with snow. There hasn't been any evidence to prove that this increases strength, but it will prevent the ski from popping out of the slot when loaded.

Take time to get this anchor right, as the life of everyone who is attached to the system depends on the integrity of the anchor. If it fails someone will probably be killed.

Creating a direct haul system

Clip a screwgate karabiner into the anchor; if you have used the cord tie an overhand knot in it to create a loop. Take the end of the rope, tie an overhand knot in it and clip it into the karabiner. Now attach yourself to the rope using a Klemheist knot as described above.

Top Tip

> A Klemheist works best with the longer tail being in the direction of pull; it will work the other way round but not as well.

Attach the rope to the anchor with an overhand, then attach yourself with a Klemheist.

Throw the end to the victim.

Work your way down to the edge of the crevasse, establish communication with the person in the crevasse, and throw them the end of the rope. You need to get the rope tight on the victim as quickly as possible in case the snow bridge they are on collapses, which could shock load the anchor. Snow and all other mountaineering anchors don't like being shock loaded.

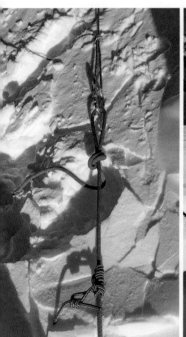

Back at the anchor, leave the end clipped in as a back-up and clip a HMS (pear-shaped) karabiner into the anchor with the narrow end pointing towards the victim. Take a prusik loop and wrap it round the rope leading to the victim then clip both ends into the karabiner. This is known as a French prusik, and its job is to hold the rope so you can haul then rest, without the rope slipping backwards. The French prusik should self-manage if the narrow, pointed end of the karabiner is towards the victim. This is often known as an autobloc. Dig out the snow from under the prusik so that when tensioned it is floating; this stops snow from impeding smooth operation. Once the French prusik is clipped into the karabiner, clip the rope through the karabiner, do up the screwgate and pull the rope through until it is snug on the victim.

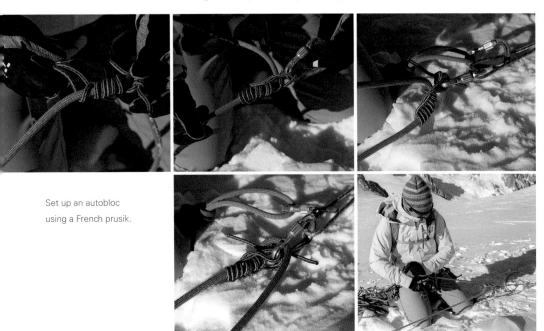

Set up an autobloc using a French prusik.

It is worth securing this using a slippery hitch, also commonly known as a mule hitch.

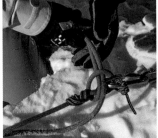

Lock off with a slippery hitch.

This knot backs up the French prusik while you work at the edge, but it can be released under load should the prusik slip. Here you could use a mechanical device instead of French prusik, which we will look at shortly.

Still using your Klemheist for safety, you can go back to the lip and prepare the edge of the crevasse.

The next stage is to set up a haul system. Take a second prusik, tie a Klemheist round the rope going to the victim between the anchor and the crevasse, and attach your DMM Revolver karabiner, clipping the dead rope coming from the anchor through the Revolver. You have now created a 3:1 pulley system. Untie the slippery hitch and you are ready to haul out the victim; if there are enough people just pull on the rope. If there is just you, then tie the dead end of the rope into your harness, close to the Revolver, then you can push with your legs, away from the crevasse, while pulling on the rope coming from the anchor.

Set up a 3:1 haul system.

If this is still too difficult you can increase the mechanical advantage to 6:1. To do this, tie an overhand knot in the dead rope next to the Revolver, and clip in a karabiner, then take the rope that you clipped into the anchor at the beginning of the rescue and clip it into the karabiner. Pull on this rope and you will feel how much easier it is to move the victim. As you pull up the victim you will need to reset the haul system, by sliding the prusik next to the Revolver back down the load rope towards the crevasse.

You can replace the French prusik autobloc with a mechanical device such as a Petzl Micro Traxion or a Wild Country Ropeman; this reduces friction by having a bigger radius than a karabiner, and reduces slippage when you stop to rest. When you are building the system just use it instead of the French prusik.

Micro Traxion in use.

6:1 haul system.

You need to make sure you know how to release these devices if you need to lower someone down due to any problems. Although these mechanical devices are much easier to use I think it is essential to learn how to use all the systems.

Using a drop loop

An alternative to the direct haul system is the 'drop loop'. The main advantage is that the victim can help with the haul system as opposed to hanging like a sack of spuds.

Start off the same as above, creating an anchor, clipping in the end of the rope and moving to the edge, but instead of throwing the end down, throw down a loop with a screwgate karabiner on it. The karabiner is clipped to the victim's harness and done up.

Victim helps pull themselves out.

The rope now runs down from the anchor, through the victim's harness and back up. This rope is now attached to the anchor using an autobloc, a device like the Petzl Micro Traxion is particularly good here. When you are ready to haul, the victim pulls down on the rope coming from the anchor and the rescuer pulls on the rope coming from the autobloc.

The mechanical advantage is only 2:1 but you have two people pulling. It is easier for the victim to help if they have put crampons on, as soon as they can reach the wall they can stay stable and push.

Roped crevasse fall

Falling into a crevasse roped up is infinitely preferable to doing so unroped, but it creates some different problems for the rescuers. If we start with a team skiing as a three with a person at one end of the rope falling in, the most important thing is to hold the fall. Get down on the ground, get your skis across the direction of pull and dig your edges in; use your ski poles as a brake.

Once you have stopped, which should hopefully not be too difficult with two people holding the fall, the person closest to the victim becomes the anchor while a belay is created. If they sit up and sink the tails of their skis

Holding a fall.

into the snow this should be pretty solid. The other person then comes forward, probing to check for other crevasses and digs a ski anchor as described above. If they position the anchor just in front of the sitting person it will be easier to transfer the load onto the anchor.

When the anchor has been rigged, attach an autobloc to the rope that is going to the victim and clip it into the anchor. If you choose to use a French prusik, tie it off using a slippery hitch as soon as you have enough rope. The person who has been acting as the anchor can now slowly slide forward to transfer the load to the anchor.

This should be done as slowing and carefully as possible to avoid shock loading the anchor.

With three people the back person can dig the anchor, while the person holding the fall can use an axe to increase security.

You can now decide if you are going to haul the victim out on the rope, which is currently loaded, or if you are going to use the drop loop method. This will almost certainly depend on how deeply the rope has cut into the edge of the crevasse.

Attach the rope
to the anchor and
transfer the load.

Using a Klemheist attach yourself to the rope and work your way to the edge; if this is going to be really awkward you can do this on the end of the rope that isn't under tension. You can now communicate with the victim and prepare the edge. If the rope hasn't cut in too far you can slide your ski poles or an ice axe under it to stop it cutting in any deeper, then cut the edge away round the rope so that it is easy for the victim to get over the lip.

If you can do this, you now set up the direct haul system as described above and haul out on the loaded rope. If the rope is cut so deeply into the edge that it is going to be impossible for the victim to climb over the lip, you will need to create an alternative haul line. Depending on the rope available you can drop the other end of the rope to the victim which they can then clip that into their harness, and you can then prepare the edge and haul them out on a direct haul, or set up a dropped loop. You may have to work reasonably close to the edge to get started. As soon as you start hauling the original load rope that held the fall becomes redundant.

Go to the edge with a
prusik on the tensioned
rope, use ski sticks
to stop the rope from
cutting in any further,
prepare the edge.

The most difficult situation to deal with is the 1:1 rescue. Here you will have to hold the fall, then while you are still supporting the victim's weight, dig the anchor and transfer the load. It is probably easiest to keep the downhill ski on to give purchase while digging the anchor; bury the other ski as described above. If you are comfortable holding the fall with your skis off, bury both skis as described above.

Be careful where you position the buried ski, as if it is too far behind you it is difficult to transfer the load. When you are comfortable that you have created a good anchor, attach the autobloc and slide it as far down the rope as possible – this reduces the distance you will have to shuffle forward. Now gently move forward slowly weighting the anchor. Let the load come onto the anchor progressively to check it is holding. If you are not happy that you can create an anchor, start screaming for help or get your phone out and call for rescue.

Once the anchor is happily laden, untie from the rope. As soon as you have enough rope, lock off the autobloc with a slippery hitch, and you can use the second ski to back it up. You could do this by sliding it in vertically in front of the first ski to make a cross; alternatively you could bury it as well and join it in to the first one using a sling.

If you are worried about being dragged into the crevasse, plant one ski vertically between your legs as an anchor.

If you are the person in the crevasse, take your skis off and clip them to your harness with a sling or cord to make it easier to climb out.

Crevasse rescue using a Hyperstatic rope

If you choose to use a Hyperstatic rope like the Petzl RAD system for glacier skiing all the techniques described above are exactly the same except that you will need mechanical devices to climb or haul on the rope. The best combination is the Petzl Micro Traxion and Petzl Tibloc; the Micro Traxion is used as the autobloc then the Tibloc is used to set up the haul system.

If you have to climb out of the crevasse yourself you just replace the prusiks described above with the Micro Traxion, Tibloc combination. This works best with the Micro Traxion on the harness and Tibloc for the foot loop. Although it has the advantage of being lighter, you need to practice using any Hyperstatic rope system as it is not as easy to use as a classic mountaineering rope. You will need to keep it stuffed in its bag if you don't want a bag of knitting every time you try and use it.

Navigation on Skis

Navigation on skis is much more difficult than navigating on foot. We travel much faster through the mountains on skis, so it is difficult to measure distance accurately. The quantity of snow varies from year to year and at different points in the season, so the landscape can be difficult to relate to the map. As the Earth warms up, the glaciers are receding and changing so a glacier may be marked on a map but it may no longer be there. In addition, winter weather and conditions can make the visibility change very quickly, and you can go from great visibility to whiteout conditions in minutes.

We don't have the space in this book for a back-to-basics navigation school, so I would like to assume certain skills that you can learn when you are not on skis, then we can look at those skills in a ski touring context. There are key navigational skills that we use time and time again on skis, so we will go through them to make sure we have a good understanding of how and when to apply them.

We now have the advantage of modern technology in the form of GPS. As long as you have fresh batteries you can turn the unit on, press a button, and it will give you your position.

The latest units have maps, so they will flag your position to give a quick visual of your location. On top of this there are a number of smartphone applications that can give you a super-accurate position on a map, which can be much better than the maps available on many GPSs. There is of course the obvious limitation of battery life, and you don't want to use all the battery life navigating on your only means of emergency communication.

A mapping GPS.

A mapping app
on an iPhone.

While the use of electronic navigation tools is a bit controversial in outdoor community, I think we could be churlish to not embrace the technology as it makes our life much simpler. If you have preprogrammed your route into a GPS or are using the mapping function on your smartphone, many of which can be used in 'Airplane' mode to save battery, you just download the map then use the phones GPS to mark your position. You will have more brain capacity to look around you and concentrate on all the other aspects of your day. On a good day this may just be enjoying the view, but on a difficult avalanche hazard day it could make a huge difference. If you are fully focused on the navigation you may not notice the signs of instability, the fact that the wind has changed direction and the slope you want to ski down is now becoming wind loaded. You may not notice that one of your team is tiring or needs some food, if you are counting paces it is really difficult to do any of this.

If you have preprogrammed your route on your GPS you will have already done much to mitigate your avalanche risk and you will know which key places you need to be extra aware of. You can now use this aid to make your navigation slicker and you can use more of your brain capacity to focus on your situational awareness.

I am not suggesting that we head into the mountains armed only with electronics you still need the ability to navigate with a map and compass in case you run out of battery. We are now going to look at these key skills.

Navigation tools

Let's start with the essential navigation tools:

Map – and something waterproof to keep it in. Maps are expensive and letting them get wet will shorten their lifespan, if you don't look after them they will usually disintegrate when you most need them. The case can be as simple as a zip lock bag or a purpose-designed map case. Whatever you do, under no circumstances should this be worn round your neck; apart from the risk of strangulation in a wind you will risk ridicule from other hillgoers.

Although it may appear sacrilege to some people, I will often cut up my maps to make them more user-friendly. Tours usually fit into sections of map, so chopping means that they are easily stored in a pocket as opposed to in your rucksack, where they tend to live if you have a bulky map.

Navigation tools.

Don't be afraid to annotate your map. I will often draw on bearings with the three figure compass bearing written next to the line, this makes navigation much quicker and simpler on the hill.

Compass – A compass with a large baseplate like the Silva Type 4 is much easier to use than small ones. It is easier to hold and operate with a glove on, and the larger baseplate eases the process of taking bearings on the map and on the ground. A romer scale also makes taking grid references much easier. I would suggest attaching the compass to your jacket, as it is very easy to lose when trying to ski and navigate at the same time.

When using the compass and the map you will need to adjust your bearing for the magnetic variation; you can find this on the edge of the map, but make sure you look for it before you go on the hill. Some models of compass are available with a facility to dial this in, just remember to change it when you swap areas. It is also worth noting that the bias on the compass needle is different for different areas, so a European compass will not work properly in South America as the needle will dip and drag on the compass housing. The Suunto M-3 Global has these features.

A Silva Type 4 compass.

An altimeter watch.

Altimeter – Measuring distances travelled is very difficult on skis. On foot we may use a compass bearing and measure distance using pacing or timing, but this is difficult to do on skis, so we will often ski on a compass bearing, and use an altimeter to give us this extra dimension required to pinpoint our position. The easiest type of altimeter to carry is the type in the style of watch, which includes all the usual watch functions. Altimeters work by measuring changes in air pressure.

In the mountains air pressure changes with the weather, so it is essential that you calibrate your altimeter regularly to known altitudes. Points such as huts, cols and summits are usually accurately marked on the map and can be used at the beginning and during each day. If you calibrate your altimeter on arrival at the hut you can use any change in altitude as an indicator to weather trends. A decrease in altitude overnight would be caused by an increase in air pressure, which is usually associated with improving weather. An increase in altitude is associated with a decrease in air pressure, which is usually associated with deteriorating weather.

Those coming to ski touring from the UK hills probably haven't used an altimeter that much, the big changes in air pressure we find in the UK make them difficult to use. In the Alps the air pressure is more constant so an altimeter is easier to use and more reliable; it is an essential tool for ski touring navigation.

GPS – Global Positioning System. A hand-held GPS has become an essential piece of navigational equipment. As mentioned earlier it can give you an instant position anywhere in the world, as long as you have a clear view of the sky and hence the satellites. The most basic units that just give you this position can be integrated into standard map and compass navigation as a check. Where GPS is particularly good is, when you are planning your ski tour, you take the time to mark key waypoints on the map and input their grid reference into the GPS. If the navigation is getting difficult and the weather deteriorating then you have the information ready to use. Many units allow you to do this on a computer before you leave home, making the process even easier. Units with mapping are particularly good.

When choosing a GPS I wouldn't look for anything too fancy as having too many functions uses batteries quickly. If you choose a unit that is too big you will stop carrying it with you; my preference is for a unit that will fit comfortably in the palm of my hand. A touch screen makes inputting waypoints in a hut or on the hill much faster. If you are going to use a unit with mapping make sure you have the correct maps. Some areas require you to download these maps in sections, so make sure you have the sections that surround your planned tour, as you may change your plans. I will always try to have the same map in my hand as on my GPS, as this makes it much easier to use on the ground.

Smartphone with Mapping – As mentioned above I wouldn't rely on this, as most smartphones are limited by battery power but they do make life easy. I have used maps on my smartphone from Arctic Norway to New Zealand and I know guides who have used them in as remote places as Svalbard. Most of the national mapping agencies have their own apps and there are number of global apps like View Ranger that will get you a map wherever you are.

A further app to consider is Fatmap which by the time of going to print will offer 3D mapping all over the world with the ability to highlight different slope angles and gradients. This can make terrain planning and management significantly easier.

Navigational skills

Now that you have the tools we need to think about the basic skills you should have to use them. You need to be able to look at a map and relate the map to the landscape. This is all about contour interpretation, being able to look at the map and work out what the land should look like.

Top Tip

The contour intervals on different maps are not the same – a bigger contour interval will make terrain appear less steep than it is on the ground. Make sure you check!

You need to be able to take a compass bearing on the map and use it on the ground, and be able to take a bearing in the landscape and use it on the map. Remember the magnetic variation in the Alps will not be the same as it is at home. It is currently almost zero, but it changes each year and in different parts of the world. If you have these basic skills you just need to be able to apply them.

Taking a compass bearing on a map.

When I am skiing, most of my position fixing is done by terrain interpretation. As I ski I am constantly looking at the mountains, I am choosing features and relating them to the map, then using those features to pinpoint my position, studying the contours on the map, and relating their form to the shapes I see on the ground. If you make a habit of this it soon becomes second nature. You need to do this every time you are out in the mountains, so that when the weather does come in you know where you are. It is all too common to come across parties who have been happily skiing along not paying attention, the cloud comes in and all of a sudden they are lost. If your levels of concentration and navigation practice are on top form in good visibility, dealing with poor visibility will be much easier.

Navigation tactics

We are going to look at the techniques and tactics that are commonly used while navigating on skis.

Where am I?

When you are skiing and lose track of where you are it can be pretty worrying, so you need some tactics to re-establish your location. If you have been keeping track of where you are and have just lost concentration, you should be able to sort it out pretty quickly. You could even follow your tracks back to the last known position.

If you have a GPS or smartphone app you can just ask it, then plot that position on the map. If you don't, or your batteries are flat you will need to use your map and compass. Look carefully at the terrain around you; even if the visibility is poor you can often gain clues from the landscape, look for shapes and changes that you can relate to the map. If you can see a recognisable feature take a bearing to it, subtract the magnetic variation then place the edge of your compass on the point and rotate the whole unit to line up the lines on the baseplate with the grid lines on your map. You will be somewhere on that line. If you have two known points you can do this again with the second point, where the bearings intersect is your location, this is commonly known as resection.

If you don't have known points that you can take bearings from, you can use your map and compass and a technique called 'aspect of slope' to home in on your position. Imagine the direction a football would roll from your current position, this is the fall line. Take a compass bearing down the fall line, then subtract the magnetic variation and go to your map. Align the lines on the compass housing with the grid lines then move the compass around until the edge of the baseplate is sitting at right angles to the contour lines. You are positioned somewhere on that slope, and you can then use your altimeter to gain a position on that slope. This is a great technique, it isn't as accurate as a resection but it does work. The only danger with it is if you are miles off the position you thought you were in, then you could convince yourself that you are on a different slope altogether, which just happens to have the same orientation. This technique is a really useful way of checking if you are about to ski down the right slope at the beginning of a descent.

Following a handrail

There are many occasions where you can see some big features around you but the immediate landscape is difficult to read. You can use these features as handrails, a classic example would be skinning up the Punta Calabre above the Benevolo hut (see guidebook section). The initial ascent

Kate Scott and Mike
Austin use a handrail to
navigate in poor visibility.

The route marked in red
from the Benevolo hut to
the Punta Calabre shows
a number of features that
can be used as handrails.

follows the edge of a river, you then head up a shallow valley heading for a set of cliffs. You can now handrail the bottom of these cliffs until they change direction (this point is pretty easy to spot), you then take a bearing for a kilometre across the glacier to the base of some rocks, from where you can then take a bearing to the summit. By using a handrail in this way we can complete a full day ski tour in more marginal conditions than we would have attempted in more open terrain. You still need to be aware of the objective hazards, such as crevasses, avalanche etc. but the navigation will be easier to deal with.

Following a compass bearing on skis

If there are no handrails to follow and the visibility is poor you will have to rely on your ability to follow a compass bearing. You can use these techniques in ascent or descent although they are more difficult to use in descent. When you have the bearing dialled into your compass, look along the direction of travel arrow and see if you can spot any distinctive features on that line. You can then ski to a specific feature, then choose another feature and repeat. This will keep you moving in a straight line on your bearing.

Kate Scott following
a compass bearing.

If there are no obvious features, send someone out ahead in front of you and direct them so they are on the correct line, they need to be far enough away that you can keep a good line but close enough to communicate. You can then ski to them and repeat. A much more efficient method is to move together with both of you following the compass bearing, the back person is checking the direction and can shout corrections. On a glacier it is worth using your rope, as crevasses will be difficult to spot if the visibility is bad enough that you need these techniques.

You can look back along your tracks to check that you are travelling in a straight line, and you can also check this using a back bearing. To do this, instead of lining up the red arrow in your compass, spin it through 180 degrees and use the white arrow. You can easily keep a check on your direction.

When skinning this is pretty easy, but in descent you will be limited to a racing snowplough to keep things moving in a straight line.

Using GPS on skis

As discussed earlier, GPS is a great tool but you must be able to navigate with a map and compass as well. The US government owns the system, so they could switch it off, it could have a technical issue, your batteries may run out, you may drop your unit, or it might just break. All these possibilities will mean you end up with no GPS, so you will have to go back to map and compass navigation.

When you are using your GPS you need to be aware that the map datum and coordinate systems vary from country to country. You can usually find the details on the map sheet, but the standard European ones are:

Country	Grid/Coordinate system	Datum
Switzerland	Swiss Grid	CH-1903
France	UTM-UPS	WGS-84
Italy	UTM-UPS	European 1950

There are three main ways to use GPS on the mountain:

1. Just ask the unit for your position. This is a great way to relocate yourself if you aren't sure where you are, or as a check against your map and compass navigation.

2. When you head out for the day with a mixed forecast, you can leave a trail of waypoints as you go. If the weather turns bad you can retrace your steps joining the waypoints together. You know the route is safe as you travelled it earlier in the day.

   Most GPSs have a track back facility, which does this automatically. The problem with track back is that you have no control over where the waypoints are positioned, as it's the GPS that decides where to position them, not you. If you are skinning up a glacier and detour round a crevasse you would almost certainly choose to record waypoints accordingly. If you rely on track back it may put a waypoint on either side of the crevasse then join the dots between the two. In descent, in poor visibility, this could lead you straight into the crevasse.

3. Input waypoints before you set out. This is the most efficient way of using GPS. With many GPS units you can mark all the waypoints on your map on your computer then download them to the unit. This is the most efficient method and the least prone to error.

   If you don't have this facility, or if you are in a hut, you will need to input the waypoints manually. The best way I have found to do this is to use the romer scale on my compass to gather the waypoints, write them down in a list, check them back against the map, then input them to your GPS, then check them again. The two places where an error is most likely to occur is gathering the waypoints in the first place, and then inputting the coordinates into the unit. Many modern units have touch screen functionality so you can easily mark waypoints on the map on your GPS unit. This significantly reduces the chance of error.

While you are gathering the waypoints, mark their position on your map with a pencil, this makes relating everything, when you're on the hill, much faster and clearer. If you have the ability to input waypoints via a touch screen on a map you have to be pretty careful where you touch, doing it with a pencil increases accuracy. Be sure to double check the coordinates against the map to make sure you have really placed the waypoint where you think you have.

With all these navigational tools and tactics, they are no use unless you practise them. Practise on a clear day so that all these tools become second nature for when the weather does close in, and you need to use them in anger.

Navigation is an integral part of everything we do in the mountains, and preparing for bad weather navigation is part of tour planning, which we will look at in another chapter.

Skiing in bad visibility

When the visibility or light is so poor that you can't see how steep the slope is, or see any obstacles, you will need to modify your skiing style. You need to become much more conservative, as you can't risk falling over something and getting hurt. In the Alps, if a helicopter can't fly, there isn't much chance that anyone will be coming to help you.

Whipping the rope
forward allows you
to see the terrain.
Photos – Andy Perkins.

If the visibility gets so bad that you can't read the terrain ahead you can use a technique that I call 'whipping'. Take your 5 metres of 7mm cord that I described earlier and tie one end onto the basket of your ski pole, then tie an overhand knot in the other end. You can now whip the cord forward using the ski pole. Where the cord lies on the snow you can ski only its length then repeat. It is a pretty slow way to make progress, but it is better than falling over or into something.

Planning a Ski Tour

Neil Stevenson leads a team ski touring in the Lyngen Alps, Norway.

I have given you all the solid tools that you need to operate safely and efficiently in the backcountry, and now we'll talk about how you can use them when planning a ski tour.

Right at the start of this book we talked about the scope of ski touring, which is massive. It takes in everything from a short skin from a lift to a multi-week expedition in a remote part of the world. Although all the techniques we have discussed are transferable to any group of snowy mountains all around the world, we are primarily focused here on the European Alps. When we are discussing huts and hut-to-hut trips we are considering huts that have a guardian and staff for the main ski touring seasons. We will discuss using unguardianed huts, but the main focus will be ones with a guardian who will provide food, drink and a warm bed for the night.

Remember you don't need to be an amazing skier, or be able to navigate through complex glacial terrain with a white bag over your head, or break trail in metres of snow for days on end, to go ski touring. You just need to choose objectives that are realistic for you and your group, and will be fun. If you don't feel comfortable skiing on a glacier, then don't choose a tour or a time of year where you will need to. If you don't want the hassle and weight of skiing with an ice axe and crampons, choose a tour that doesn't need them. Though, if you are at all unsure, it is worth having a light set just in case. The mountains are so extensive and the options so many that you don't need to commit to tours that you are not ready for. As you develop your skills, knowledge and experience you may choose to ski steeper terrain and climb more challenging summits with crampons, or you might not. Personally I love hut-to-hut tours without glaciers, as they are more relaxing and your rucksack will be lighter without the extra weight of crevasse rescue kit.

We are now going to look at how you gather information about ski tours, where they are, and what would be fun to do, in any specific area. We'll also look at how we judge the conditions and choose an appropriate tour, starting with day tours then moving on to multi-day, hut-to-hut adventures.

Ski tours through the season

As soon as the first snows of winter hit the ground there will be people out ski touring – my first time on skis most winters will be in ascent rather than descent. It always takes time for the ski areas to get organised and open, and with the exception of the really high resorts like Tignes, Zermatt, Saas Fee and Hintertux, they very rarely open before early December, and often not until the weekend before Christmas. If you are planning early season skiing you need to bear this in mind.

Mike Austin ski touring in Salvan, Switzerland.

It is usually possible to ski in the Alps somewhere from early December if you go high or watch the snow forecast. However, from Christmas onwards things are a bit more reliable. The best touring options early in the winter are usually at lower altitudes. The high mountains can be really cold, suffer from strong winds, and the crevasses on the glaciers are not well bridged. In addition, high mountain terrain is often quite rocky, so it requires a significantly larger volume of snow to fill in and cover rocks, whereas a lot of the lower hills are summer meadows, with grass, which needs much less snow to make the terrain skiable. This terrain is often the classic chocolate box image of snow-laden trees with farm buildings to ski through, as the temperatures are usually much colder so the snow line is correspondingly lower. You can often create tours by skiing up one side of a mountain and down the other, then use public transport to get back, which isn't practical later in the season.

There are some hut-based touring opportunities from New Year onwards, with some of the Silvretta (Austria), Queyras (France), Mont Thabor (France and Italy) huts being open. These areas are non-glacial so you can enjoy ski touring without the full weight of crevasse rescue kit.

This early part of the season offers the best opportunity for powder skiing, so I think some of the best options are tours near lifts where you can maximise your skinning to skiing ratio. When you are thinking about a trip it would be worth looking at an area where you could make a number of ski tours, as well as enjoy some off-piste skiing from a valley base.

As we move to late February more huts begin to open, with the Silvretta being one of the first glacial touring areas for all the huts to be open.

In early to mid-March the higher huts start opening. This is traditionally the time when the glaciers have filled in enough to be safe to ski on, and the snow is more stable. The high huts will usually stay open until mid-May or until the ski conditions dictate that people stop skiing. The high tours in the Bernese Oberland and the Valais Alps of Switzerland can be good right into June, and this is usually the best time to ski tour Mont Blanc.

If you are going to more exotic destinations, then you need to research the optimum time to visit. As you know, the conditions in the mountains don't follow a calendar, so you can get good or bad conditions at any time of the year.

Information gathering

We live in the internet age so a lot of initial research about an area can be done in the summer when all you can do is dream about skiing. The second part of this book is dedicated to a selection of ski tours, so hopefully you will find some ideas about where to start there. If you would rather spend your time leafing through guidebooks and maps, then there are guidebooks to most popular ski touring areas. Often these are in the local language, but a few elementary language skills can give you the basics, and many of the books have maps and photographs to help. There are some books in English, so between them and what we have here you should be able to ski for years.

Ski touring guidebooks.

Most books are arranged geographically, with each tour having a grade and a rough time to complete it for an average party. As you know there is no such thing as an average party, and the snow conditions can make a huge difference to the length of a tour, but at least it gives a guideline idea of timings.

Another source of inspiration can be blogs of where people have been skiing, or the websites of guides and guiding companies. A further great source of ideas and general ski touring information is the annual journal of the Eagle Ski Club. The Eagles offer courses, plus guided and member-to-member ski tours all over the world, and is a great club for those interested in ski touring but don't know where to start.

We will now go through the pieces of information that will help decide what tour is most appropriate for you, be it a day tour or a hut-to-hut trip. We will then look at the details of planning a tour and choosing a team – this is as important as selecting the right tour.

Ski tour grading

Most guidebooks use a grading system to help you select an appropriate tour for your level of experience, the weather and conditions. Any scale is extremely subjective and the same tour will never feel the same on any two different days, so the grading is given for average conditions. Average conditions would mean the average conditions that a particular ski tour would be done in, so if it's a glacial tour then mid-season with a good covering of snow on the glacier.

There are a number of tour grading systems out there that all end up in roughly the same place, so rather than presenting the systems we can look at the terrain and then give the grade that will match. The three grading scales we will look at are the Blanchère, Traynard, and that used by the Swiss Alpine Club (CAS). This can be particularly confusing if you are a mountaineer, as they use the same nomenclature as the Alpine Mountaineering grading system. To make life easier we will describe the terrain, then mark up all the possible grades that it may equate to, although the Traynard scale is usually used to describe the steepest section of skiing on a tour and is often combined with the Blanchère. I have included the Blanchère here in French, German and Italian as these are the languages that many of the ski texts are in.

Terrain		CAS	Traynard Scale	Blanchère Scale
	Terrain up to 30 degrees: skier should be able to ski this with basic off-piste techniques. Skinning usually not too challenging. Undulating terrain. Limited chance of a slip becoming serious.	F-PD	S2	SM – Skier Moyen MS – Mittlere Skifahrer MS – Medio Sciatore
	Terrain 30–35 degrees: skier can make controlled turns and cope with all types of snow. Consequences of a slip may be serious.	PD	S3	BS – Bonne Skier GS – Gute Skier BS – Buon Sciatore
	Terrain 35 degrees and above in ascent and descent: a slip would be very serious. You should know how to use an axe and crampons on this terrain.	AD The grading continues beyond this but you are getting into extreme skiing and mountaineering terrain.	S4	TBS – Très Bonne Skier SGS – Sehr Gute Skifahrer OS – Ottimo Sciatore

When you move into ski mountaineering terrain where you need crampons, ice axe, use of a rope and crevasse rescue knowledge, the Blanchère Scale extends to:

Terrain up to 30 degrees with basic mountaineering skills.	SAM – Skier Alpiniste Moyen MAS – Mittlere Alpineskifahrer MSA – Medio Sciatore Alpinista
Terrain 30–35 degrees and more, advanced mountaineering terrain that may require short pitches of climbing.	GAS – Gute Alpineskifahrer BSA – Buon Sciatore Alpinista BSA – Bonne Skier Alpiniste

The scale does extend into TBS and SGAS, but that is technical climbing with skis on your back. The Traynard scale also extends into S4, beyond which is terrain about 45 degrees. Both of these are outside the scope of this book.

Ski maps

Once you have done some basic research and decided on an area you would like to visit, it is time to get hold of the maps. Again the internet can be a big help in sourcing these before you leave home. The quality of mapping varies around the Alps and, without casting aspersions on national mapping agencies, the Italians are the worst and the Swiss the best, with the French followed by the Austrians in between.

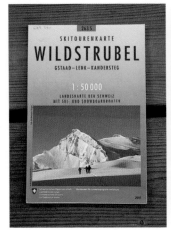

Swiss ski touring map.

This has a real influence on my decision-making on the hill, as I know there are many inaccuracies on Italian maps, such as unmarked cliff bands, so I will be much more careful about the conditions in which I would be prepared to navigate in.

In France the classic ski tours are marked on the 1:25,000 scale IGN maps, this is great if you are new to an area and want to quickly identify the classic tours. A dashed purple line marks the tour. If the line is dotted it means that you may need mountaineering equipment, or that section is not always passable on skis.

In Switzerland, there is a separate set of 1:50,000 ski touring maps, which are blue in colour. They have all the classic ski tours marked in red, with dotted lines indicating mountaineering or sections completed on foot, and a dashed line showing that that particular line isn't always skiable. There is also a direction arrow on some tours to indicate the best direction. The tours are numbered which corresponds to the list of tours on the back of the map, where a grade and average times are given. There is also a lot of other useful information on the back of the map, such as hut and rescue numbers.

The Austrian Alpine Club has ski version maps of the most popular areas in Austria, but you need to look after them carefully as the paper is pretty fragile. They are their standard maps with the classic tours marked in purple, again dashes for sections that are not often in condition, and dots for on foot/mountaineering.

Italy is not as simple as any of the above; different areas are covered by different map series, and they are all slightly different. The Kompass map series covers the biggest geographical area. In the Val d'Aosta the maps are better than in most other areas. As I said earlier you need to treat the information with a bit of suspicion, some of the maps have ski routes marked, but not all.

Planning the tour

Once you have decided on an area and a rough tour itinerary, be it a day tour from the top of a lift or a multi day hut-to-hut tour, you can start the next stage of planning.

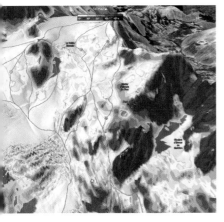

Using the avalanche terrain overlay on Fatmap to plan a ski tour.

Look at the map and guidebook in detail

Get the guidebook and map out and start looking at it in detail. This is where you can really get to grips with the terrain. Good map interpretation will allow you to visualise the terrain in 3D so you can picture skiing through the landscape. The internet can again be a great help – 3D mapping software like Google Earth or now Fatmap (much higher resolution) allowing you to look at an image of your terrain from loads of different angles and really get a feel for the landscape. By the time this edition is published it will be possible to use Fatmap anywhere in the world; you will be able to shade all the avalanche terrain, then plot a route through the mountains and upload the route to your GPS.

This is the time to note key navigational features that will help if the weather turns bad. I will often mark the key compass bearings with a ruler and write the bearing next to it on the map, making navigation much faster on the hill should the weather change. As we discussed in the navigation chapter I would also mark any GPS waypoints I have prepared at home on the map.

At this stage it is worth identifying a number of options within the tour. Is there a way to cut it short if the snow is really bad, or you aren't travelling as fast as you thought you would, or the weather has changed? Having these options in your head before you go on the hill saves standing scratching your head when you should really be getting on with it. The plan may be as simple as to turn around and head back the way you have come, but if you haven't at least thought about it you are less likely to do it.

Marking bearings
on the map ready
for the next day.

When you are studying the map, have a look at how close together the contour lines are to get an idea of steepness – the closer the contours, the steeper the slope. What you are most interested in are the slopes around or greater than 30 degrees, as these are most prone to avalanche. They usually give the best skiing, but if you can identify them before going on the hill, you are armed with key piece of knowledge about potential avalanche terrain when you start making decisions on the ground. The latest versions of the Swiss ski touring maps shade areas over 30 degrees in a pink-red colour. There are a number of tools that you can use to measure this on the map, for example Mammut and Brooks-Range have a clear card with gradations on it, for different scales of map. You hold the card against the contours and you can read off the steepness. If you don't have one then, as a guide, on a 1:50,000 map with a 10m contour interval, if the contours are closer than 0.5mm apart then the slope is steeper than 30 degrees. Identifying these slopes as a potential avalanche risk does not mean avoid them completely, as they usually offer the best skiing. It just means note them and be aware of them in relation to the avalanche risk.

This is also an opportunity to look for other hazards, such as whether or not you are going to be on a glacier. If so, judging the shape of the terrain, can you work out where the crevasses might lie? The terrain can also give you clues about what kit you may need at different points in the day. For example, if you are going to skin over a col that you know has been a windward slope for some time, it will probably be scoured offering hard snow, which may require you to use ski crampons. The lee slope may be loaded with wind slab. Does the guidebook indicate climbing a couloir? If so, make sure your crampons and axe are to hand, so you don't have to empty your sack at the transition.

How to calculate how long a tour will take

Timings are a key element to any tour, and pretty difficult to estimate accurately as there are so many variables. If the weather is nice, the snow good, you are feeling fresh and there is a well-set track to follow, then you will fly along. If you have to break trail and navigate then it is unlikely that you will travel at the same speed.

There are all sorts of complicated ways of calculating the timings. If you have a guidebook with a time given, that is a reasonable starting point, and as you do a few tours in the book then you will get a feel for where you are in relation to the author's times. I find a good rule of thumb is about 300m of height gain per hour, unless it is a long, horizontal distance with not much up, then I use about 3km per hour. In descent I usually allow 1000m per hour unless the terrain is complicated. If there is a short descent I don't count it. I then adjust it once I see how we are moving.

This is way too vague for lots of people, so if you prefer you can use a more scientific method, developed by Werner Munter. His system involves breaking your tour into legs, which you will do anyway when looking at the navigation. He assigns units for distance travelled and height gained or lost:

- One unit is assigned for each 1km travelled horizontally.

- One unit is assigned for each 100m of height, gained or lost.

- Add the units up to gain a total for ascent and descent.

- Divide the uphill total by 4, and multiply by 60 (minutes) to get an uphill time.

- Divide by downhill total by 10, and multiply by 60 (minutes) for a downhill time.

Example in ascent

If we use an example of a ski touring leg where we skin for 2km with a height gain of 300m, then we have total of 5 units. Divide this by 4, to give us 1.25 then multiply this by 60 (minutes) to give a time, in this case 75 minutes.

Example in descent

We are going to ski down 400m over 3km, so 7 units divided by 10, which is 0.7, multiply by 60 (minutes) is 42 minutes.

You do this for all the legs, then add them together to get a time for your day out. As we discussed earlier, the conditions and the team will affect the timing dramatically, so these numbers are just a starting point that you can then vary as you develop a sense of your speed through the mountains.

It is always worth building a contingency into your timing, planning to finish the tour as it gets dark doesn't leave any margin for error. If you plan to finish an hour or so before dark you will have that time spare if you need it.

Timing a ski tour

We talked earlier about the seasonal variations in where you may want to ski on any given day, but you also have to think about the timing of the tour within that specific day. Earlier in the book we talked about a ski tour I had done where the snow was super-crusty, but by timing the day correctly the sun had softened the crust allowing a good ski down. This is vital for this and many other reasons. If we think about spring ski touring, where the mornings are cold and the afternoons warm, you want to be finished skiing before it gets warm. Physically it is much harder work skiing in the heat, but also, safety-wise there is an increased avalanche risk and there is a higher chance of having a slow twisting, injury-inducing fall in soft afternoon snow.

As well as safety, you need to think about the quality of the skiing. If you arrive at the top of your main descent of the day and it is still bullet hard, you will have to wait around until it softens. Arrive too late and it will have turned to soup, so you want your tour timing to allow you to arrive on top, have a brew, take your skins off, then ski perfect, spring snow all the way home. This just takes a bit of thought at the planning stage, for such things as: what aspect is the slope facing, what altitude is it, and how strong is the sun? Earlier in the season when it is cold this is less important, but powder is usually best in the morning or in the shade.

Brian O'Connor skiing down from the Col d'Argentière.

If you are skiing on a glacier late in the season, the sun's power has an effect on the strength of the snow bridges, so making sure you are over any possible problems before the heat builds up is important.

Mark Charlton making some big turns on perfect spring snow, Finnmark, Norway.

Who to tour with

Choosing a team to ski with is important, and how you work together can make or break a ski holiday. You obviously want to ski with your mates, but I would suggest not having too many of them in a group. The more people involved in a decision the longer the decision will take to make. It has also been clearly proven that the bigger the group the worse the decision and the more difficult it is to communicate within that group. I would start with four or five as a maximum, any more than six and everything becomes too unwieldy.

Make sure everyone is of a similar fitness, skiing standard and has similar aspirations, as any misalignment in these three things can spell disaster. If people can't keep up, keep falling over, or want different things from the trip, then you are going to have problems. Making sure these things have been discussed before you leave home, so everyone is on board with the plans and options. This will also save time on the trip and prevent possible issues.

Having the right team can have a significant impact on the quality of decision-making on the hill. If the most experienced person in terms of avalanche awareness is the least fit, then there is a good chance they will be at the back. This means they won't be feeling the snow or making the route choice. If the fittest, least experienced person is at the front, they could be blindly leading the group into danger. If the pace is so quick that everyone is working so hard that all they can do is keep up, they will not be looking around and absorbing the information from the landscape. This is essential for good decision-making in the mountains. Being able to look at the bigger picture, where your route fits into the landscape, and the effect of the weather and conditions are all essential, so you need to work together to ensure nothing is missed.

The leadership issue is always worth considering, and in many groups a natural leader will emerge, through experience or personality. While most groups of equals don't need a leader, decisions often need a leader to at least lead a discussion. No decision at all can often be as bad as the wrong decision.

Here are some good ways of minimising these problems:

- At the planning stage make sure everyone has looked at the map and discussed the possible options for the day; this leads to informed choice.

- Discuss what you see around you and encourage discussion to foster openness and group decision-making.

- I often think out loud which often leads to discussion about the route, the skinning track and the conditions.

- Use that day's avalanche forecast as a lead-in to discussing what you see while you are on the mountain. What the team absorbs can then feed into the following day's decision-making.

What to book before you go

There are certain things that you will need to book before you leave home, such as transport to the mountains. Flights are easy, but you could also travel by train ensuring your kit arrives with you.

Top Tip

> Fly with your ski boots in your hand luggage. You can often hire skis etc. in resort if they go missing, but boots are a nightmare to replace.

Tour planning check list

Before you leave home it is worth having a check list to make sure you have gathered all the information. If we start with the conception of a tour and finish at the airport hopefully this will help you run through all the essentials:

- Where are we going to go? Country? Area? Specific tour?

- When are we going to go? Early season for powder and day tours with some lifts, or later for hut-to-hut tours?

- Who are we going to go with? Build the team.

- Plan the tour, or in the case of day tours, a number of tours, before you leave home.

- Book the huts. If you are going to try a hut-to-hut trip you will need to book the huts in advance. On popular tours like the Haute Route this may have to be done months in advance. You can always change the plan if the weather dictates. Most huts have no problem changing your bookings if possible, but it can be more difficult making a last minute booking. We will talk more about using huts later.

- Collect as much prior weather and avalanche information before you go. You can then see how this fits with the reality when you hit the ground.

- Create a tour folder with all the hut numbers, hotel details, taxis, bus timetables etc. before you go. There is no point arriving in the airport to discover the last train of the day has just left. The logistics of getting to a ski tour can be as important as the actual tour planning.

- Don't be afraid to change the plan if the weather or the conditions are not good. There is always something good to be done in the mountains, it just might not be what you had originally planned.

Food and drink on tour

The food and drink you take with you is an integral part of the planning of each day. What you take on a tour in minus 20°C in December will be quite different to what you take with you in early May. You need to plan your fluid intake for the day. In cold weather you don't feel like drinking as much as you would on a hot day, but the air is dry in the mountains so your body is losing fluid just by breathing. I always start the day by drinking as much fluid as possible, so I am hydrated going out the door. I then try and drink something every hour or so on the go to keep topped up, then make sure I hydrate well when I get back at the end of the day.

How I carry the fluid depends on the point in the season. Early season I have a one litre flask that I fill with hot blackcurrant juice; as the season warms up I will often take a half litre flask and a litre flexible water container that I can fill as much or little as I think the day dictates. Having a flexible container means that it packs really small in my sack when it isn't in use.

Top Tips

Put a slice of fresh ginger in with your hot blackcurrant juice for a warming bite.

If you fill the cup of your flask with snow before pouring in the hot liquid you get more fluid for the weight of water you are carrying.

Some people like using energy powders in their water. It's really personal preference; I prefer to use water or juice, then have an energy gel or bar if I want a specific energy product. I have tried hydration systems on and off over the years and they don't work very well in cold environments. The tubes freeze even with an insulated cover and the bladders often split or leak. If the tube freezes, most of them are no good to drink out of so you have no accessible water for the day. It is also very difficult to keep track of how much you drink. Suddenly running out part way through the day is much worse than having to take your sack off every time you need a drink. I will never carry more than two litres of water even on the hottest days, the weight just slows you down too much – remember, one litre of water weighs one kilo.

When it comes to food I just take what I like to eat. You can live on energy bars and gels, but they aren't very much fun to eat day after day and they are expensive. There are few things more comforting on the hill than a good sandwich, but don't bother with tomato or lettuce as they always freeze and go soggy. Foods that have slow-release energy are great, so nuts, oatcakes, cheese and that type of thing are much better than chocolate and sugary foods which give you an energy spike then a crash.

On a day trip I will usually have a sandwich or some oatcakes, cheese and sausage, with a couple of energy bars and gels in my bag just in case. On a hut-to-hut trip I will have something like that at the start of the trip, then have a bag of nuts and raisins made up that I can snack on throughout the day. I will usually have a bowl of soup or something to eat when I arrive at a hut, to get some glycogen back into my muscles as soon as possible, then eat normally in the evening.

Altitude

When ski touring in the Alps, the effect of altitude is usually not that much of a problem, unless you are planning to ski Mont Blanc or some of the other 4000m peaks. However it is worth being aware of the risk of altitude sickness as it affects different people in different ways, and at different altitudes, and is an important element in tour planning.

As we gain height, air pressure is reduced, so every time you breathe there is less pressure to force oxygen-rich air into your lungs, so less oxygen gets into your bloodstream. Your body needs oxygen to keep you alive, operate your muscles and keep the brain functioning, making good solid decisions. Most fit people will not notice the effect of altitude until they are between 2500 to 3000m. As height is gained, if no effort is made to acclimatise, then your body may rebel and you may develop altitude sickness.

At its most basic level, Acute Mountain Sickness (AMS) will result in you feeling tired, lethargic, out of breath, loss of appetite, you may have difficulty sleeping, and you may also feel nauseous. The first signs are usually a feeling that doing an activity that you would normally find easy is more difficult. If that's all you feel don't worry, you will feel normal as soon as you descend. If you feel like that on the way to a hut, but don't feel any worse, you will probably have a poor night's sleep then be fine, as your body adjusts (acclimatises).

If you have a selection of the above symptoms that don't get better, or you continue to feel worse, then you need to descend to a lower altitude and let your body recover. At European ski touring altitudes it is unlikely that you will become more ill than what we have discussed above, but on rare occasions where you don't get better and don't descend, then the situation can get much worse. AMS can develop into High Altitude Pulmonary Oedema (HAPE) or High Altitude Cerebral Oedema (HACE), which is fluid on the lung and/or brain. This is incredibly serious and can be fatal. You are unlikely to come across this, but it is worth being aware. Encouraging anyone with these symptoms to carry on is an extremely bad idea.

One of the many drawbacks with the human body is that until you go to altitude for the first time, you have no idea how your body will behave. Some people feel ill at 2500m, some can climb to the summit of Mont Blanc

Kate Scott ski touring at over 5000m on Mt Elbrus; careful acclimatisation is required to ski safely at this altitude.

(4808m) and higher with no real effect; there is no way of telling and fitness plays no part. Fit people can often be more seriously affected as they can push on when less fit people need to rest and let their bodies catch up with the altitude. You need to let your body adjust – we call this acclimatisation. The human body will quickly produce more red blood cells to counteract the lack of available oxygen; this will allow you to feel pretty normal while exercising at altitude.

The speed that your body acclimatises is also difficult to predict, so taking it easy on your first forays to altitude is a good idea.

When you are planning a ski tour, look at the altitudes. It is unlikely that you will be much above 3000m on a day tour unless you are using the Aiguille du Midi lift in Chamonix, or the Klein Matterhorn lift in Zermatt. On these tours you will probably be up and on your way down to lower altitudes before your body realises what is happening.

On a hut-to-hut tour you do need to think a bit more about the acclimatisation process, as you will be staying at altitudes in huts. On a tour like the Haute Route or in the Bernese Oberland the huts are almost all above 2500m, so you won't drop below this altitude until the end of the tour.

When I structure a tour I will try and have the higher sections and the higher huts later in the tour, so the team will be more acclimatised. On a tour like in the Bernese Oberland where you may start from the Jungfraujoch railway at 3600m, I would not suggest spending the first night at the Mönchsjoch Hut at 3658m, but getting the first train up in the morning and spending the first night at the Hollandia or Konkordia huts, which are lower. Using a bit of common sense will allow you to avoid the risk of altitude sickness in the Alps. On many tours I will program in a warm-up day where I will use the highest lifts available to get my body to trigger the production of some extra red blood cells.

One thing to be aware of if you ski further afield, is that some of the areas you may visit have a high base altitude. If you go ski touring somewhere like Colorado in the USA, then you fly into Denver at almost 2000m and go up from there. A day's gentle skiing from the lifts would be a good idea to allow your body to adjust before heading for the backcountry.

On Tour

We have looked at tour planning, so you now have the skills, the team and a plan. The next stage is to take this onto the mountain. We are going to have a look at some general things to think about before any tour, then look at things specific to a first tour, then a first overnight tour. If you have done your research, then you should have an idea about what the snow is doing and what the avalanche conditions should be like. You can start adding real, on the ground information to this matrix as you travel to your start point. As you are travelling, ask yourself: Is the snow line where I thought it would be? Can I see any fresh snow on the trees or by the road? Is there any wind? Can I see snow plumes blowing off ridgelines? Is there any sign of avalanche activity?

It always pays dividends to have an extra day at the start of a multi-day tour so you can recover from the journey, check your kit, buy any food or extra kit, and go for a ski. This can be a day tour or just a bit of lift-accessed skiing; either is a great warm-up and you then know that you are starting the tour ready to go. I always use this as an opportunity to go through avalanche rescue procedures with the team. Even if you have all practised already that season, it is good to go through it as a group, to make sure you all have the same ideas.

If you are starting from a lift it is worth finding out where it is, and what time the first lift leaves. If you can buy your ticket the night before you should do so, as this will save you queuing in the morning. If you are starting from the road it is worth checking out where the parking place is, so you can have a slick get-away in the morning. It is always worth phoning the huts to make sure they have your booking and to get up-to-date local conditions.

The first day tour

Your first ski tour is pretty exciting. You will have all this new kit and you're about to step out on a new chapter in your skiing life. Let's use the Petit Croisse Baulet near Megève as an example.

The avalanche forecast says Category 3 – Considerable, with some fresh snow from the previous evening. There is the risk of wind slab on northerly aspects after recent wind, and the possibility of easily triggered slides as the snow warms up in the afternoon sun.

The weather conditions are good, clear and cold, and you spoke to someone who has done the tour recently, so you know there is plenty of snow, and no strange snow or navigation issues to worry about.

You have all the information you need and have studied the map, so have the different descent options pencilled onto the map.

There are two possible lift access points, The Jaillet lift in Megève or the main lift access in Combloux. It would be worth using the piste map to find the Sommet Salles at the top of the Pertuis lift, where a number of lifts meet and is the starting point for the tour. Starting at the Sommet des Salles, head down the Jorace piste for a few hundred yards then cut left into the trees where there is a pisted snowshoe track. This forms a nice, flat spot for your first transition into skinning mode, so wipe your ski bases dry and face them to the sun, then get your skins on and turn your bindings into touring mode.

The first section of skinning is along the snowshoe piste to the Col de Jaillet; here you leave the piste and head up through the woods on the blunt south-east ridge. Depending on the conditions you may need to make a couple of kick turns, but even if you don't need to, it is always a good idea to practise a couple to make sure they are nice and smooth. Ask yourself as you skin, "How is the snow feeling?" If there is a track, dive off it to get a feel for the snow at the side, and do some ski pole tests to see if the snowpack feels like you expected from the avalanche reports and the weather forecasts you have been tracking. Have a dig about with your hands to see how easily the new snow will slide.

As you reach the east ridge you may notice some cornicing on the north side, which would fit with the avalanche forecasts, an indication of wind loading on that aspect. As you approach the summit, it is often worth taking a small dogleg to the west to avoid the steepest slopes directly below the summit, making the skinning easier.

The view from the summit is amazing with the Mont Blanc Massif on one side and the Aravis range on the other. If you are moving well the ascent should have taken you about an hour. This is the perfect place take in the view, have something to eat and drink, and make your second transition of the day. It's skins off, so first turn your bindings into downhill mode, then peel off one skin at a time being extra careful not to get snow on the glue, as you may want to use them again. This is also the time to make a final decision about the descent.

The options from the summit are: to retrace your line of ascent – you can ski a similar line but slightly to the south on the other side of a stream, which feeds back into your line of ascent; you can ski a line to the south via the Rocher de la Combette and meadows heading for Orat then Le Plan; or my favourite route which is down the ridge to the Tête de Ramadieu. At a col you can head south down some beautiful open meadows heading for Orat. You may need to be careful if the sun has warmed the snow too much as the final section is a bit steep, so you may want to ski one person at a time and follow little ridgelines. You then pick up the road that leads back to the lifts in Le Plan.

Mike Austin skiing down from the Petit Croisse Baulet in perfect powder.

The lift system can then take you back to your starting point. You have just completed your first ski tour, loads of skiing and only an hour of skinning. There are loads of other variations you can make in this area, which we will look at in the guidebook section.

If you think back to our discussions earlier, when you have finished for the day remember to review what you have done: What was good? What was bad? What could you do better? This is the best way to learn and will set you up for the next day.

Your first hut-to-hut tour

The Silvretta

When you have made a few day tours, the logical progression is to move on to a hut-to-hut tour; this allows you spend nights out in the mountains, remaining high to take advantage of the best snow conditions. It also allows you to pass through bigger alpine terrain, as you don't need to return to the valley each evening.

As we mentioned earlier the hut network in Europe is superb, but in the touring season huts can get busy, so make sure you have booked your huts before leaving home. Let's use a five-day tour in the Silvretta region of western Austria as an example.

The logical starting point is Galtür; this pretty little village is high in the mountains, tragically made famous by the avalanche that killed 31 people in February 1999. Having got your kit sorted and decided that the weather and avalanche forecast are okay, you need to sort your hill food. This is always a dilemma for me, as if you take lunch for five days your sack will be really heavy, go too light and you will compromise your performance. I usually strike a balance and take lunch for the first two days, then snacks that I can supplement from the hut for the rest of the trip. The Silvretta area is particularly easy in this regard, as lunch is included in the hut price (it isn't in most other parts of the Alps).

The first day uses the Ischgl lifts to gain height, this is the scariest part of the tour for me, negotiating my way through hoards of barely in control piste skiers is much more dangerous than the backcountry hazards. You are heading for the top of the Pauliner Kopf. It's worth spending a minute with the piste map to plan the fastest route through the system. Once you have escaped the ski area, the world seems a nicer place. A short descent to the south-west for a transition to skins, then a nice skin to the col below, or the summit of the Piz Val Gronda for the second transition of the day. I was skinning up here once and could hear the Scissor Sisters playing a concert in the ski area behind me, very bizarre. You now have two choices. You can take a descending traverse and ski towards the Heidelberger hut, or climb the Piz Davo Sasse which has a nice north-facing bowl, which often holds powder, before heading for the hut.

Using an alpine hut

When you arrive at any hut you need to work out how that particular hut is run. Most ski huts have a ski room where you can leave your skis overnight; if not you will leave them outside. There will also be a boot room where boots can be left and where you can pick up slippers.

Louise Baltez ski touring
in the Silvretta, Austria.

The ski/boot room
in the Similaun hut
in the Ötztal.

I would suggest that you leave your kit in the ski room or the boot room to start with, and one person goes and checks in with the guardian. The guardian will tell you where all your kit needs to go, where you can hang your boots and skins to dry, leave your ice axes, etc. This is your opportunity to remind the guardian if you have any vegetarians or anyone with any food allergies, and also check what time dinner and breakfast are. All huts seem to have slightly different payment systems for drinks and extras on top of the half board price, so find out when you check in what they would like you to do. The guardian will often assign you a table that will be where you sit in the dining area for the duration of your stay. Once they have explained that, they will assign you a bed space. This is often really specific especially if the hut is busy, and you probably will be given numbered beds that you must stick to.

Most huts ask for payment in the evening following dinner and they generally prefer cash, so make sure you have enough with you. In 2018 a half board deal in a hut plus a few extra drinks was about €70 per person per night.

Huts, by their nature, will have a lot of similar kit lying around, so you need to make sure you keep track of your belongings, having your name or a marking on your boots, liners and skins will help. I usually pack my skins away as soon as they are dry. It is unlikely that your kit would be stolen, but it is possible that someone may take it thinking it is theirs.

The washing facilities in huts vary dramatically. In the Silvretta, many of the huts have hot showers, whereas on the Haute Route you will be lucky to get running water at all. In huts with showers or running water I usually take a small travel towel and hotel-sized shower gel, plus my toothbrush and paste. On a trip with no running water I will just take my teeth cleaning kit and save the weight.

Hut meals are fairly standard in format, but variable in quality, dinner being usually three courses, consisting of soup followed by a main course and dessert. Drinking water will depend on the altitude of the hut. Higher huts will generally charge (quite a lot) for bottled water, lower huts will often provide it. If you arrive at a hut at lunch time or early afternoon, which is usually the case in the spring when you will need an early start to get the best quality snow, you can buy lunch. You can usually buy snacks and get your water bottle filled for the following day. You will need to hydrate after the day's exertions, and the cheapest way to purchase water in huts is to buy litre jugs of boiling water, this is usually much cheaper than bottled cold water. I usually carry a few fruit or herbal tea bags to flavour it. While hydrating it is worth getting the map out and starting to plan the following day. The hut guardian will be able to supply you with a weather forecast and often an avalanche forecast as well. If you do arrive early then you have perfect opportunity for an afternoon nap. Almost all huts insist on sheet sleeping bags for hygiene – silk is definitely the best as it packs the smallest in your rucksack.

When you check in at the hut, the guardian will let you know what time breakfast will be. If you have a specific objective in mind there may be a particular breakfast time, but most ski touring huts will have a 'between x and y time'. The breakfast system varies from hut-to-hut with some huts having a self-service style buffet, and some where the guardian will bring things over to your table – again you should check this. Breakfast is usually pretty simple, just bread and jam with tea, coffee or hot chocolate. Some huts have muesli, cheese and cold meats but I wouldn't rely on it. Fussy eaters don't usually get on very well in huts! If you do have any food allergies it is always worth discussing this with the guardian when you make the reservation.

Back on tour

Back to your arrival at the Heidelberger hut; you can enter the hut through the ski room, which is at the front right of the building where you can leave your skis and ice axes, then take everything else upstairs. Boots go in the boot room, and it's worth pulling your liners out so they dry more easily. You may want to consider swapping a boot with a mate so that no one will take yours by mistake in the morning.

The Silvretta is unusual in that most huts in the Alps supply hut slippers, but the Silvretta huts don't, so you will need to take something with you to wear in the hut. Keep them as light as possible, flip flops or crocs are good.

After check-in you can get washed, have something to eat, and make sure everything is drying ready for the next day. Once you are settled and have started to rehydrate you can talk to the guardian about conditions, and chat to other hut dwellers to find out where they have been. This is a great way of finding out how the conditions are; remember to keep your options open and have a number of alternative plans if at all possible.

The Heidelberger hut,
Silvretta, Austria.

The Silvretta is great for this as all the huts have day touring options as well as the opportunity to ski to another hut. The next logical hut from the Heidelberger is the Jamtal, one of the most modern huts in the Alps, and the classic way to get there is via the Breite Krone, then the Kronen Joch and down to the hut. This gives you the opportunity to climb a peak, maybe using crampons, cross a col, and arrive at a new hut.

Mornings in the boot room can be a bit chaotic as everyone is trying to get ready at the same time, so I usually put my skins on my skis and sort my boots out before breakfast, then I can put them in a quiet corner for when we are ready to go. If you haven't collected all your drying kit the night before, I would again suggest organising this before breakfast when the drying area is quiet. You can then enjoy breakfast not having to worry about these other jobs. Putting your skins on before breakfast allows them to cool a bit. Having been in a warm hut all night their warmth can melt the snow, and if you head straight outside and start skinning, the snow under your skis will immediately turn to ice causing your skins to ball up.

When you have finished eating, set a time for everyone to be outside with their skins on ready to go, which will avoid some of the team standing about in the cold waiting for the rest of the team. When you are outside, move away from the hut and carry out a transceiver check for the group – you are now good to go. You will have studied the map the night before and, if the light allowed, scoped out which direction you are going to head so you can get away from the hut smoothly.

If you are planning the Breite Kroner, you will have a nice steady skin. Concentrate on getting a steady rhythm and try not to stop too often. Leaving the hut feeling a bit cold will save you stopping within 20 minutes of the hut to change clothing. I usually try and stop every hour to have a drink and a snack, this is the time to adjust clothing or attend to anything else. Try not to stop for too long, as people will start to get cold and want to put on layers that they will only have to stop and take off again later. You should make the flat area between the Breite Krone and Kronen Joch after a couple of hours skinning. Here you can decide if you are going to cross the col or climb the peak. Turn left for the peak and right for the Joch (German for col).

If you are heading for the peak you skin up the east face/ridge to a point where it gets too rocky or awkward to skin. You can depot your skis here and continue on foot. You may decide to wear crampons, it depends on the quality of the snow, but if you are at all in doubt I would put them on. I would suggest leaving your skins on your skis and put the bindings into ski mode, then should they be blown by the wind they are less likely to slide away. You will see lots of people heading up just using ski poles, but I would get into the habit of using a pole and an ice axe, at a minimum take your axe with you.

After a great view from the top it's back to the skis, where you can stow away your crampons, and take your skins off and pack them away. You can now ski down before a short shuffle over the col. The descent to the Jamtal hut is down a beautiful valley which faces north-west then west. By working the terrain and looking for the shady snow you can often find powder on one side of the valley and spring snow on the other. As you progress down the valley the easiest skiing is on the right bank (northerly side). When you arrive at the hut, the ski and boot room are down a slope on your left facing the hut, where you can find boot warmers, before heading up to the sun-baked terrace for a well-deserved beer.

You are now two days into your first hut-to-hut tour. We will suggest how to keep going across the Silvretta in the guidebook section, but for now you should have a good idea of the daily rhythm and how the huts work. Some touring days are longer or shorter than others, some are more technical than others, but they all follow the same general theme. As the season progresses the afternoons become warmer so the snow is of a poorer quality later in the day. The way to avoid this is to be out early, so instead of leisurely 7am breakfast you may end up with a 5am breakfast instead.

Skinning to the Breite Krone, Silvretta, Austria.

When It All Goes Wrong

Aftermath of a skier-triggered avalanche in Riksgränsen, Sweden. The victim was dug out alive in 10 minutes from 1.5m down. Photo – Bruce Duncan.

When we head into the mountains we always hope that things won't go wrong, but if you spend enough time in any hazardous environment then something might happen to you. Hopefully by good training and judgment the problem won't be with your party, but you may come across a team in difficulty that needs your help. If you are near a ski area then the best course of action is to call the ski patrol, look after the injured party, and wait for help to arrive. If you are skiing in, or close to, a ski lift system take the time to get the number for the ski patrol, it is usually printed on the piste map. Even if they are unable to rescue off-piste they will be able to coordinate a rescue for you. The first thing the ski patrol will ask you is, "Where are you?", so making a mental note of where you are can save a lot of time. When we are ski touring we spend a lot of time away from lift areas, and even a short tour in marginal weather can put you in a remote situation a long way from outside assistance.

We have talked a lot in this book about avalanche awareness and rescue, but this is not the only thing that can go wrong on a ski tour. A simple fall that results in a twisted knee on a sunny, windless day can be a simple rescue. A call to the rescue services with a position and description of the problem, and a helicopter can often be on scene in less than an hour. The exact same incident on a cloudy day with cold weather and wind can be a much more serious incident. If the visibility is poor then a helicopter can't fly, and rescue teams in the Alps are not able to respond if they can't fly due to the distances involved. If the casualty can't ski then you either have to stay put, or build a stretcher that will allow the casualty to be dragged to safety.

The problem doesn't have to be an injury to a person. A broken ski binding that you can't fix, or rig a 'get me home' repair, can be equally as serious, and if the team can't fix the problem you may have an epic extracting yourself from the situation.

Emergency procedures

It is worth having a check list in your mind in case an incident occurs. The first and most important thing is to ensure the safety of the rest of the party. If you or members of the party take risks to help an injured person you may end up with more victims, which will only make the situation much worse.

In my mind I always consider the following:

- Assess the site of the accident and the position of the casualty in relation to any danger.

- Is it safe to approach and conduct a rescue or render assistance?

- First focus on basic ABC first aid (Airway, Breathing and Circulation), then worry about other injuries and treatment.

- Do you need outside assistance? If so call as soon as it is practical to do so.

- If you can evacuate the person with the problem or injury, make sure you have a plan and discuss it with the team.

- If the casualty cannot evacuate themselves, keep them warm – they will cool very quickly if not active.

- If you are going to have to wait for rescue consider the types of shelter available; you may have to move the casualty.

- Look after the whole group. If people are standing about they may become cold, and if the accident is serious witnesses may be in shock.

First aid

We are not going to write a first aid manual here, but encourage you all to take a first aid course with a mountain component; this will put many of the common injuries that you may come across in context, and give you some practical tools to deal with them. It is often the simple things that will keep someone alive until help arrives. Remember your ABCs – Airway, Breathing, and Circulation. It is also worth remembering that if anyone has been buried or even caught in an avalanche they should go and get a hospital check-up. The risk of secondary drowning as the result of breathing in cold snow is real and should not be treated lightly. Having a first aid kit in the party is essential, we have suggested a basic first aid kit in the Appendices.

Group shelter

The next piece of essential kit is the group shelter; we talked about these in the kit section. You should have enough capacity to get all your team out of the weather should a problem arise. Having a shelter that is big enough for everyone to fit in is warmer and better for morale than having the team split between a number of smaller shelters. We cannot emphasise enough how this simple bit of kit can save your life and the lives of your team. If you don't have a shelter we will talk about ways of digging in later in the chapter.

Treating a broken leg in a group shelter in the High Arctic.

Calling for help in the mountains

If you do need to call for outside assistance you need to have the means to do this, and the correct numbers available. A mobile phone is great in most situations, but you need to be aware that if you don't have line of sight on a mast then you are unlikely to get a signal. Most ski areas have masts on top of the higher lifts, so it is surprising where you can get a signal. When you are planning your tour it is worth thinking about your options if you can't get a signal. Personally I carry an Iridium Satellite phone but this is an expensive peace of mind. While most people ski with an 'it won't happen to me' attitude you should carefully consider how you would call for help if you needed it. The standard rescue number from a mobile phone in Europe is 112 but this doesn't work in every country; for example if you are Italy the number is 118, and if you are in the Valais region of Switzerland the number is 144. I have outlined the numbers below country by country, they are correct at the time of going to press but it is worth checking. An alternative if you are on a hut-to-hut ski tour is to call the nearest hut. This can often save time as they can often best explain to rescue services where you are.

The author using an
Iridium Satellite phone.

When, as an aspirant guide, I had to call a rescue on the Weissmies, I had to lose about 500m in altitude to get a phone signal. I called the Almageller hut and explained the problem and asked them to call for a rescue. I explained that there was no phone reception at the site of the accident, and that I would re-ascend to the casualties. They then called and helped coordinate the rescue services.

There is an excellent app called Echo 112 that will call the rescue services and send your GPS coordinates from your phone. This can greatly speed rescue.

France

In France the Gendarmerie du Haute Montagne (PGHM), the police force in the area, carries out rescues. The service is completely professional with its own helicopters. You can dial 112 and ask for mountain rescue, or even better dial one of the direct rescue numbers outlined below. This number will put you through to the rescue centre directly; the numbers vary in different parts of France.

Savoie

PGHM de Modane: +33 4 79 05 18 04
PGHM Bourg St Maurice: +33 4 79 07 01 10

Haute Savoie

PGHM de Chamonix: +33 4 50 53 16 89
PGHM Annecy: +33 4 50 09 47 47

Hautes Alpes

PGHM de Briançon: +33 4 92 21 58 58
Isère et Drôme
PGHM de Grenoble: +33 4 76 77 57 70

Switzerland

In Switzerland rescue is coordinated by REGA who employ local guides to perform the rescue. In some areas they use their own helicopters and in others they use those from local companies, for example Air Zermatt or Air Glacier in the Valais.

144 in the Valais
1414 for Swiss Rescue Service REGA

REGA has also produced an app that will allow you to request assistance and automatically sends your GPS position (assuming you have phone reception).

iREGA for iPhone http://itunes.apple.com/ch/app/irega/id415358154
iREGA for Android https://play.google.com/store/apps/details?id=ch.
rega.Rega&hl=en

Italy

The rescue services in Italy use a variety of agencies depending on the region.

118 or 112
Valle d'Aosta +39165 238 222

Austria

112 for general emergencies
140 for Austria Mountain Rescue Services
144 in Vorarlberg

Essential information when calling a rescue

When you call a rescue there are some pretty standard pieces of information that the rescue services will ask for. Remember that this will almost certainly be in the local language so you need to have the information ready to go. It is worth writing it down so there is no confusion when you are on the phone:

- Name and phone number.

- What's happened, nature of injury, number of people injured, number of people in the party.

- Where you are, GPS position (local map coordinates are best), and description including altitude.

- When did the accident happen?

- Weather, visibility, wind speed and direction are all very important if a helicopter is going to be sent to help.

When you are speaking to the rescue services it can often feel like they are getting hung up on the details, but the above information will help them make the correct response. They will often call you back once they have decided what to do, and may call back regularly to see how you are getting on.

A top tip from the PGHM in Chamonix: if you are involved in an avalanche incident and the operator is getting bogged down in detail just shout avalanche at them and they will skip straight to your location and get help dispatched as soon as possible.

Help the rescue team to find you

If you do call a rescue make it easy for the rescue team/helicopter to find you. It is almost certain if a rescue is to take place that a helicopter will be involved, so make your team easy to spot. Find an area that has as much space as possible away from any obstructions that may affect the rotors. When you are calling for rescue make sure you give as much information about your location as possible. If it is dark, flash your headtorch, it is amazing how far away it can be spotted from the air. If a team is approaching on foot, or you need to attract attention, make the international distress call. Six short blasts on a whistle followed by a minute, then another six followed by a minute, repeat as required.

As the helicopter approaches make the international distress signal. Stand with your arms in the air spread apart in a Y symbol with your back to the wind, this lets the pilot know that it is your team who need help and indicates the wind direction. If a helicopter does appear and you don't need assistance make the symbol for NO, one arm up and the other down to make the diagonal of an N.

As the helicopter approaches, kneeling down with your back to the wind and your hands in the Y can help the pilot as it provides a visual reference.

Yes I need help, No I do not need help.

Working close to a helicopter

If a helicopter is going to arrive on scene you need to be ready for the downdraught; secure any loose items, keep all the kit together so it is obvious to the pilot, and if you have been using a group shelter make sure it is packed away. The downdraught can be enough to blow skis and rucksacks away and can make it difficult to see, so would be worth putting on goggles. In most situations a winchman will be lowered or will get out of the helicopter, which will then move away to allow the winchman/medic to assess the situation and carry out any first aid or packaging, prior to the helicopter returning and

A rescue helicopter
above Chamonix, France.

removing the casualty. Most helicopters operating in the Alps can only carry a couple of people, so don't expect the whole team to be lifted out. In many situations the casualty will be removed and the rest of the team will have to ski out. If they are to be lifted out it may take a few rotations.

If you need to approach the helicopter only proceed if indicated to do so by the crew, and approach as per their directions; this is usually from the downhill side. You need to be aware of 'rotor sag' so stay low if you want to keep your head. Once on board follow the crew's instructions.

Waiting for rescue

Often the most difficult things to decide in bad weather with a casualty is to know if you should stay put and wait, try and move to a more sheltered position, or try and get to the nearest hut. If you have reported your position to the rescue coordinators you need to inform them if you plan to move; it will not make rescue any easier if you aren't at the position you reported.

If you have to wait it is important to look after the whole team not just the injured person; there is no point increasing the number of casualties. Keep everyone warm, put on spare clothing, drinking and eating will help keep everyone warm. If you are going to be there for a while, eat and drink a little at a time to spread out your supplies.

Get the team in a group shelter while everyone is still warm, once people start to get cold it is difficult to warm them up. If there isn't much shelter consider digging an emergency shelter in the snow.

Emergency snow shelter

If you do have to sit out some bad weather there is no better place to hide than in a snow shelter or snow hole. The air temperature in a snow hole is usually just below freezing and there will be no wind. If you are on a glacier have a good probe for crevasses before taking your skis off or start digging. The best place to dig a snow hole is in a bank of snow. Start by probing the bank to make sure it is deep enough, if the probe doesn't hit anything solid at its full depth then there is enough snow. Move a few steps up the bank so it is easier to clear the excavated snow. Start digging slowly into the bank making sure you work slowly as you don't want to get sweaty and damp. Change the digger frequently, so that everyone keeps warm but also stays dry. If you were digging a planned snow hole you could start at two points, digging into the hillside towards each other, then block up one of the entrances. When digging an emergency shelter you just need to dig a hole big enough to get the team out of the weather.

Dig an entrance about shoulder width apart and dig a corridor into the snow bank, you can make the floor slope slightly up to allow the cold air to drain out the door. Once you have gone in a metre or so you can dig out the snow to create benches, this will allow the team to sit up off the floor keeping away from the coldest air. Once you have a hole big enough for everyone to sit on their rucksacks for insulation you could stop there. Continuing slow improvements can help you to keep warm, smoothing off the roof will prevent any drips.

A snow hole; this one was planned so we had food and sleeping bags, but the principle is the same in an emergency.

If there is only flat snow you can dig a trench in the ground, lay skis across it then cover this with the group shelter. You can then pile snow on top to insulate and keep it in place. This is pretty grim and a last resort for shelter as it feels like you are in a grave.

An alternative is to build a 'shovel up'. Start by piling all your rucksacks together then covering them with the group shelter. Next shovel snow on top to make a big mound, this needs to be big enough to allow you to tunnel into it to create a space for the team inside. Once you have a big enough pile, pat the snow down, and the shovelling will have caused the snow to bond to itself. Now dig a low tunnel into the middle of the pile where the rucksacks are and pass these out down the tunnel. This will create a cavern which can then be enlarged to give enough space for everyone to shelter.

If you have never seen this done you are probably a bit sceptical but it works really well, try making a mini one to convince yourself of the principle. One of the advantages of a shovel up is that you can build it on the flat, so you can construct one away from avalanche-prone terrain whereas a snow hole requires you to have a slope to dig into.

Another alternative if you are really desperate is to dig a trench in the snow, lay skis and poles across the trench, then lay your group shelter on top of this, and shovel some snow on top of it to hold it in place. You can then crawl in for one of the most miserable nights of your life. It is as bad as it sounds, but it will get you out of the wind and weather, and may save your life.

Self evacuation

If the weather is too bad for a rescue, and you need to move a casualty to a more sheltered location or to a hut, you will need to work out how to move them. Lots of first aid books talk about the importance of not moving the casualty, but this would be in a situation where help is definitely coming. You have to think to yourself, "What will happen to the casualty if I don't move them?" The answer is often simple, they will die. If that is the alternative, no matter how grim it may be, you need to move them. Having appropriate pain relief at this point can make life easier and reduce the screaming; if you don't have anything strong enough you just have to work with the casualty.

Extra emergency kit

It is easy to keep adding this and that to your ski touring kit and you end up with a rucksack that is too heavy to ski with. Keep things focused and spread the kit between the party, and you should be able to deal with most situations.

If we think about common emergencies or situations that might crop up, and what kit we should take along, we have already covered crevasse rescue kit in detail and you should carry this any time you are on a glacier. Being caught out because you are too slow, or have a medical or equipment issue, you should have a group shelter and know how to construct a snow shelter.

I always carry a small repair kit in case there is a binding or other equipment problem. It's amazing what you can fix with a Leatherman-type multi-tool, some tape and cable ties.

In everyday skiing situations I carry a multi-tool, a few stout cable ties and a roll of physio-type tape. Duct tape is great when it is warm but it goes brittle in the cold and does not stick. If you need to use tape to secure your skins, physio tape lasts better than duct tape as well. A scraper and some Glop Stopper-type wax to rub your skins with if they are balling up is also really useful.

Spares kit.

If I am heading out on a hut-to-hut tour I usually carry a bit more, but my normal kit is:

- Carrying bag

- Leatherman/multi-tool

- Binding tool/screwdriver

- Cable ties (heavy-duty plastic ones)

- Rubber ski straps

- Wire

- Physio tape

- Scraper

- Emergency skin glue

- Spare ski pole basket

- Binding mounting screws

- Nut and bolt (small diameter)

- Skin tip

- Spare transceiver batteries

- Five metres of 7mm cord; you can use this for repairs, crevasse rescue or to help deal with flat light

On a longer tour I will add:

- Araldite epoxy glue

- Fritschi binding toe piece – easy to replace in the field but a nightmare to cobble together if you break one

- Silicon ski wax

- Skin proof – a longer term solution to balling up skins

Evacuating an injured skier

If your party has to evacuate an injured skier you are not going to be able carry them out; you will need to be able to build a sledge from their skis and drag them out.

You can improvise a stretcher or you can use a kit stretcher that you brought with you. It is worth practising the construction of a stretcher in the comfort and warmth of your own garage; being on a windy mountainside with an injured person is not the place to do this. Practising it will also allow you to fine-tune the kit you take with you. The key elements in sledge construction are how you are going to fix the skis together and give the sledge rigidity, and how to make it strong enough so the whole thing will not disintegrate as soon as the casualty sits on it and is towed.

There is a clever ultra-light sledge from Brooks-Range that I often have in the party if we are on a remote tour. K2 have a shovel in their Backside range that can be used to construct a sledge. Even with these kits it is essential to practise prior to going into the mountains. Once you are happy with your design and construction, try dragging your sledge on snow. It is particularly worth practising going across and down a slope, you will often need someone with a rope at the back to control the speed.

A Brooks sledge
in action.

An improvised stretcher.

Improvised stretcher

If you don't have a stretcher kit and need to move someone you will need to improvise a stretcher. This can be easier if you have a set of skis with holes in the tips and tails. If not, and you were stuck, I'm sure you could make a hole with a multi-tool if you had to. There are loads of potential sled designs but the following suggestion does work.

Start by laying the skis side by side then using ski straps, tie shovel handles or bits of ski pole between the bindings. This can then be braced diagonally using ski poles and more straps/cord to keep the sledge more stable and strong. Once you have the structure the victim can be lashed on top. This isn't as solid or as comfortable as the likes of the Brooks Ultralight sledge but it will allow you to get someone out of a difficult situation.

The BCA Shaxe system (see kit chapter) can be used to construct a very effective rescue sled, this is something I carry with me pretty much all the time as the ski straps are so useful for lots of other ski touring uses.

Neither of these improvisations is as solid or as comfortable as the likes of the Brooks Ultralight sledge but it will allow you to get someone out of a difficult situation.

Guidebook

Skinning up the Periades glacier, Chamonix.

One of the most difficult things to get to grips with when learning to ski tour is deciding where to go. This book has focused just on the European Alps which is itself a huge area of mountains, and knowing where to go for your first trip, and the type of ski tours to try, is a real minefield. I would like to help make that decision-making process easier for you by suggesting some great tours to get you started. The tours I have included begin with day tours, then build to multi-day hut-to-hut trips.

There are dozens of great ski touring possibilities in the Alps and further afield, so making a selection to include in this book was really difficult. My criteria were that they must be classic tours, that I and people I know have skied regularly and thought they reached that classic status. The selection also includes tours having enough challenge to help you develop the skills needed to move through the mountains safely, but none of the routes are overly complicated, so they are achievable at this stage of your ski touring career. Most of the tours have a number of options to make things harder or easier so you can modify them as you see fit. I have included the grade for the tour using the three grading systems that you will come across if you look in different guidebooks. This is the grading system described in the 'Planning a Ski Tour' chapter.

The final criterion is that I have completed all the tours recently, so the information is accurate and as up-to-date as it can be at the time of publication.

In the introduction to each tour you will find: the best time of the year to complete the tour, the maps you will need, possible alternative guide books, web links to huts, local avalanche information and booking numbers. All the points referred to in the text will match the features marked on the recommended maps. We will start off with some day tours, some using lifts, others where you just skin from the road, before moving onto multi-day adventures.

I have made a conscious decision not to include GPS coordinates and things like that. I want to encourage you to get the map out and do the tour planning, to work out how long the legs will take you, and to identify which slopes to be careful of. By doing this yourself, and not just plugging a set of coordinates into a GPS and pressing go, you will learn to read the map, relate it to the terrain, and develop your skills as a ski tourer.

In many respects choosing day tours was more difficult, as there are so many great options right across the Alps. After long consideration I decided to focus the day tours around alpine centres where it is easy to rent and buy good-quality ski touring kit. It is possible to rent ski touring kit in most alpine centres but the quality is incredibly variable. What seems to happen is that ski hire shops get it into their heads that hire kit should be lightweight, skinny ski touring skis with Fritschi bindings. While the bindings are fine, the narrow, lightweight skis are not easy to ski on, especially if you are new to ski touring and are getting to grips with lighter, softer boots.

I have centred the day tours round the alpine centres of the Mont Blanc Massif (Chamonix) and Verbier. This gives access to a huge selection of off-piste terrain to get your ski legs, lots of touring options and a great selection of shops to hire or buy kit. Before we get onto the actual tours it is worth mentioning if you are going to rent kit, or want to buy boots, you will need to reserve the kit to get the best of what is on offer, and should make an appointment to have boots correctly fitted. At the time of writing, the boot rooms in Sanglard Sports in Chamonix and Mountain Air in Verbier have worked well for myself and my clients.

Angus Pearson skiing the Periades glacier, Mont Blanc Massif.

DAY TOURS

Mont Blanc Massif

Weather Forecast

http://chamonix-meteo.com

Avalanche Forecast

http://france.meteofrance.com/france/montagne?MONTAGNE_
PORTLET.path=montagnebulletinneige/DEPT74

Maps

Chamonix Massif du Mont Blanc IGN 3630OT. This will cover you for
most things in Chamonix including the Vallée Blanche, Grands Montets
and any tours you may do in the Aiguille Rouge. There are also a couple of
Mini Maps for Mont Blanc and Argentière which are very useful as they
fit in your pocket really nicely.

Megève IGN – Mini Map M3531OT Megève (1), covers all the other tours
mentioned.

Alternative Guidebooks

Mont Blanc Ski Tours – Eric Delaperriere and Franck Gentilini

Mont Blanc - Toponeige

Aravis, Bauges, Chartreuse - Toponeige

Useful websites

www.chamonix.com – Tourist office website, useful lift info, weather and
accommodation. They also have a good app.

www.chamonix.net – A portal website that has an accommodation
finding service along with, lift, weather and general information.

www.ohm-chamonix.com – Mountain information including conditions,
links to huts etc.

www.evasionmontblanc.com – Lift information, Saint Gervais, Les
Contamines and Megève.

Many of you may be surprised by the inclusion of Chamonix in a selection of day tours to help you develop your ski touring skills, as the mountains are steep and glaciated, but the Mont Blanc Massif has a huge variety of terrain. Within a short drive of Chamonix there are more than 20 ski areas with all types of terrain, both lift-accessed and natural. There are glacial off-piste skiing options, including the world famous Vallée Blanche, as well as great non glacial touring. Importantly for those trying ski touring for the first time, there are some great shops where you can hire as well as buy ski touring kit.

It is always worth trying to get a day's skiing in before heading out touring, to remind your muscles how to ski and to reacquaint yourself with your equipment. There are five ski areas within the Chamonix Valley which all offer great skiing, but in my opinion skiing on the back of La Tour is probably the best place to warm up for off-piste, to check your skins work, and to practise your avalanche rescue skills prior to heading onto a glacier or out there touring.

The Grands Montets is a great place to ski off-piste, though it is not the place to seek out fresh untracked snow as it is a bit too popular with good skiers. Having said that there are few more spectacular places to ski in the Alps than the glacial runs from the top station down onto the Argentière glacier. The surrounding lower ski areas of St Gervais, Megève and Les Contamines are all great places to ski on powder days as there aren't so many off-piste skiers. The terrain is generally of a shallower angle, so on high avalanche risk days it is easier to find suitable terrain where you can still ski off-piste, when many of the lifts in the steeper Chamonix valley will be shut. There are also a number of great ski touring options, so we will start our guidebook there.

Petit and Grand Croisse Baulet

Grade – F SM S2

Season – December - March

Map – Megève, Mini Map M3531OT Megève (1)

Access point – Jaillet lift in Megève or the main ski lift in Combloux.

Starting point – Using the piste map find the Pres and Pertuis (high-speed quad coming from Combloux) lifts.

Equipment – Standard ski touring kit, no need for ice axe and crampons.

Sitting above the villages of Megève and Combloux, the Petit Croisse Baulet is as close to a perfect first ski tour as you can get: easy access, great skiing, lots of options, and amazing views all combine to give a tour that I do a number of times every season.

Starting at the top of the Pertuis and Pres lifts, ski down the Jorace (red) piste for a couple of hundred metres, then as the piste bears right you cut left on a pisted track through some woods. Put your skins on here and skin along the track to the Col du Jaillet, where you leave the pisted track and head into the woods. There is usually a track, but if not head up through the woods in a westerly direction heading for the east ridge, then when you reach the ridge head left, keeping back from the often corniced edge. As you approach the summit, skin a few metres past it to avoid some steep snow, before heading onto the summit ridge.

Martin and Roy Goodlad skiing down from the Petit Croisse Baulet.

There are a number of options from here depending on how much time you have, and the conditions. You can carry on along the ridge to the Grand Croisse Baulet which adds about another hour of skinning. If you choose to do this, ski down the ridge, it's up to you if you take skins off to do this or leave them on. It will depend on the snow; it is often easier to leave them on in soft snow, but easier to take them off in hard snow. Skin up the right-hand side of the face to an amazing summit position.

Descent options

Descents from the Petit Croisse Baulet in red, the green line is the ski line to the Grand Croisse Baulet.

You can now ski the face back to the col where you will have to fit skins and climb back to the summit of the Petit Croisse Baulet. There are a couple of skiing options from here; you can ski back to the Col du Jaillet and then back into the ski area where you started from, or you can ski down the ridge towards Le Plan, then at a col head south. This slope can be very crusted so I wouldn't advise it if there has been warm temperature or lots of sun. If the snow is good here, ski down through meadows until some steeper terrain leads into the valley bottom, then follow the line of the stream, then a road which leads you to the village of Le Plan. You can now use the lift system to get back to your starting point. An alternative is to head south, then at a flattening of the ridge head west through some trees to a steepening in the terrain. Now head south and ski down past a small cliff band, then down a meadow and some steeper terrain to join the track leading to Le Plan. If either of these options look crusty you can work the northerly aspect from the summit. This is in the shade and often holds powder when the other aspects on the mountain have transformed. Ski down and left traversing towards the col mentioned earlier. If the snow is good you could use your skins to get an extra lap in. When you are at the col mentioned earlier, you can follow the ridge crest, then pick up a track leading onto the north side of the ridge, then ski some more meadows to reach a track which leads through the trees to Le Plan; this can be awkward but doesn't last too long.

With so many options you can vary the length of the day to suit and get in some great skiing.

Les Contamines Montjoie – Col de la Fenêtre, Col de la Cicle, Col des Chasseurs and Rochers des Enclaves

Season – December · March

Map – Megève, Mini Map M3531OT Megève (1)

Access point – Notre Dame de la Gorge lift station

Starting point – Top of the Bûche Croisée lift

Equipment – Standard ski touring kit plus crampons, as the Roman road that is skied in descent can be icy, and at times it is impossible to descend without them. The Col des Chasseurs requires an ice axe as well. The Enclaves just requires standard kit.

Les Contamines is at the head of the Val de Montjoie about 35 minutes drive from Chamonix. The ski area of Les Contamines has some great off-piste skiing, but unlike the neighbouring areas of St Gervais and Megève it does not have much tree skiing, so it is best in good visibility.

Les Contamines will sell you a discounted randonnée (ski touring) lift ticket before 10am, this gives you access to the essential lifts needed to start all of the following tours.

There are two access points to the ski area, the best one to park in is at Notre Dame de la Gorge at the head of the valley, which allows you to ski back to the car after a number of the ski tours. All the tours start from a lift and all, bar the Rocher des Enclaves, can be accessed by buying a randonnée ticket which allows a single up on the lifts. The Enclave requires a day ticket so you can use the lifts to get back at the end of the tour.

Ski tours in Les Contamines L-R Col de la Fenêtre. Col de la Cicle and Rocher des Enclaves.

Les Contamines tour descents L-R Col des Chasseurs, Col de la Cicle and Col de la Fenêtre.

Use the piste map to locate the Bûche Croisée lift; to find this use the main access lift (Signal), then ski the Gentianes piste and ride the lift. All four tours described start from this point. It is a good place to work out where you are heading. The Col de la Fenêtre is the first col, the Cicle and the Chasseurs are out of sight. The Rocher des Enclave is visible in the distance, and you can see the ski descent for this route in profile to below the Lac de la Girotte dam where you rejoin the ski area in the village of Hauteluce.

Col de la Fenêtre

Grade – F S2 SM

This is a great little tour with about an hour's skinning and some nice skiing. Leaving the top of the lift take a descending traverse heading south-west. There are often some big glide cracks in the snow here that can be as big as crevasses. The traverse leads to a nice flat area where you can transition to skins; you can often get a few extra turns here before attaching your skins.

You can see the col above you. Look at the terrain and look for the easiest route that will allow you to skin at as low an angle as the terrain will allow. The best route heads towards an obvious gully, then swings to the right before arriving at the narrows. Depending on the snow you may need to take your skis off and boot up the gully, or you may be able to make a series of kick turns up the gully. The angle eases above the gully to allow more relaxed skinning towards the col. A rising traverse right to left is usually the easiest way to arrive at the col. It is easy to confirm you are in the right place as there is a signpost.

The col is nice and flat for a transition to ski mode. The first couple of turns off the col can feel a bit steep, but the angle eases quickly, then there are two skiing options; you can head left or right. I would only suggest the left-hand route if there is good powder as the lower section is through some tight trees. This is pretty easy in soft, untracked snow but isn't much fun once the snow has been skied out. The classic descent heads right on a long traverse until you are under the Col de la Cicle here you turn left and ski down a series of nice bowls heading for the chalets at La Balme. Here you start heading north-west and join the Roman road. In summer this is the line of the Tour de Mont Blanc. This road usually has a ski track across it for most of the winter, and is pretty flat so it is worth letting the skis run. Follow the track into the trees; this is quite popular with snowshoers so watch out. The track leads through a meadow then where it rejoins a track you cross a bridge, which dates from the Roman period and crosses a gorge, and is well worth stopping to look at.

Carry on down the road. As it gets steeper towards the valley floor, water ice sometimes forms across the track, which is why I carry crampons on any of these tours. If the track is icy it is impossible to get round the ice. At the base of the steep section of the track cross a bridge and join the cross country ski track which leads back to the car.

Col de la Cicle

Grade – PD S3 BS

If you are going to ski to the Col de la Cicle put your skins on at the same point as the previous tour, then head south using the terrain to keep the angle low. There is a bench feature to follow which keeps you off the steeper terrain. After 2km you will come to a col marked 2283 on the map, turn north-east here and head for the Col de la Cicle. The initial section can become icy and you may need to put on ski crampons. When you get to the col transition to downhill mode and ski north-east until you join the descent from the Col de la Fenêtre.

Col des Chasseurs

Grade – AD S4 TBS

When you reach the Col de la Cicle transition to crampons, put your skis on your pack, and climb the steep snow to the south-east. When possible put your skis back on and follow the ridge to the south-east; this can be tricky and may require ski crampons and intricate skinning. At the col transition to downhill mode and ski the gully; the first section is 40 degrees so requires good technique. The descent is north-facing and often has great snow; ski down until you join the descents from the other routes at La Balme.

Rochers des Enclaves

Grade – F S2 SM

This tour doesn't have any particularly steep skiing and so is a great option in difficult avalanche conditions. It also has great views and is often less frequented than some of the other tours described.

Start at the same point as the previous tours. Begin as for the Col de la Cicle then head for the Col de la Gitte, pass point 2389 and head south-west to the summit of the Rochers des Enclaves. When you are ready to descend, ski back to point 2389 then head north and a bit east down the ridge. If you are short on time you can join this ridge straight from the Col de la Gitte. There are lots of possibilities on or around the ridge crest. At the Chalet de Berger under the power cables head north-east then join the summer road which leads past Colombe where you should be able to cut through the trees back to the piste without putting your skins back on.

Chamonix – Vallée Blanche

Map – IGN Chamonix Massif du Mont Blanc 3630 OT

Equipment – Classic ski touring kit plus glacier travel kit

Grade – PD S2-S3 SM-BS depending on variation

This is one of the most classic glacial ski descents in the Alps, with lots of variations and a great possible short tour to the Italian side of the Vallée Blanche. While this isn't really a ski tour (unless you go to Italy) it is a great introduction to glacial skiing.

The start of any Vallée Blanche adventure starts at the Aiguille du Midi. The descent of the famous arête can be a circus with inexperienced people being guided down and slipping about, desperately trying to hold onto their skis. A handrail is in place for most of the season, so it isn't as bad as it looks, but wearing crampons and carrying your skis on your rucksack will make the experience much more pleasurable.

When you find a comfortable spot put your skis on. There are lots of variations but today we will start in the direction of the classic Vallée Blanche descent which takes us under the south face of the Midi, past the Cosmiques hut, and round to the Col du Gros Rognon. You have two choices from here; if you just want to ski the Gros Rognon variation, contour round the Gros Rognon then ski west then north-west, skiing and working left as you go, and eventually you will reach a traverse track that leads round to the top of the Geant Icefall. If you want to ski the classic Vallée Blanche, carry on skiing under the east face of Mont Blanc du Tacul to the flat area below the Pyramide du Tacul, then ski west, then north, to join the tracks described above. There are lots of crevasses in this area so watch out. In most years the left side of the icefall is well filled in and you can ski down this, but don't hang about as this area is threatened by seracs from above.

As you ski down the side of the icefall you will notice the Requin Hut ahead of you on the left sitting above the glacier – you can stop here for lunch or a coffee. In most seasons the route drops down below the hut then crosses the Salle à Manger to the other side of the glacier. This area is heavily crevassed even if you can't see them, so take care. When you have crossed to the other side of the glacier the line now heads down the main line of the Mer de Glace, the exact line varies from year to year depending on the snow and the crevasses.

Vallée Blanche descents L-R Classic descent, Gros Rognon, Petit Envers.

There are two ways to the valley; you can ski all the way to the valley in the earlier part of the season or take the Montenvers railway to the valley. If you want to ski down, carry on down the glacier past Montenvers until it is possible to ski right off the snout of the glacier. You now need to put your skis on your pack and hike up for 20 minutes to reach a track leading to a little buvette (hut selling drinks). Put your skis back on and follow the track down through the woods back to the valley until you pop out at the top of the Planards piste. The track can be quite narrow and icy, and often is the most difficult part of the descent.

If you are going to take the train, head left towards the train station – the building you can see is the Montenvers Hotel. Watch your line at the end as there is a steep drop-off on the left side of the glacier. You often have to ski a bit further than you think so you are actually passed the base of the cable car that leads up to the train. When the terrain allows cut back to where you can get off the edge of the glacier. This is where the tourist attraction of the Grotte du Glace (Ice Cave) is. Steps now lead up to a cable car that takes you to the Montenvers train.

John and Fiona Fells skinning across to the Italian side of the Vallée Blanche.

A really nice extension to this day is to take a skin across to Italy. Start the skiing as described, but instead of heading round the Gros Rognon, carry on skiing under Mont Blanc du Tacul until you reach an obvious flattening just beyond Pointe Adolphe Rey. Change to skins here, remember you are on a glacier so change your skis one at a time. The route now heads through a band of crevasses that can often be spectacular heading for the Col du Flambeau. As you come through the col you will see the Helbronner lift station. At the time of writing this was closed for renovation, but it was a perfect place to stop for an Italian coffee. When you reach the Italian border the coffee halves in price and doubles in quality compared to France.

The classic ski from here is to shuffle back over the Col du Flambeau then ski down until you join the classic Vallée Blanche. Alternatively you can ski towards the Dent du Géant (big pointy thing) then cut left and ski down the Combe de la Vierge. As the terrain eases in angle you can cut across the flat area to the classic descent, or keep on the right side of the glacier and ski down the Combe Noire. You need to find out about conditions here before you set off as there are lots of crevasses, some of them running parallel with the direction of travel. There is also steep terrain above some of the crevasses.

Routes on the Argentière Glacier L-R Col du Tour Noire, Col d'Argentière.

Col du Tour Noire, Col d'Argentière

Tour Noire – Grade – F S2 SM

Argentière – Grade – PD S3 BS

These tours start from the top of the Grands Montets lift. They are both a great introduction to ski touring on a glacier, and have one of the most spectacular backdrops of any ski tour. The tours both start from the top of the Grands Montets ski lift – this lift can be incredibly busy, and being at the back of the queue could easily ruin your day. It is usually worth buying your ticket the night before.

When you have got to the top, walk down the stairs and put on your skis. You are on a glacier as soon as you start skiing, so eyes open. Ski down over the steepening then cut right and duck under the rope. Ski down the Glacier des Rognons in an easterly direction. Ski to the right of the Rognon (it's not very clearly marked on the map, but is really obvious when you are there), then when the ground steepens head right, ski round some crevasses, and down onto the Argentière glacier. Change to skins, remembering you are on a glacier, then head up the glacier. The safest route through the crevasses is usually up the middle, then across to the left towards the Argentière Hut. Carry on up the glacier until you reach the bottom of the Glacier des

Améthystes; if you are heading for the Col du Tour Noire turn left here. The glacier is initially steepish, then rises in a number of steepenings and easings. As tours go it is pretty straightforward, but the terrain and the scenery is spectacular and you can relax and focus on your techniques.

If you are heading for the Col d'Argentière carry on a bit further then head up the Glacier du Tour Noire. Keep on the left to start with to avoid crevasses, then trend right weaving through some crevasses and steepenings to the col. This tour is steeper than the Col du Tour Noire so there are a few more kick turns, its aspect also means that it gets a lot of sun. In the spring, after fresh snowfall, this can create some fantastic breakable crust. It might be worth waiting until the crust has softened before starting your descent. I did this exact thing one April day, we could feel the crust on the way up and timed our descent to enjoy some challenging, but fun, skiing on the descent. If you get it wrong this a great place to work on Alison's crust tactics in the downhill skiing chapter.

Brian O'Connor on the way to the Col d'Argentière.

Verbier Val de Bagnes, Grand St Bernard Hospice

Weather Forecast

www.meteoswiss.ch

Avalanche Forecast

www.slf.ch

Maps

GD St-Bernard 1:25000 1365 Topo Suisse

Martigny 1:50000 282S Topo Suisse – Ski touring map with routes marked.

Useful websites

www.verbier.ch – Tourist office site with links to ski lifts, accommodation etc

www.gsbernard.net – St Bernard Hospice

Kat Congleton
skiing in Bruson.

Verbier is a huge ski resort, it has a reputation for being expensive but you don't have to stay in Verbier itself, you can stay in Le Chable or one of the other villages in the bottom of the valley, then use the fast lift from Le Chable into the system each morning. There are some great shops where you can hire and buy ski touring kit, Mountain Air is probably the best.

There are lots of marked itinerary runs and short skins within the ski area which you can do to get to grips with your ski touring kit. When you are comfortable with the kit I would recommend heading across the valley to Bruson, a small village with four lifts and great off-piste skiing and touring options. The access lift has been replaced since the first edition so you now park in the main ski car park in La Chable and a continuous lift takes you into the Bruson system. In spite of the new lift Bruson is still surprisingly quiet.

As a venue Bruson is better earlier in the season due to its altitude, making it a great place to tour from December through to mid-March. You can tour later but some of the runs that reach the road can melt out so you would need to walk the last bit.

Bruson

Grade – F S2 SM

Season – December – mid March

Equipment – Standard ski touring kit

Map – Martigny 1:50000 282S Topo Suisse

There are load of great off-piste options and Bruson is the perfect place to combine some off-piste skiing and a bit of touring. The main area is north facing so it tends to keep the quality of the snow pretty well. The classic tour in the Bruson area is the Tête de la Payanne and it is one of my favourite short tours. Start by taking the Grand Tsai T bar (drag lift), then at the top shuffle up a blunt ridge for a bit (they didn't quite finish the lift in the right place) before sliding down and across to a flat area where you can put skins on. You are heading for a col marked 2331m on the map between the Six Blanc and the Tête de la Payanne. This is a nice, rising line with a couple of kick turns to gain the col.

Andy Congleton skiing in Bruson.

There are a couple of options from here; you can turn right and climb the Six Blanc which has a steep north face that leads back into the ski area, in cold snow you can ski the south-west face to Commeire from where you can get a taxi back to Bruson, or in low altitude snow conditions, you can ski all the way to Orsières where you can get a bus or a taxi back to Bruson.

Our plan is to turn left and climb the Tete de la Payanne. The best skinning line is to follow the ridge crest, then when it gets steep and a bit rocky take a rising traverse across the south-west face. This is exposed to the sun so you need to consider the avalanche risk. If there has been a lot of freeze-thaw make sure you have your ski crampons to hand. The best line takes you past the summit, so you will need to cut back left if you want to visit the summit cairn. There are a few little tops on the ridge, so it is often worth keeping skins on and heading along the ridge to the south to a point where you are sure you can ski from without any re-ascent.

When you are ready to ski you can ski off in a northerly direction. The ground just below the summit is a bit steep, so if you want an easier-angled ski (and one that often has fewer tracks) head south towards the col at point 2365. The descent from here is often fantastic, low-angled powder skiing; there is a lot of space to ski so you can usually find fresh tracks. Ski in a north-easterly direction past a band of trees and into a clearing marked Le Tseppi on the map. Ski across this to the bottom left-hand corner where you pick up a track. Before the new lift you could join clearings and roads to get back to the car. If you do this you end up in Bruson where you can't join the lift so unless you have left a car you need to follow one of the forest roads that traverse from Renarosse back into the ski area.

Grand Saint Bernard Hospice – your first overnight

Grade – PD S2-S3 SM-BS There are a couple of short steep sections but nothing to worry about.

Contact / reservations – www.gsbernard.ch – 0041 27 787 1236

Season – December - March/April depending on the temperatures

Map – GD St-Bernard 1:25000 1365 Topo Suisse

The Grand Saint Bernard Hospice has sat on the Grand Saint Bernard pass between Italy and Switzerland for over 1000 years. It was built to care for travellers crossing the pass, and still does this today. The monastery is inhabited all year round and is run in a similar fashion to a mountain hut with dormitories and small rooms available. Booking is just like a hut where you can book half board. It is still a working place of worship, so guests do have to be mindful of this, but are invited to take part. The church and the museum are both fascinating.

Since the closure of the St Bernard ski area access is on skins from the road head. As you approach the Grand St Bernard Tunnel keep a lookout for a turn-off, this is signposted 'Col' as the road is open over the col in the summer months. A car park is usually cleared to allow for parking.

The ascent to the hut follows the summer road. When the road climbs onto the north side of the valley stay on the south side and the valley floor. The last section is particularly avalanche prone and is known as the Combe Mort so check the conditions with the monks before setting off.

It takes about two hours to get to the monastery, and on the way you will pass two small huts which can be used as emergency shelters if you get the weather wrong; they both have emergency telephones and a stove. Depending on your timings, you can arrive, settle in, then do some training round the hut or go for a short skin. Just north of the hut there is a little knoll which can make for a nice, short outing. If you have a bit more time then you can take in the Col Est de Barasson, which is a detour on the approach. Just head south under some power lines shortly before the valley narrows. The ascent to the col is north facing so often holds good snow.

Kate Scott and Mike
Austin arriving at
the monastery from
the Italian side.

Classic ski tours
from the monastery
L-R Mont Fourchon,
Fenêtre d'en Haut.

There are a number of great options from the monastery, so you can vary
the amount of time you stay there, my favourite option is to stay for two
nights. This would involve arriving at the monastery and spending the night.
The next day make an ascent of Mont Fourchon, spend a second night, then
on the following day traverse the Fenêtre d'en Haut and another col on the
way back to the car.

You could of course just stay for one night, climb Mont Fourchon, then
ski out. It just depends on the time you have available.

Both these tours leave the monastery and head west round the lake,
you can do this without skins. Pick up the road and follow it to an avalanche
tunnel, ski through this, or in stable snow you can ski a few turns below the
tunnel. The routes split after the tunnel.

Mont Fourchon

Put your skins on then climb up past some buildings at spot height 2356m, skin round a ridge, then head north into a small valley. You then ski west in an arc, you can use the steep ground to the north as a handrail in bad visibility. The easiest line is to stay north of the rocks at spot height 2771m. The ground steepens as you approach the summit, and in most conditions you will need to leave your skis and climb on foot to the top. You may need crampons but that will depend on the snow conditions. From the summit descend back to your skis. If you fancy another summit, head south-east and climb the north-west ridge on the Pain de Sucre, this will almost certainly require crampons.

There are a couple of options on the ski descent; you can go back down the way you came up, or alternatively at point 2582 at the lake head south-east then south, passing to the south of the Tête des Fous, then ski down the valley in an easterly direction. If the snow is good just keep heading down, I have often skied as far as the Maison de Refuge. When you have had enough skiing skin north to the avalanche tunnel entrance and back to the monastery.

Fenêtre d'en Haut

This is my favourite way back to the car, but like so many tours it has a bit of steep ground, so be mindful of the avalanche conditions. Use the same start as Mont Fourchon to the end of the tunnel, from here head north-west skinning up between two blunt, rocky ridges. At about 2650m you skin up a bench leading west and then to the col. This line keeps you on the lowest angle terrain which is safest and offers the easiest skinning. Once you are on the ridge, head north-east towards point 2861m and as the ground steepens take a rising traverse to the north heading for another col. You will have to put your skis on your back and crampon at some point, so choose a good point where is not too exposed.

Once you reach the col it is back to ski mode for a great north-east facing ski back to the car, the route is obvious so the only thing you have to consider is where to cross the river to regain the road.

This three day trip, combined with a warm-up round Verbier (1 hrs drive) or Chamonix (2 hrs drive), is a perfect introduction to the delights of overnighting in the mountains. It will set you up for longer tours where you will spend a number of nights in the high mountains travelling from hut-to-hut.

HUT-TO-HUT TOURS

What follows is a selection of hut-to-hut tours – there are loads of tours that we could have chosen from, and this is only a small selection of tours that we have done and enjoyed. All the tours are five or six days so fit nicely into a week's holiday. If you have the time it is often nice to have a warm-up day to give your legs a work out and to check out the snow conditions.

I have tried to include options where possible, some of them to increase the difficulty and length of days, and others to make life easier.

As with the day tours I have made a conscious decision not to include GPS coordinates and things like that. I want to encourage you to get the map out and do the tour planning, to work out how long the legs will take you, and to check which slopes to be careful of. By doing this yourself and not just plugging a set of coordinates into a GPS and pressing go, you will learn to read the map, relate it to the terrain, and develop your skills as a ski tourer.

Silvretta Tour – Austria

Louise Baltez ski touring in the Silvretta.

Grade

F S2 SM

Season

Late February to late April, early May is possible depending on the snow.

Map

Alpenvereinskarte 26 Silvrettegruppe Skiroten edition printed by the Austrian Alpine Club

Weather forecast

www.weatheraustria.net

Avalanche forecast

http://lawine.tirol.gv.at/en/

Hut bookings / contact

Heidelberger Hut – www.heidelberger-huette.at – 0043 664 425 30 70

Jamtal Hut – www.jamtalhuette.at – 0043 54438408

Wiesbadcner Hut – www.wiesbadener-huette.com – 0043 5558 4233

Useful information

www.galtuer.com – Tourist office site, links to accommodation, lifts and bus information.

www.ischgl.com – The next town down the valley Ischgl offers more accommodation and you can find the lift and bus times to start the tour here.

Equipment

Classic touring kit plus, ice axe and crampons if you want to summit any of the peaks. Glacier travel kit as some of the days are on a glacier.

The Silvretta Alps in western Austria is one of my favourite places to introduce people to hut-to-hut ski tours. The huts are great, the mountains of are an achievable size, and there are lots of great options to link huts together. An important thing to consider when planning a trip there is that the access and exit valleys to two of the huts mentioned are long and steep-sided, so they are an extremely serious place to be in high avalanche conditions. If in any doubt about the conditions call the hut guardians before setting off to get the latest information.

The huts in the Silvretta are superb – all of them have showers so it is worth taking a small wash kit. The Heidelberger Hut which is the first hut you will visit does not provide hut slippers, which is a bit out of keeping with the rest of the Alps and worth thinking about. The Jamtal sells slippers for about €2 and the Wiesbadener provides them.

The small town of Galtür is a great place to be based, with a small ski area at Wirl where you can get your legs warmed up, and you can make a short ski tour to the Breiter Spitz to check all your kit is working properly.

The tour I am going suggest is a circular tour which has a great aesthetic appeal.

Day 1 Galtur – Heidelberger Hut

Take the free bus from Galtur to Ischgl then use the lift system to get to the top of the Piz Val Gronda lift. You can now ski from the summit to the Heidelberger Hut (2304m) heading south-west and contouring round the hillside. If you have the time you can take in the Piz Davo Sasse which has a great north-facing bowl. In certain snow conditions it is also possible to ski straight from this summit to the hut.

The Heidelberger Hut is a great old hut with a mix of dormitory (lager) accommodation and smaller rooms. If you want a small room you will need to reserve one when you book. It is open from early January so it's a great place to do some early season ski touring, using the hut as a base and touring out and back every day.

Arriving at the Heidelberger Hut.

Day 2 Heidelberger – Jamtal

There are a number of day tours that you can do from the hut but our itinerary heads from the Jamtal Hut via the Breite Krone (3079m). Leaving the hut in the morning head south through a small valley, then south-west heading for the Kronen Joch. Just before the col, cut back on yourself towards the Breite Krone. You can usually ski some of the way before rocky ground forces a transition from skis to feet. You can leave your skis here and you might want to put on crampons depending on how hard the snow is. I usually just go with ski poles in my hands, but have an ice axe to hand just in case. It is a short hike to the summit where you can enjoy the view over the Silvretta peaks and beyond. When you get back to your skis leave your skins on, slide down then skin to the Kronen Joch where you can make the last transition of the day. The valley that leads down to the Jamtal Hut is roughly east/west, so you can often find spring snow on the southerly aspects and cold powdery snow on the northerly aspects. As you ski down the lower section of the valley it is worth keeping to the right bank of the stream, which leads you to the hut. Jamtal is a modern hut that was renovated and extended after it was damaged by an avalanche. It has rooms or dormitories with beds for 200 people and can get very busy, so make sure you keep track of your kit.

Route to the
Breite Krone.

Day 3 Jamspitze

We can ski with lighter packs today and make a day tour from the Jamtal Hut. The Hintere Jamspitze (3156m) is a perfect objective involving about 1000m of skinning with a nice summit, then a great descent on a north-facing glacier. When you leave the hut in the morning there is a short downhill section. Some people will leave with skins on and accept the awkward start, others will ski down then put skins on. You will be on a glacier about an hour into the day, so I would put my harness on in the hut.

Andy and Kat Congleton skiing down to the Jamtal Hut.

The route to the Jamspitze in red, the route to the Obere Ochsenscharte is in green.

Head south following the main valley, where a rock barrier exists you can go round it left or right; I would suggest left as you will skin up the right-hand side tomorrow. Shortly above the rock you will skin onto the glacier. The peak straight ahead of you is your objective for the day, and the Jamspitze to the left is also a great objective. Skin up the glacier heading for the Urezzas Joch, then bear right heading for the col between the Hintere and Vordere Jamspitze. Like the Breite Krone, skin as high as you are comfortable, then leave your skis and carry on to the summit on foot. If you are feeling adventurous you can also climb the Vordere Jamspitze via a steep snow couloir, then some roped scrambling along a ridge.

When you are back on your skis you can head due north, being on a north-facing glacier the snow usually stays cold and powdery for a long time after a snow fall and often gives great skiing. You will need to make a short skin to get back to the Jamtal hut and apple strudel.

The hut guardian brings in supplies by snow cat up the valley from Galtur, so if you need to cut the tour short you can ski and skate down a pisted track that leads all the way back to Galtur.

Day 4 Jamtal – Wiesbadener

Taking everything with us we head off in the same direction as yesterday heading for the Obere Ochsenscharte which is the col below the Dreilander Spitz. This beautiful rocky summit takes you into the world of ski mountaineering and requires crampons and a rope. If you don't fancy this, then you can enjoy the great run down to the Wiesbadener Hut (2442m). If you want to make the day longer you can stop part way down and skin to the Vermuntpass (2797m), which has a small bivouac hut where you can get out of the weather before skiing the north-facing glacier to the hut.

If you arrive early at the hut and still want some skiing, you can check in, have a bit of lunch, then skin up to the Tiroler Sch (2935m) to the east of the hut which gives another really nice ski.

Day 5 Piz Buin

There are a number of options from the Wiesbadener Hut. If you are happy with crampons and a rope the Piz Buin is a great ski mountaineering option, if you don't fancy getting the rope out, the tour to the col at its foot is a great day out. Some people finish the classic Silvretta tour on day five and head for the valley. I will include a couple of options then you can choose what you fancy.

Route to Piz Buin from the Wiesbadener Hut.

Leaving the hut, head south then take a rising traverse round the ridge of the Grüne Kuppe (2479m) to gain the Ochsentaler Gletscher (short decent on skins). There are some seracs above you, so keep a bit spread out and don't hang about. Head straight across to the west side of the glacier then skin up the edge close to the rock wall. Once you are above the band of obvious crevasses, take a curving line across the glacier heading for the Buin Lücke. This can be your high point for the day where you can strip skins and head back to the hut. Alternatively, if you are making this your last day, ski down the valley below the hut. Keep going to the Silvretta Stausee, skate across the lake, then climb up to the Hotel Piz Buin at Bielerhöhe. You can get refreshments here, then to get to the valley you can either ski and skate down the cross country ski track, or for a small fee the hotel will take you out in a snow cat or behind a skidoo.

If you fancy the Piz Buin itself this is real ski mountaineering. Change into crampons, ice axe and, depending on your confidence, rope at the col. Climb up and left to enter a gully via a few tricky moves, follow this with the odd bolt that can be used for protection, to where a steep chimney gives access to the upper ridge and snow slope. There is a fantastic old wooden cross on the summit. Go back down the way you came up.

The route to the summit of the Piz Buin.

Day 6 Wiesbadener – Galtur

If you have decided to spend another night in the hut the nicest way I have found to finish the tour is to ski the Rauher Kopf (3101m) which gives a great final summit and a north-facing ski. The first bit of skinning above the hut is pretty steep and will often require ski crampons. As the angle eases head north then southeast to reach the Rauhkopfgletscher. Climb the glacier to the col to the east of the summit, where you can leave skis and climb to the summit. When you are back on the skis head north, following the valley all the way to the edge of the small ski area at Bielerhöhe. You can turn right here and follow the cross country ski piste to Wirl and Galtur. Alternatively if you want to enjoy a final bite to eat in the mountains you can take the drag lift to the hotel (there is a small charge). You can then descend as described above.

Ötztal Tour – Austria

Kate Scott arriving at
the Martin Busch Hut.

Grade

PD S2-S3 BS

Season

March – early May

Map

Alpenvereinskarte 30/1 Ötztaler Alpen Gurgl

Alpenvereinskarte 30/2 Ötztaler Alpen Weisskugel

Weather forecast

www.weatheraustria.net

Avalanche forecast

http://lawine.tirol.gv.at/en/

Hut information

Martin Busch – http://www.hotel-vent.at/erlebnis/martin-busch.html – 00 43 52 54 81 30

Similaun – http://huetten.alpenverein.at/huettenHome/DE/Home/index. php?huetteNr=1206 – 0039 0473 669711

Bella Vista also known as Schöne Aussicht – http://www.goldenerose. it/en/mountain-hut-bella-vista

Hochjoch Hospice – http://huetten.alpenverein.at/huettenHome/DE/ Home/index.php?huetteNr=0566 – 0043 676 6305998

Vernagt – http://huetten.alpenverein.at/huettenHome/DE/Home/index. php?huetteNr=0648 – 0043 664 1412119

Useful information

www.vent.at Tourist office site with links to buses, accommodation, etc.

If the Silvretta is a great first tour then the Ötztal is a great consolidating tour. Again it has lots of options, so you can complete the tour crossing cols and enjoying some great skiing, or you can ascend some of Austria's most classic ski mountaineering peaks.

The Ötztal is a long valley that runs north/south, a short drive or train/ bus journey from Innsbruck. The tour I have included here is a circular tour from the small village of Vent, the last village in the valley. Like the Silvretta, the access and egress routes are down a narrow valley so you need to check the avalanche conditions and forecast. It is possible to access the area from the Italian side of the range via the ski area of Kurzras at the head of Schnalstal, so you can avoid being in the bottom of steep, narrow valleys if there is a lot of fresh snow. In the spring ski touring season this is very rarely necessary, but it is worth keeping in mind.

Day 1 Martin Busch

Assuming conditions are good we will start in Vent. The first day needs a bit of timing to get to the Martin Busch Hut before the steep west-facing slopes you are skinning under heat up. The route finding is pretty easy as you just keep on the west side of the gorge. If the track has been baked by the sun you may need ski crampons as, depending on the line of the track, there are a few spots where you are skinning above a bit of a drop. The hut sits on a nice promontory, it is a really lovely spot and has plenty of space for some transceiver or crevasse rescue practice, as this is a fairly short day. If you want a longer day you can stop for a coffee, then carry on up the valley to the Similaun Hut, though this is at 3019m so it may be a bit high for some folk for a first night.

Day 2 Similaun

The plan for today is to climb the Similaun, one of the classic ski peaks of Austria. Set off from the hut following the wide valley south-west, then at about 2800m you can head south-east up the Niederjochferner, the route is generally on the left side of the glacier. As the glacier eases in angle at about 3000m head for the summit block. Skin up this as far as you are comfortable, then swap skis for crampons and head up the ridge. The west/north ridge is reasonably narrow so I would use an ice axe instead of ski poles. The summit has a superb cross with great views all round. When you have your skis on there are two options. You can take a direct line for the hut by skiing down the left-hand side of the glacier, but this misses a lot of the best skiing. The best line is to ski back down the Niederjochferner to about 2850m where you can bear left, then put your skins back on and climb to the hut.

The Similaun ascent from the left and descent towards the hut.

Day 3 Similaun – Bella Vista

Leave the hut without skins heading north, then as soon as the terrain allows turn west and put your skins on. Climb west up a small glacier heading for an unnamed col to the south of the Hauslabjoch; you will pass a monument to Ötzi, the ice man who was found preserved in the ice on this spot in 1991. Climb north to the Hauslabjoch, above the joch if you are confident in crampons you can climb the north-east ridge on the Fineil Spitz. Once you are back on your skis head north-west to the base of the rock ridge at 3100m, then head south passing under the Fineil Spitz until it is possible to head north down the Hochjochferner. There is a steep section on the glacier, so keep left then find your way through a band of crevasses before skiing left to join the ski area. You are heading for the Bella Vista Hut also marked as the Schöne Aussicht on the map. You can either skin up to the hut, or pay a small fee and take the Hintereis lift and ski down to the hut. The Bella Vista is more like a hotel in the mountains with a sauna and a hot tub, and small rooms if you want one.

The Hauslabjoch.

Summit of the
Weisskugel.

Day 4 Weisskugel

You can start early, but it is much easier lying in and getting the first Hintereis lift in the morning, then skiing round to the col to the east of the point marked Egg on the map (3163m). Ski down to the Hintereisferner where you put your skins back on. Skin up the left side of the glacier to the Hintereis Joch, then skin through the col which is a huge wind scoop, then towards the south-east ridge of the Weisskugel; access to the ridge is guarded by a steep slope. The snow conditions will dictate if you can skin up this or if you have to swap to crampons. The south-east ridge above is broad, and most people stop where it narrows, but if you are feeling good on the crampons then the narrow ridge ahead leads to an amazing ski mountaineering summit. Retrace your route back through the col then ski down the glacier and the valley beyond. It is tempting to try and take a high line toward the Hochjoch Hospiz, but the snow usually runs out and you end up on a rocky hillside. Ski down to below the hut, then skin up heading east beyond the hut until the terrain allows you to cut back left to the hut.

Day 5 Fluchtkogel – Vernagt Hut

Leaving the hut, head north-west heading for the Kesselmandferner. The track leads through a cliff band that doesn't often hold much snow, so you might need to take your skis off for a short section. The route through the snout of the glacier will vary from year to year depending on the snow and crevasse conditions. Once the angle eases, keep on the right side of the glacier all the way to the summit. Skins off then ski back down to the col at 3361m Winterjochl also marked as the Ober Guslarjoch, then ski down the Guslarferner heading east and south-east leaving the glacier at 2950m, where you can ski along a valley created by a moraine until you can cut north-east to the hut.

Day 6 Guslar Spitz – Vent

The last day of a tour is always difficult as you need to allow enough time to make it to the valley before the conditions become difficult or dangerous. The final descent to the valley has large south-facing slopes above the trail, so you need to time the day to get to the valley before conditions become dangerous. Leaving the hut, head due south passing a rock ridge to the east, then climb to a col at 3073m, and turn north to the summit. Retrace your track skiing under the hut then cross the river and ski down the south-facing valley. Keep your height looking for the summer track which is followed through some steep ground, and round the corner past the Auf Plattei. Head north-east following the terrain until it lets you ski into the valley floor, which is followed back to Vent.

If you want a bigger final day, it is also possible to climb the Wildspitze (3770m) then descend through the Mitterkar Joch at 3468m using the via feratta cables before skiing past the Breslauer Hut, cutting east until you can join the ski area.

Haute Route – The High Level Route – Chamonix to Zermatt

Grade

PD S3 BS skiers should be able to confidently kick turn in exposed places.

Season

Early March to mid May

A team on the classic traverse of the Pigne d'Arolla, one of the best views in the Alps. Photo – Andy Teasdale.

Maps

You will need a number of maps. The following maps will get you across the tour, but you may want to consider adding the 1:25,000 maps for the sections round the Prafleuri hut, and the descent to Zermatt, where navigation can be difficult if the weather is poor.

1:50,000

Swiss Topo 282 S Martigny

Swiss Topo 283s Arolla

Swiss Topo 284s Mischabel

1:25,000 more detail as suggested above.

Swiss Topo 1326 Rosablanche

Swiss Topo 2515 Zermatt Gornergrat

Avalanche forecast

www.slf.ch

Weather forecast

www.meteoswiss.ch

Hut bookings

Albert Premier Hut – http://refugealbert1er.ffcam.fr/ 0033450540620

Argentière Hut – http://refugedargentiere.ffcam.fr/ – 0033450531603

Trient Hut – www.cas-diablerets.ch – 0041 27 783 14 38

Mont Fort Hut – www.cabanemontfort.ch – 0041 27 778 13 84

Prafleuri Hut – www.prafleuri.ch – 0041 27 281 17 80

Dix Hut – http://www.section-monte-rosa.ch/fr/cabanes/cabane-des-dix – 0041 27 281 15 23

Vignettes Hut – www.cabanedesvignettes.ch – 0041 27 283 13 22

Col Collon Hut – 0039 0165 730047

Bertol Hut – www.bertol.ch – 0041 76 711 19 22

Useful Information

www.chamonix.com – Accommodation in Chamonix

www.zermatt.ch – Accommodation and information for Zermatt

Alternative guidebooks

The Haute Route by Peter Cliff, Menasha Ridge Press Inc., 1993, 978-1871890211.

Haute Route Chamonix - Zermatt : Ski Touring by Didier Lavigne and François Damilano, JMEditions, 2012, 978-2918824091

The Haute Route is probably the most famous ski tour in the world, joining the two major alpine centres of Chamonix, at the foot of Mont Blanc, and Zermatt at the foot of the Matterhorn.

There are many possible variations to the route. What we are going to describe here is the classic Verbier variation, this is probably the route with the biggest chance of success. It includes elements of many of the other variations, but generally takes the easiest line, crossing passes and a couple of peaks, to end with one of the best day's skiing you will find anywhere – the final descent to Zermatt skis down the spectacular Stockjigletscher under the north face of the Matterhorn, all the way to Zermatt.

There are a number of possible options on this route which we will highlight, some of which can make certain days longer or shorter.

As we mentioned earlier the Haute Route is very famous and hence popular, and at times very busy. If you are contemplating the route I would suggest booking the huts months ahead to guarantee a reservation. If you have the flexibility to avoid starting on a weekend this can make the whole experience much quieter. Most people leave Chamonix on the weekend, with most guided groups setting off on a Sunday, so the huts will be busy as that wave of people ski across the Alps. If you can, set off a few days after the weekend then the experience will be more pleasant as there will be far fewer people.

Day 1 Argentière – Trient Hut

The first day of the Haute Route begins in Argentière at the head of the Chamonix valley. The Grands Montets lift takes you to 3300m, this lift can be very busy so make sure you find out what time the first lift is and be there early. An alternative is to spend the first night in the Argentière Hut which would allow an early start the following morning.

Route to the Col
du Passon.

The traditional first col on the Haute Route was the Col du Chardonnet. With glacial recession getting off the Argentiere glacier has become much steeper and will often require a short section on crampons with your skis on your back. When you get to the col there can be a real bottleneck with lots of people using ropes and side slipping all the way from the col leaving a deep un-skiable trench. You could end up waiting for quite a long time. In recent years I have started using the Col du Passon instead, which doesn't have the same number of hold-ups and is still a nice start to the trip.

Once you have reached the top of the Grands Montets descend the steps onto the snow, ski north off the col, then trend right and duck under the rope onto the Rognons glacier. There is a big rock, Le Gros Rognon, in the glacier, ski to the right of this, then when the ground steepens cut right above some crevasses under some steeper ground and ski down to the Argentière Glacier. Ski down the left-hand side until you are through a band of crevasses, then track right across the glacier. Climb up off the glacier, you may have to boot this as the glacier has retreated. Don't be tempted to take the high traverse to get to this point, as it is not very nice and doesn't usually save any time. Skin up the wide slope; the easiest-angled terrain is on the right, then traverse back across below the col. You will need to transition to crampons here and put your skis on your pack. Climb up the gully then transition back to skis. You could take your skins off for the next short section, it will depend a bit on the snow conditions, or just slide downhill for a bit then head east across the glacier heading for the Col du Tour. You will probably have to take your skis off to get through the col and may need to put on crampons. When you have crossed the col you can now head across the Trient plateau for the Trient hut. When you can see the hut you can get to it by skinning round on the left.

Day 2 Trient Hut – Mont Fort Hut

Leaving the Mont Fort Hut with the Mont Blanc Massif behind. Photo – Andy Perkins.

The start to this day is really pleasant as it is downhill. Leave the hut keeping the rocks on your right and ski down to below the Col des Ecandies, you will need to make a short hike to reach the col. Ski down the Combe Ecandies and the Val d'Arpette to Champex, although you will probably have to walk the last bit.

You now need to get from Champex to Verbier, the easiest way is by taxi and you can organise this beforehand. Taxi des Combins www.taxi-des-combins.ch is particularly reliable, or ask the hut guardian to make a reservation for you the night before. Alternatively you can arrive in Champex, have a bit of lunch, and get the restaurant to organise it for you.

When you get to Verbier there are a number of different lift combinations that you can use to get to the Mont Fort Hut. If you aim to get to the Col des Gentianes you can ski easily down to the hut.

An alternative first two days of this tour is to go over the Col du Passon, then ski across to the Albert Premier Hut for the first night. This is a lower hut and a shorter day so there is less time pressure. On the second day cross the Col Superieur du Tour then ski round to the Col des Ecandies joining the route as described above, You will still have plenty of time to the get to the Cabane du Mont Fort. This makes for a more balanced two first days instead of one massive day then one short day.

Day 3 Mont Fort – Prafleuri Hut

Leaving the hut, skin up the piste heading south-east heading for the Col de la Chaux. The route climbs gently, then there are a couple of kick turns to get to the col.

Skins off, then ski east-south-east contouring round a rock buttress then down to a snow-covered lake. Skins back on and climb to the Col de Momin where you join the glacier, then head east for the col between the Pt M Calme and Rosablanche. If time allows you can climb the Rosablanche, which will usually requires a short section on foot. Ski down the Glacier de Prafleuri. There are a few options for getting off the end of the glacier to the hut, the easiest takes a swing to the north before heading for the hut.

The approach to the Prafleuri Hut is particularly difficult in poor visibility as there is a lot of steep ground and cliff bands to negotiate. It is really avalanche prone as well, so in difficult weather or a high avalanche risk I would not push through to the hut. It is also very difficult to escape from if conditions are bad, so I would think carefully before completing the day.

If you decide not to push on when you pass through the Col du Momin turn left, skiing across the Grand Desert to the north, then along the east side of the Lac de Cleuson to the village of Nendaz.

Day 4 Prafleuri – Dix Hut

Setting out from the Prafleuri Hut, head south and cross the Col des Roux. Ski south round a rock band, then take a descending line south keeping height for as long as possible paralleling the Lac des Dix. When you can slide no more put on skins and skin along parallel to the lake. This section is really exposed to avalanche after fresh snow fall or in warm conditions, so judge it carefully. At the head of the lake you need to ascend some steep ground at the Pas du Chat. This can often feel exposed, and you are a long way from anywhere if you decide that you don't like the conditions (the only option is to turn round and return to the hut). Although this isn't considered a very serious day, I think, due to its location, the Pas du Chat is one of the most serious places on the tour.

Above the Pas du Chat the angle eases and you follow the side of the glacier to the Glacier de Cheilon, passing under the Dix Hut until you can cut back up to it.

Day 5 Dix – Vignettes Hut

In good conditions the traverse of the Pigne d'Arolla (3790m) on this day can be one of the highlights of the tour. Leave the hut in downhill mode and ski as far as you can, then follow the glacier under the Pts de Tsena Réfien heading for the Col de la Serpentine. When the glacier flattens at about 3500m head east; you will now need to climb a steep section of glacier often referred to as the Serpentine. In good snow this is a steep skin, but you will often have to use ski crampons, and on occasions boot crampons, and the rope to protect from crevasses. Above this skin to the Col du Brenay and then to the summit. The Pigne has got to be one of the best viewpoints in the Alps with peaks stretching away in every direction. The ski descent to the Vignettes Hut is nice and open for the first section, then steepens and becomes crevassed at about 3500m. Trend right here to ski past the steepening, then cut back left (north) to the Col des Vignettes – the hut sits on the ridge just along from the col.

This day can often be quite short so it is worth considering carrying on over the Col de l'Évêque and Col Colon to the Refugio Col Colon, from where it is a much shorter day to Zermatt.

Day 6 Vignettes – Cabane de Bertol

It is easily possible to ski from the Vignettes to Zermatt, we will describe this shortly, but it is always a long day, and the snow is always terrible skiing into Zermatt, so a nice way to do this day is to take a slight variation and spend the night at the Bertol.

No matter where you finish the day you have to head back through the Col des Vignettes then cross the Col de l'Évêque then ski down onto the Haute Glacier d'Arolla. If you are heading for the Bertol then ski down here until it is possible to cut off the glacier and climb past the Plan de Bertol and on to the Col de Bertol. The hut sits on the ridge above the col and is one of the most spectacularly positioned huts in the Alps. Leave your skis securely at the col then climb the ladders and chains to the hut.

Alternative day 6 Vignettes – Zermatt

Take the same start until you reach the Haute Glacier d'Arolla, then as soon as the glacier begins to level off at about 2900m head east and climb to the Col du M Brule. This is quite steep at the top, so you need good snow conditions to manage it all on skis. It is barely worth taking skins off to traverse round the Haute Glacier de Tsa de Tsan to the Col de Valpelline.

Last transition of the day, then ski under the Têtes Blanches where you will join skiers coming from the Bertol Hut. Ski down the left side of the Stockigletscher; this has some huge crevasses and is no place to be in bad weather. At about 3000m turn south and ski down the section of glacier that links the Stockigletscher and the Tiefmattengletscher. Keep on the left side under the Stockji to join the Zmutt Gletscher. Find your way down the glacier looking for the best snow; the right is often better as it has been in the shade longer.

How far you will get on skis will depend on the snow cover, but it is usually possible to get to Furi where you can either get the lift to Zermatt or join the piste to town.

Day 7 Bertol – Zermatt

On the spectacular last day of the Haute Route.

You can see the Tête Blanche when you leave the hut across the Mont Miné glacier. Head for it and if you have time, skin right to the top. It is definitely worth it and what better a way to start your descent to Zermatt than by skiing from a summit?

Ski north then cut south to join skiers coming from the Col de Valpelline. You now follow the Stockigletscher as described on Day 6.

If you have the time I would recommend spending the night in Zermatt, you can then go and climb the Breithorn (4164m) before travelling back to Chamonix.

If you do have to head straight back you can do this by using a pre-booked taxi, one of the local taxi companies, or by getting the train.

Gran Paradiso – Benevolo

Iain Muir enjoying great snow on the descent from the Punta Calabre.

Grade

PD S3 BS

Season

March, April and early May.

Equipment

Classic ski touring kit including glacier travel kit.

Huts

Benevolo – www.rifugiobenevolo.com – 00390165936143

Vittorio Emanuelle – www.rifugiovittorioemanuele.com – 0039016595920

Valley accommodation – http://www.lovevda.it/turismo/dormire_e_mangiare/dove_dormire/default_e.asp?ricid=22&dd=1

Maps

Valgrisenche, Val di Rhemes Carte dei Sentieri 3 by L'escursionista editore

Val Savarenche, Gran Paradiso Carte dei Sentieri 9 by L'escursionista editore

Italian maps are to be treated with a degree of suspicion, so be very careful about setting off with them in poor visibility.

Alternative guidebooks

Orizzonti Bianchi Itinerari scelti di sci-alpinismo in Valle d'Aosta (ski touring in Valle d'Aosta) by Alessandro Mezzavalla and David Pellissier – in Italian but great maps and diagrams.

The Gran Paradiso is the highest mountain completely in Italy and is a great ski tour in its own right, but it is also gives its name to the national park it sits in. The area is a series of parallel valleys that run south from the Val d'Aosta. There are a number of tours that link huts across the head of these valleys, and another tour that goes round the Gran Paradiso. They are great tours but they do have many logistical challenges, especially if the weather and conditions don't behave. I think the best way to explore the area, and keep logistics as easy as possible, is to spend a couple of nights in the Benevolo Hut, then a night in the valley before climbing the Gran Paradiso.

The approach to the Benevolo Hut is up a steep valley, so check the avalanche conditions carefully.

Day 1 Benevolo Hut

How far you can drive up the Val di Rhêmes to Rhêmes-Notre-Dame will depend on the snow, and the council's enthusiasm with a snow plough. Some years you have to park at the village, others you can drive to Thumel. Skin up the valley initially on the right side of the valley, crossing a river as you go, then at 1950m altitude cross the river via a bridge and skin up the left side. Don't be tempted by the summer road above the river on the west side, it crosses lots of avalanche chutes, and can give difficult skinning with serious consequences if you slip.

The Benevolo Hut.

If you get to the hut early enough, and it isn't too warm, you can check in with the guardian, dump some kit, and skin up the Pointe de Lavessey in the afternoon. This is a really nice little ski tour and gives a great view point where you can spy out your objectives for the next few days.

There are loads of great objectives you can ski from the Benevolo. I have spent five days there in one trip and skied a different peak or col everyday, but I will describe two of my favourites. If you have time for three nights at the hut you can visit both, if only two then you will have to pick which one.

Day 2 Punta Calabre

This is great ski tour in any conditions, but it works in mixed weather with difficult visibility. Leave the hut and head west to a bridge, cross the river then skin up on the west side of the river – there is a shallow valley that makes the skinning easy. Eventually you turn a corner and head west up a small valley climbing steeply out of the end, placing you under the cliffs of the Granta Parei. In poor visibility these make a great handrail. Follow the cliffs to about 3000m, where you are now on a glacier. Cross the glacier, heading south for a rock ridge descending north from the summit of the Punta Calabre. In poor visibility this is an easy compass bearing and a definite point to head for. Climb more steeply up the glacier which then eases, before a final kick lands you on the summit. This is one of the great summits that you can skin to. The ski area you can see to the south is Val d'Isère, you are looking right down into Le Fornet.

Routes to the Punta di Galisia on the left and Punta Calabre on the right, also see the route marked as a handrail in the navigation chapter.

When you ski down, initially follow your line of ascent, then when you reach the point where you arrived under the cliffs, instead of following your ascent tracks, carry straight on. Contour along under the cliffs for about 1km passing the Lago Granta Parei on the way, until you can see a clear way down an open slope towards the river, a bridge and a short shuffle back to the hut.

Punta Galisia

I have skied this as often as Punta Calabre and in terms of enjoyment there is nothing between them. You can leave the hut as we did for Punta Calabre, or skin up the other side of the river, there are pros and cons to both; the hut guardian will be able to advise you about the conditions. With either start the plan is to end up on the right side of the glacier to the right of point 2955m. This is marked on the map as a little bump, but a combination of glacial recession and suspicious Italian cartography means that there is a big rock rognon at this point. Keep to the right of this and skin across to the Col Basagne. You now cross the border into France and skin up the Glacier de Basagne to the summit.

When you ski down you can retrace your steps, or if the snow is good you can ski off the summit and head north. There is some great skiing and, as the aspect is north, the snow is often cold and powdery. As you descent there are loads of options, but eventually you will have to choose one side of the river to follow back to the hut.

Day 3 Gran Vaudala – Rhêmes-Notre-Dame

The descent of the Gran Vaudala.

Leaving a hut when you have skinned up a long valley to get to it can often feel like an anticlimax, but we have a cunning plan for getting back to the car. It is possible to skin over the Col du Gran Vaudala, and ski a beautiful valley to rejoin our approach track at the bridge we crossed on our way in. This descent is a bit condition dependent so try and scope it out on your approach, and ask the hut guardian about conditions before setting off.

Leave the hut and skin up the east side of the river, there are a few places where the terrain is steep and you will often need to put on ski crampons. Once you are past the gorge, head up left over a series of steepenings and small valleys. When you can see the col you will notice a bit of a cliff band barring direct access, but you can go round this on the left. It's skiing time from here all the way to the car (with a bit of shuffling). Just head down the valley – there are few steep slopes and some great skiing. Where the valley flattens and you can see some buildings on the east side of the river at 2338m; head towards them. The terrain will then feed you down into the stream bed, you then follow this for 350m of descent to join your skinning track. This can need some precise skiing later in the season if the stream bed has started to melt out, so check conditions carefully. When you are back on your approach track, cross the bridge, then shuffle and skate to get on the main descent track back to the car.

It is possible to stay in Rhêmes-Notre-Dame for the night.

Day 4 Gran Paradiso – Vittorio Emanuele hut

After a night in the valley you will be raring to go. There are two huts on the Gran Paradiso, the Chabod and the Vittorio Emanuele. It is possible to go up from the Chabod and descend to the Vittorio Emanuele, but the glacier is much more heavily crevassed going that way, so I generally go up and back from the Vittorio Emanuele.

If you choose to go this way, leave the car at Pont and follow the summer track up the valley floor then more steeply towards the hut. The ground through the forest is pretty steep and doesn't hold snow that well. Sometimes you can skin up but you wouldn't want to ski down (don't worry you don't have to come back this way), and you may even have to carry your skis for a section. As the terrain levels off more snow will appear and you can skin to the hut, which looks like a World War Nissan hut, but is really comfortable and welcoming.

The summit of the Gran Paradiso.

Day 5 Gran Paradiso

Fuelled with pasta from the night before, leave the hut heading north then north-east into a valley that leads to the Ghiacciaio del Gran Paradiso. The snout of the glacier is quite steep, but a rising traverse usually avoids the need for any kick turns. There are then a series of rises and easings until a col is reached between the Becca di Montcorve and the Paradiso itself. The next section towards the summit is a lot steeper than it looks on the map, and can be icy as it is exposed to the wind. You will often need ski crampons, and on occasions boot crampons, to climb this. After the steepening, head for the Finestra del Roc which is a notch in the ridge that joins Il Roc and the Paradiso. Leave skis here and put on crampons, you will also want the rope if you plan to climb all the way to the Madonna on the top. Many people just ski down from here, but if you don't mind a bit of exposure the scramble to the summit is well worth it. The last section is particularly exposed, but there are some bolts in place that you can clip the rope into to protect yourselves. Retrace your steps back to your skis then ski back down the line of ascent.

When you reach the hut you have three options depending on the time available. If you are tight on time you can head for the valley by following the route of ascent to the hut, which will probably involve carrying skis for a bit. Alternatively you can spend the night in the hut and have another day's skiing ending up at the car.

Day 6 Mont Tresenta – Pont

Having enjoyed Italian hospitality for another night there are a couple of options; you can skin up to the Colle del Gran Paradiso, or skin and then crampon up Mont Tresenta. If you do either of these, when you start skiing head down and left to cross a moraine below Il Ciarforon, there are two large cairns on this so they are an obvious thing to head for. You can also reach this point on skins directly from the hut.

Descent from the Vittorio Emanuele Hut, the left line goes to the Col du Gran Paradiso and La Tresenta.

Take a traverse line down and across, heading south-east under the Becca di Monciair and Denti del Broglio until you are below the Ghiacciaio del Grand Etret. If you still have the legs you can skin to the col at the top of the glacier, or you can ski down the valley back to the car. Don't be tempted to cut down to the valley early, as the ground is much steeper and more complicated than it looks on the map.

APPENDIX 1 – VARIATIONS ON THE MANUEL GENSWEIN TRAINING MODULE

The object is to train people in 15 minutes to be able to perform a companion rescue.

1. Ask everyone to pull out their probe and assemble it. Take it apart and repeat a total of three times. Research has shown that much time can be wasted not knowing how to assemble a probe. When they have done this get everyone to gently probe each other to see what a body feels like.

2. Ask everyone to pull out their shovel and assemble it again, do this three times for the same reason as above. You can make this a race to introduce the concept of urgency.

3. Basic transceiver handling. As a group get everyone to turn their units from 'off' to 'send' to 'search' on command. Repeat at least three times so everyone is comfortable with the operation of his or her unit. Also check that everyone knows how to get their unit out from under their clothing in an incident.

4. Practical search of one buried unit at 35m distance. Talk the group through the search as everyone performs it. Whole group on receive, then follow their unit to the buried unit. Focus on following the unit walking in a curve, distance number decreasing.

5. At 10m slow down and, following the arrow, bring the unit in closer to the snow, slowly and accurately. Find the lowest distance reading and mark that point in the snow.

6. Pinpoint search using a probe in a spiral fashion.

7. Repeat the search again, but start far enough away that a signal search is required.

8. Short explanation of tactical/conveyor shovelling, then get the group to start shovelling in formation. Practice rotation.

9. If time allows use two buried transceivers so that the concepts behind multiple burials can be covered.

APPENDIX 2 – KIT LIST

Day tours non-glacial personal

Skis

Skins

Ski crampons

Boots

Poles

Rucksack

Avalanche transceiver

Avalanche probe

Metal shovel

Boot crampons – itinerary dependent

Ice axe – itinerary dependent

Mobile phone/communication

Sun cream, skin and lips

Knife/multi-tool

Water bottle/flask

Personal first aid – blister kit, painkillers

Insurance

Camera

Clothing

Base layer bottom

Softshell or Gore-Tex trousers

Base layer top

Softshell top with hood

Waterproof jacket – Paclite

Waterproof trousers if wearing softshell – Paclite

Synthetic insulated jacket with hood

Down jacket if really cold

Thin gloves

Thick gloves

Warm hat

Sun hat

Sun glasses

Goggles

Glacier tour personal

Harness

Personal or group glacier travel/crevasse rescue kit

Hut-to-hut

Headtorch

Book/Kindle

Toothbrush and toothpaste (some huts have showers but some don't even have water)

T-shirt to wear at the hut

Sheet sleeping bag

Change of socks depending on the length of the tour

Group kit

Group shelter

First aid kit

Spares kit – see below

Map

Compass

GPS

Brooks sledge – depending on venue

Spares kit – see Appendix 4

Crevasse rescue kit

There should be TWO of these in the party, even if it's a party of just two.

2 x 30m 8mm rope

2 x ice screws – about 17cm. These should be clipped together with a snaplink karabiner, and should have rubber caps on the teeth to protect the teeth and your trousers

2 x 8ft slings (120cm doubled length)

3 x screwgate karabiners, at least one should be an HMS (pear-shaped) design

2 x prusik loops and 1 mechanical device such as a Wild Country Ropeman or Petzl Micro Traxion

1 x pulley-style karabiner – such as a DMM Revolver

30m of 8mm rope – there should always be two ropes in the party

I usually add 5m of 6mm cord, which can be used in anchor creation, but also can be used to help reading the terrain in poor visibility (see navigation chapter)

Personal crevasse rescue kit if not carrying above

1 x ice screw – about 17cm in length

1 x 8ft sling with two screwgate karabiners

APPENDIX 3 – FIRST AID KIT

2 pairs non-latex surgical gloves

1 face shield to act as a barrier if giving CPR

1 pair tough-cut scissors

2 triangular bandages

2 large wound dressings

2 10 x10cm non-adherent dressings

Roll of surgical tape

Small selection of plasters

A few antiseptic wipes

1 100mm wide crepe bandage

2 packs steristrips to close wounds

Personal painkillers – paracetamol/ibuprofen

APPENDIX 4 – SPARES KIT

Rubber ski straps x 4 (30cm ones work best)

Cable ties – a selection of lengths and thicknesses

Metal scraper

Small block of wax

Binding mounting screws

Physio-type tape – much better than duct tape in the cold

Spare transceiver/GPS batteries

Screwdriver

Emergency skin glue

On longer tours I add

Araldite

BMG
BRITISH MOUNTAIN GUIDES

Where ever you are headed, we'll be right with you...

As qualified members of the International Federation of Mountian Guides our members hold the world's highest possible qualification for leading groups in the mountains and the only UK qualificatiion valid abroad for climbing, off piste skiing and ski touring on glacial terrain.

So if you are planning an adventure from skiing powder to climbing a Himalayan giant, you will find a British Mountain Guide who will be able to help.

www.bmg.org.uk

ARC'TERYX

Photo: © Ian Sherrington BMG

AvalancheGeeks

We take avalanche education seriously.

We're passionate about what we teach and what we ski. We take pride in delivering informative, hands-on avalanche courses.

American Avalanche Association courses run in the Alps and Scotland.

www.avalanchegeeks.com

Mountain Adventure Company